NEGOTIATING LEGALITY

Despite escalating geopolitical rivalry, the United States and China continue to be economically intertwined. Numerous Chinese companies have made substantial investments in the United States and are reluctant to exit this strategically important market. While the global expansion of Chinese companies has ignited intense policy and academic debates, their interactions with complex host-state legal systems have largely escaped systematic examination. To fill this knowledge gap, *Negotiating Legality* introduces a dual institutional framework and applies it to analyzing multiyear survey data, 176 interviews, and a substantial corpus of US lawsuit records, thereby shedding light on how Chinese companies develop in-house legal capacities, engage with US legal professionals, and navigate litigation in US courts. As the first comprehensive investigation of these crucial topics, this book is an indispensable resource for those seeking to understand China's rise, its global impacts – especially on legal systems of developed nations like the United States – the intricate dynamics of US–China relations, and the strategies multinational companies employ to mitigate increasing legal and political risks amidst shifts in the global order.

Ji Li is the John S. and Marilyn Long Professor of US–China Business and Law at the University of California, Irvine School of Law. He is an interdisciplinary scholar who has spent a decade researching the rise of China and its global impacts, with a focus on the United States. His earlier book, *The Clash of Capitalisms? Chinese Companies in the United States* (2018), explores Chinese investors' adaptation to the complex, stringent US regulatory system.

CAMBRIDGE STUDIES IN LAW AND SOCIETY

Founded in 1997, Cambridge Studies in Law and Society is a hub for leading scholarship in socio-legal studies. Located at the intersection of law, the humanities, and the social sciences, it publishes empirically innovative and theoretically sophisticated work on law's manifestations in everyday life: from discourses to practices, and from institutions to cultures. The series editors have longstanding expertise in the interdisciplinary study of law, and welcome contributions that place legal phenomena in national, comparative, or international perspective. Series authors come from a range of disciplines, including anthropology, history, law, literature, political science, and sociology.

A list of books in the series can be found at the back of this book.

CAMBRIDGE STUDIES IN LAW AND SOCIETY

NEGOTIATING LEGALITY

Chinese Companies in the US Legal System

Ji Li
University of California, Irvine

CAMBRIDGE
UNIVERSITY PRESS

CAMBRIDGE
UNIVERSITY PRESS

Shaftesbury Road, Cambridge CB2 8EA, United Kingdom

One Liberty Plaza, 20th Floor, New York, NY 10006, USA

477 Williamstown Road, Port Melbourne, VIC 3207, Australia

314–321, 3rd Floor, Plot 3, Splendor Forum, Jasola District Centre, New Delhi – 110025, India

103 Penang Road, #05–06/07, Visioncrest Commercial, Singapore 238467

Cambridge University Press is part of Cambridge University Press & Assessment, a department of the University of Cambridge.

We share the University's mission to contribute to society through the pursuit of education, learning and research at the highest international levels of excellence.

www.cambridge.org
Information on this title: www.cambridge.org/9781108845229

DOI: 10.1017/9781108954891

First published 2024

A catalogue record for this publication is available from the British Library

Library of Congress Cataloging-in-Publication Data
Names: Li, Ji, 1976 October 8–
Title: Negotiating legality : Chinese companies in the US legal system /
Ji Li, University of California, Irvine.
Description: Cambridge, United Kingdom ; New York, NY : Cambridge University Press, 2024. | Includes bibliographical references and index.
Identifiers: LCCN 2023047134 | ISBN 9781108845229 (hardback) |
ISBN 9781108954891 (ebook)
Subjects: LCSH: Business enterprises, Foreign – Law and legislation – United States. |
Investments, Chinese – Law and legislation – United States.
Classification: LCC KF1419 .L56 2024 | DDC 346.7307–dc23/eng/20231012
LC record available at https://lccn.loc.gov/2023047134

ISBN 978-1-108-84522-9 Hardback

To my family

CONTENTS

FIGURES

TABLES

ACKNOWLEDGMENTS

Embarking on the journey of writing this book has been a privilege, made possible by engaging with an incredible community of friends and colleagues whose unwavering support and astute insights have been essential. I am particularly grateful to Rachel Stern, Matthew Erie, Benjamin van Rooij, Taisu Zhang, Benjamin Liebman, and Sida Liu for their invaluable critiques and thoughtful suggestions on earlier drafts of the manuscript.

Feedback on specific sections has also been helpful. For Chapters 1 and 2, I extend my thanks to Ann Southworth, Swethaa Ballakrishnen, Bryant Garth, Jacques deLisle, Emily Taylor Poppe, Alejandro Camacho, Carrie Menkel-Meadow, Gregory Shaffer, Kenneth Simons, Robert Solomon, Shauhin Talesh, Christopher Whytock, and other participants at the workshop hosted by the UCI Center for Empirical Research on the Legal Profession. Additionally, I am grateful for enriching exchanges with Tom Ginsburg, Matthew Erie, Eve Darian-Smith, and others at the Chinese Law and Development panel during the 2019 Law & Society Annual Meeting; with Frank Garcia, Patricia McCoy, Diane Ring, Judith McMorrow, Shu-Yi Oei, and other attendees at the Law and Economics workshop at Boston College Law School; and with Andrea Wang, Paul Heaton, Tobias Wolff, Teemu Ruskola, Beth Simmons, and other faculty scholarship workshop participants at Penn Carey Law School.

Chapter 3 was significantly enhanced by comments from William Alford, Matthew Erie, Sida Liu, Weixia Gu, Mark Wu, and other panelists and discussants at the China and the International Legal Order Symposium, as well as by feedback from David Wilkins, Gregory Shaffer, Victor Fleischer, Atinuke Adediran, Peter Zeughauser, Ann Southworth, Carole Silver, Swethaa Ballakrishnen, and others at the UCI Law School's summer workshop on the legal profession.

The development of Chapter 6 benefited from the insights of Benjamin Van Rooij, Stephen Lee, Alejandro Camacho, Gregory Shaffer, Christopher Whytock, Carrie Menkel-Meadow, Richard Hasen,

Bryant Garth, Shauhin Talesh, Sameer Asher, and others at the UCI Law summer faculty workshop; of Amitai Aviram, Ralph Brubaker, Jeremy McClane, and colleagues at the University of Illinois College of Law faculty workshop; of K. S. Park, Hoyoung Shin, Summer Kim, and attendees of the 3rd UCI and Korea University Law Shuttle Symposium; of Benjamin Liebman, Sida Liu, Donald Clarke, Taisu Zhang, Carl Minzner, Margaret Lewis, Zhuang Liu, Ke Li, Jerome Cohen, Tom Kellogg, and others at the Chinese Law Workshop at Columbia Law School.

Throughout this project, UCI School of Law has provided an intellectually stimulating environment that fostered growth and learning. I am thankful for the support and critiques from my colleagues who generously dedicated their time to review parts of this book. In the past few years, some empirical findings of this book were published in *Law & Social Inquiry*, *Harvard International Law Journal*, *Yale Journal of International Law*, and *University of Pennsylvania Asian Law Review*. I appreciate the valuable input of the editors and reviewers of these journals.

I wish to extend a special note of gratitude to Candice Niu, Junchen Pan, Abby Li, Xue Luo, Sherry Qu, and the other dedicated staff members of the China General Chamber of Commerce USA. Their diligence was instrumental in facilitating the annual survey of Chinese companies in the United States and assembling the unique dataset. My appreciation also extends to the anonymous executives, lawyers, consultants, and other practitioners who generously shared their knowledge and perspectives. The writing of the book benefited from thoughtful and stimulating conversations with Sophie Wu and Edward Fan.

I express my heartfelt gratitude to the series editors for Cambridge Studies in Law and Society, namely Rachel Stern, Mark Fathi Massoud, and Jens Meierhenrich, for considering this manuscript worthy of inclusion in their distinguished series. My thanks also go to Matt Gallaway and his support team for their professionalism and meticulous attention to detail throughout the publication process. A special mention is due to the anonymous reviewers, whose keen interest, constructive comments, and supportive feedback were instrumental in shaping this project.

Lastly, and most importantly, my profound thanks go to my family, the cornerstone of all my endeavors.

INTRODUCTION

After decades of exponential growth, China has transformed from a stagnant, impoverished autarky to the world's second largest economy highly integrated in global supply chains, and numerous Chinese firms have embarked on an overseas business expansion of an unprecedented scale. Against that backdrop, many Chinese investors have ventured into the highly competitive, strategically important US market. Prior to the onset of the US–China trade war, the United States stood out as the largest national recipient of Chinese outbound foreign direct investment (FDI).[1] Though ensuing confrontation between the two countries has hampered the investment flow, most of the largest Chinese investors have been hesitant to withdraw from the US market, and some have even doubled down, further expanding their US operations despite the escalating US–China geopolitical rivalry.[2]

With business presence comes extensive exposure to the US legal system, which is notorious for its complexity and peculiarity. The multifaceted system comprises different levels of courts, each with its own set of rules, procedures, and requirements. The sheer volume of laws, regulations, and legal precedents is immense and, depending on the subject matter areas, substantive laws may vary significantly across different states. Additionally, social, political, and policy concerns may factor into

[1] Ji Li, The Clash of Capitalisms? Chinese Companies in the United States 42 (2018).

[2] 2022 Annual Business Survey Report on Chinese Enterprises in the United States 22 (June 2022), www.cgccusa.org/wp-content/uploads/2022/07/%E3%80%90FINAL%E3%80%91CGCC-2022-Annual-Report-interactive.pdf.

judicial decision-making process, adding another layer of complexity. As a result, legal disputes can take years to resolve, and the outcome is not always predictable, even for experts in the field. In brief, managing US legal risks is a daunting task even for highly sophisticated American companies, let alone Chinese investors that have survived and thrived in a home-state institutional environment where law often assumes a secondary role in business transactions and dispute resolution. However, those firms that have learned to navigate the system may leverage the complex legal framework to gain a competitive edge over rivals.[3] More importantly, Chinese investors facing an increasingly hostile regulatory environment in the United States may find litigation the only effective means to protect their investment from unfair US government treatment.[4] One question naturally follows: How do they negotiate the omnipresent and consequential US legal risks and opportunities?[5]

As the US–China rivalry escalates, Chinese companies operating in the United States have captured a great deal of public attention, so there is abundant media coverage when they show up in US courts. Lawsuits filed by or against Huawei and TikTok, for instance, regularly make the front pages of major international news outlets.[6] But what appear to the public as stories that stimulate their curiosity are often matters of life and death for the Chinese companies. When the federal government took action to exclude Huawei from the US market, the company sought legal remedy, and its loss in court resulted in substantial downsizing of the company's expansive

[3] Bruce C. Rudy & Stephanie L. Black, *Attack or Defend? The Role of Institutional Context on Patent Litigation Strategies*, 44 J. MNGT. 1226, 1227 (2018).

[4] See Chapter 6 for more discussion.

[5] Note that, for the purposes of this book, "Chinese companies" refers to companies owned by Chinese investors that operate within the United States.

[6] *See, e.g.*, Cecilia Kang, *Indiana Sues TikTok for Security and Child Safety Violations*, N.Y. TIMES (December 7, 2022), www.nytimes.com/2022/12/07/technology/tiktok-lawsuit.html; Paul Mozur & Austin Ramzy, *Huawei Sues U.S. Government Over What It Calls an Unfair Ban*, N.Y. TIMES (March 6, 2019), www.nytimes.com/2019/03/06/business/huawei-united-states-trade-lawsuit.html; Dan Strumpf, *Huawei Sues the U.S., Says Congress Acted as "Judge, Jury and Executioner,"* WALL STREET J. (March 6, 2019), www.wsj.com/articles/huawei-sues-the-u-s-challenging-a-law-signed-by-president-trump-11551924208; Joseph De Avila, *Parents of Two Children Sue TikTok After Alleging They Died from Doing "Blackout Challenge,"* WALL STREET J. (July 7, 2022), www.wsj.com/articles/parents-of-two-children-sue-tiktok-after-alleging-they-died-from-doing-blackout-challenge-11657212025; Demetri Sevastopulo, *Huawei Challenges Its Designation as a Threat to U.S. Security*, FINANCIAL TIMES (February 9, 2021), www.ft.com/content/b7e2294d-9207-4fae-8fed-d63a80e99618.

US operations.[7] TikTok also sued after US President Trump issued an executive order to ban the app, and its legal success allowed the Chinese-owned company to continue to grow.[8] More recently, the state government of Montana took the lead in issuing a total ban of TikTok, and the company immediately filed a lawsuit challenging its constitutionality.[9] The litigation behavior and preferences of Chinese companies in the United States have direct impacts not only on their global operations but also on intricate US–China relations.[10]

US lawsuits involving Chinese-invested firms also raise novel and important legal issues. Never has the United States been so connected economically with a foreign country it so profoundly distrusts. The tensions between the economic integration of the two superpowers and their soaring geopolitical contests spawn difficult issues for courts, as the former determines that a vast number of Chinese parties maintain a normal presence in the United States and carry on routine commercial transactions. Yet because of the geopolitical rivalry, they are easy targets of suspicion, discrimination, and outright hostility, which is further aggravated by the lack of knowledge about China and the enormous institutional gaps between the two countries. To illustrate, consider the lawsuit *Ralls v. The Committee on Foreign Investment in the United States (CFIUS)*. As will be detailed later in this book, the plaintiff in this case, a US firm owned by a large Chinese company, made an otherwise mundane investment in Oregon. Because the property it acquired is adjacent to a military facility, CFIUS deemed it a threat to national security and ordered immediate divestment. Throughout the process, however, the agency gave no explanation to the Chinese investor, and due to the onerous restraints over the compelled divestment, it the investor stood to incur substantial losses.[11] Hence the lawsuit, the first one against the powerful US government agency since its creation decades before. Much to the surprise of those familiar with US law governing foreign investment review national security screening, the Chinese investor eventually prevailed.[12] The federal appellate court ruled that foreign investors are

[7] See more details about the cases filed by Huawei in Chapter 6.

[8] See Chapter 6 for more detailed analysis of the lawsuits.

[9] David McCabe & Sapna Maheshwari, *TikTok Sues Montana, Calling State Ban Unconstitutional*, N.Y. Times (May 22, 2023), www.nytimes.com/2023/05/22/technology/tiktok-montana-ban-lawsuit.html.

[10] See more details about the cases filed by Huawei in Chapter 6.

[11] Ji Li, *Investing Near the National Security Black Hole*, 14 Berkeley Bus. L.J. 1, 8 (2017).

[12] *Id.*, at 26.

entitled to the same constitutional protection as domestic parties and CFIUS must follow due process in depriving them of their property rights.[13] The unprecedented ruling put legal boundaries on the hitherto nearly unlimited discretion of the powerful federal agency. As will be elaborated, a growing number of Chinese companies have been litigating in US courts, and new legal issues abound. The United States being a common law country, court judgments generally bind future cases.[14] Therefore the lawsuits involving Chinese companies have been reshaping the contours of substantive US laws in various subject matter areas such as conflict of laws, comity, sovereign immunity, and national security review of foreign investment.[15]

Moreover, the US legal experiences of Chinese companies have become integral to the intricate and consequential bilateral relations. Facing an increasingly adverse investment environment, some of the companies have turned to their home government for assistance.[16] However, with limited human resources, the Chinese government has urged Chinese investors to exhaust available legal remedies before seeking diplomatic help.[17] Therefore, the investors' pursuit of legal action in the United States partially determines the timing, scope, and manner of possible intervention by the Chinese government. As vividly illustrated by the extradition case for Meng Wanzhou (i.e., Huawei's CFO),[18] as well as the constitutional cases against Trump's TikTok ban,[19] legal strategies figure prominently in the political dynamics of the intensifying superpower rivalry.

Furthermore, how Chinese companies negotiate US legal risks also raise important theoretical questions. By definition, multinational companies (MNCs) straddle at least two different institutional settings. If the home state and the host state share similar values, norms, and legal systems, smooth adaptation is generally expected. Canadian companies, for instance, make substantial direct investments in the

[13] *Id.*, at 8.

[14] Judges sometimes make decisions that they intend not to bind future cases. Such decisions are usually not published.

[15] See more discussion of the cases in Chapter 6.

[16] Ji Li, *In Pursuit of Fairness: How Chinese Multinational Companies React to U.S. Government Bias*, 62 HARV. INT'L L.J. 375, 397 (2021).

[17] *Id.*, at 398.

[18] Drew Hinshaw, et al., *Inside the Secret Prisoner Swap That Splintered the U.S. and China*, WALL STREET J. (October 27, 2022), www.wsj.com/articles/huawei-china-meng-kovrig-spavor-prisoner-swap-11666877779.

[19] See more details of the TikTok cases in Chapter 6.

United States, yet most of them are largely indistinguishable from local investors. However, if a stark contrast exists between an MNC's home and host states, as is the case for Chinese companies operating in the United States, the MNC's reactions to the institutional heterogeneity are both uncertain and under-explored. Of particular interest for socio-legal scholars is how differences in the companies' dual operational environments implicate their preferences and behavior as they interact with the US legal system. In addition, state-owned enterprises dominate Chinese outbound investment. Does the peculiar ownership structure, a defining feature of China's state capitalism that distinguishes Chinese companies from those based in Europe, Japan, and most other countries, have any notable effect on the way Chinese companies negotiate US legal risks? If so, how?

In summary, questions about the experiences of Chinese companies with the US legal system are of practical, policy, and theoretical importance, yet they have evaded academic attention. One may attribute the neglect to the lack of empirical evidence. After all, Chinese companies did not make substantial direct investments in the United States until around 2014 (see Figure 1.2 in Chapter 1), when data collection for this book began. For the same reason, scholars have not yet formulated an analytical framework suitable for exploring Chinese investors' management of host-state legal risks. Of course, the complexity of the topic is also a factor, as it spans multiple subject areas traditionally associated with different disciplines, thwarting any effort to devise a unified analytical framework.

Adopting an interdisciplinary approach, this book narrows the gaps by formulating a model of institutional duality and then applying it to analyze a rich body of empirical evidence including multiyear survey data of Chinese companies doing business in the United States, 176 interviews with in-house counsel, lawyers, managers, and other professionals who have served them, and many legal archives and secondary materials. To look ahead to Chapter 1, let me briefly sketch the dual institutional model. It has been well recognized that foreign companies operating in the United States are under constant isomorphic pressure from its formal rules and informal norms, thus their preferences and behaviors tend to converge with what is expected of local US companies.[20] Simply put, foreign investors generally heed the proverb

[20] See Chapter 1 for more discussion.

"When in Rome, do as the Romans do." Less studied, however, is the influence of MNCs' home-state institutions. A variety of mechanisms, ranging from intra-organizational personnel control to extraterritorial application of formal rules, may amplify the home-state institutional influence of Chinese investors and channel it to their US operations. The dual institutional pulls from the host and the home states, which converge in some areas and diverge in others, will modify how Chinese companies interact with other key actors in the US legal system.

Applying the dual institutional model, this book explores how Chinese companies negotiate US legal risks and opportunities – a broad question that spans several subject areas and research disciplines – by making four interrelated inquiries about: (1) the internal legal capacity of Chinese companies in the United States; (2) their selection of US lawyers and consumption of US legal services; (3) litigation by Chinese companies in US courts, and (4) their legal strategies for coping with government mistreatment in the United States. Each of the inquiries begins with a comparative analysis of relevant dual institutional environment, with a focus on the under-explored home-state institutions of Chinese companies. Thereafter it examines pertinent empirical evidence, interrogates key findings from prior research, and investigates new questions of theoretical and policy interest, especially those concerning the effects of state ownership and home-state normative influence on the companies when they navigate the complex, stringent US legal system. Before proceeding, a clarification of the terms will be helpful. By "Chinese companies," I mean companies that operate mainly in the United States and are owned by Chinese investors. By this definition, TikTok is considered a Chinese company, though its global headquarters is in Los Angeles and the United States is at the center of its business and the dominant source of its revenue. Wherever necessary, this book distinguishes "Chinese companies" from Chinese MNCs, which refers to China-based global business enterprises, most of which also have established US-based operations.

This book proceeds as follows. Chapter 1 provides readers with the necessary background knowledge to understand Chinese companies in the United States and the questions concerning their host-state legal experiences. It begins by surveying Chinese direct investments in the United States and their major attributes. Using descriptive survey data, the chapter then elaborates on the legal hazards Chinese investors must traverse in order to conduct business in the highly complex US institutional environment. Next, the chapter briefly reviews the cumulative knowledge and highlights its inadequacy. As noted, Chinese companies in the United States raise novel and under-researched questions, including questions about state-owned firms that tend to downplay profit-maximization and those concerning the influence of the home-state normative institutions. Chapter 1 closes by outlining a new analytical framework, which encompasses diverse corporate ownership structures and dual institutional influences, for researching how Chinese companies cope with US legal risks. This framework will be applied to all the substantive chapters to follow.

Chapter 2 delves into the in-house legal capacity of Chinese companies operating in the United States. As just noted, the US legal and regulatory regime can be confusing and cumbersome even for American companies, let alone investors from a developing country known for its relatively feeble judicial system. This chapter explores whether Chinese companies operating in the United States choose to develop internal legal capacity or instead rely on external lawyers to navigate the complex US legal landscape. It also investigates key characteristics of the in-house legal managers, such as their career bases and professional qualifications. As will be demonstrated, Chinese companies differ in their approaches to developing in-house legal capacities, and the chapter will examine possible factors that may explain such variations, with a focus on the state ownership of the companies and the cultural differences they experience in the United States.

Chapter 3 explores Chinese companies' use of US legal services. "When in trouble, find a lawyer," commented an executive of a Chinese company on succeeding in the United States.[21] Needless to say, lawyers play a crucial role in assisting Chinese companies, even those equipped with in-house legal counsel, as they cope with the US legal system. Chapter 3 studies how Chinese companies select their US lawyers and consume US legal services. The US legal market, the world's largest and most sophisticated, boasts more than 1.3 million lawyers.[22] How do Chinese investors choose their legal counsel? What lawyer attributes do they consider important: practice experience, fee rate, Chinese background, credentials, government connection, or others? Additionally, Chapter 3 will examine the quantity of US legal services purchased by Chinese companies, which determines their bargaining

[21] Li, *supra* note 1, at 106.

[22] ABA Profile of the Legal Profession 22 (2022), www.americanbar.org/content/dam/aba/administrative/news/2022/07/profile-report-2022.pdf.

power and the extent to which their lawyer selection preferences will have an impact on the US legal market. Additionally, within the dual institutional framework, the chapter assesses how their lawyer selection preferences and legal service consumption may be associated with the ownership structure of the Chinese investors and other variables of interest.

Chapter 4 explores the US litigation experiences of Chinese companies. It begins with a summary description of the data about their dispute resolution in the United States and demonstrate that a small fraction of the disputes end up in US courts. The chapter then looks at the companies' comparative litigation preferences: Are they more inclined to sue in the United States than in China? As will be shown, the empirical evidence is mixed. Though most of them regard the US judiciary as impartial, only a minority are more willing to litigate in the United States.[23] And the relative reluctance to sue reflects both cost consideration and the home-state normative influence. Next, Chapter 4 examines the decision-making power regarding US litigation decisions. Among the key players (i.e., US lawyers, in-house counsel, local managers, and the Chinese headquarters), most Chinese companies would delegate the decision to US lawyers, but a significant minority defer to their headquarters. The chapter further explores the varying roles of US lawyers and the Chinese headquarters, and the analysis focuses on state ownership, cultural differences, and other variables derived from the dual institutional model. Additionally, this chapter statistically examines the US litigation experiences of Chinese companies.

Chapter 5 continues the inquiry about litigation by Chinese companies in the United States, from two different angles. First, it presents detailed comparative case studies of three prominent Chinese companies with disparate ownership structures, from different sectors, and having different US investment experiences: Lenovo, Huawei, and Fuyao Glass. The comparison concentrates on three key aspects: the US lawyers and law firms representing the three companies in courts, their in-house counsel, and the number and types of federal lawsuits they have litigated in US courts. The case studies tie together the empirical findings from prior chapters and illuminate them in the context of the companies' US litigation. Second, the chapter analyzes hand-collected data of all federal lawsuits involving a large sample

[23] Li, *supra* note 1, at 72.

of Chinese companies. Breaking down the dataset by the role of the companies (as defendant versus as plaintiff), the chapter investigates possible associations between various institutional and firm-specific variables of interest (e.g., ownership structure, cultural challenges, and size of US investment), and the number of lawsuits they litigate in federal courts.

Chapter 6 turns to a specific type of legal action – Chinese companies suing US government entities. The US–China geopolitical tensions have led to an increasingly hostile business environment for Chinese investors. With US governments at various levels enacting rules and policies aimed at punishing, containing, or outcompeting China, Chinese investors now face an amplified risk of government mistreatment. The chapter will investigate the role of litigation as a mitigating strategy for Chinese investors. It presents detailed case studies of legal resistance by four prominent Chinese companies – Sany, Huawei, TikTok, and China Telecom – against the US government. The chapter then examines survey data about the coping measures Chinese companies would consider in response to perceived host-government mistreatment, with a particular focus on institutional and corporate factors that may modify their inclination to seek legal recourse. The analysis suggests that in this subject area the formidable coercive pressure of the host state obscures the influence of home-state institutions. Moreover, the chapter examines recent survey data on legal actions taken by Chinese companies against the US government. The final chapter is the Conclusion, which outlines the policy and theoretical contributions of this book and raises questions for future research.

CHAPTER ONE

OVERVIEW OF CHINESE COMPANIES IN THE US LEGAL SYSTEM

We invest in the US for its rule of law, yet the biggest challenge for us is also its rule of law.

—Manager of a Chinese company in the United States

In the late 1970s, China emerged from the shadows of the Cultural Revolution as an autarky steeped in extreme poverty, leaving few Chinese businesses with the means or desire to invest abroad. Fast forward to today and that once impoverished nation has since evolved into the world's second largest economy.[1] Chinese companies have channeled billions of dollars into overseas investments,[2] igniting intense debates across the globe. While some have welcomed this new influx of capital, there is a growing concern among others that these Chinese investors might export unethical business practices, show disregard for local cultures, breach host-state laws, and clandestinely manipulate host-state politics to align with the interests of the Chinese government.[3] Consequently, an extensive body of literature has emerged that analyzes the impacts of China's global economic expansion. However, no one has so far explored how Chinese

[1] World Bank, Gross Domestic Product 2022, World Development Indicators database, https://databankfiles.worldbank.org/public/ddpext_download/GDP.pdf.

[2] In 2015, Chinese investors invested in 6,532 overseas companies, an increase of 14.7 percent from 2014. *Summary Statistics of Chinese Outbound Direct Investment (Non-banking) 2015*, Ministry of Commerce of the People's Republic of China, at http://hzs.mofcom.gov.cn/article/date/201601/20160101239873.shtml.

[3] Ji Li, The Clash of Capitalisms? Chinese Companies in the United States 18–19 (2018).

companies maneuver within the sophisticated legal institutions of developed host nations, such as the United States.

Chinese investors obviously face mounting challenges in navigating the US legal system. As will be detailed shortly, corporate management and business transactions in China often relegate the legal system to a more peripheral role. Having thrived in such a home-state environment, Chinese companies encounter formidable institutional obstacles when operating in developed countries with robust, strict, and complex legal systems. Obviously, nowhere else are the hurdles as high as in the United States. How then do Chinese investors negotiate the omnipresent legal risks? Will they persist in treating law as an inconsequential or purely cosmetic aspect of their operations (inertia), adapt to mirror the behavior of US companies (isomorphism), or display mixed responses shaped by both home- and host-state institutions (dualism)? This book sets out to answer these questions by exploring a range of interconnected topics.

This chapter begins with an overview of China's outbound direct investment, particularly emphasizing Chinese foreign direct investment (FDI) in the United States. It then introduces a variety of research questions, ranging from the role of in-house legal counsel in Chinese companies to their legal responses when confronted with unfair treatment by the US government. Next, this chapter selectively summarizes and critically reviews the existing literature pertinent to the interactions between multinational companies (MNCs) and the complex US legal system. Subsequently, it formulates a comprehensive theoretical framework predicated on dual institutional influence, which will be applied consistently throughout the book. The chapter concludes with a description of the research methodology.

1.1 CHINESE DIRECT INVESTMENT IN THE UNITED STATES

Despite the scrutiny it has received, outbound investment from China is a rather recent phenomenon. In the post-Cultural Revolution decade, the Chinese government strictly limited outward capital flow due to a dire shortage of foreign exchange reserves.[4] Even after the initial restrictions were loosened,[5] Chinese outbound FDI remained at a low

[4] Yadong Luo, et al., *How Emerging Market Governments Promote Outward FDI: Experience from China*, 45 J. World Bus. 68, 73 (2010).

[5] David Shambaugh, China Goes Global: The Partial Power 177 (2013).

level of around $1.2 billion.[6] A series of embezzlement scandals and investment failures subsequently led the State Council to conclude that China was "unprepared for large-scale foreign investment,"[7] resulting in tighter controls and a 20 percent annual decrease in outward investment proposals from 1992 to 1996.

However, China's continuous economic growth, fueled in part by increasing inbound investment and a thriving international trade, boosted its foreign exchange reserves. Some government officials started advocating for less restrictive policies and encouraged "competitive" state-owned enterprises (SOEs) to invest abroad.[8] In 2000, a Politburo meeting developed a "Going Out" strategy to promote China's outbound FDI, which the Chinese Communist Party (CCP) National Congress promptly endorsed as a strategic national policy for fostering economic development.[9] Against this backdrop, the central government set up institutions to facilitate investment and ratified dozens of investor-friendly bilateral investment treaties.[10] The government also streamlined and decentralized reviews for outbound investment proposals and supplied Chinese investors with low-cost capital. For example, state-owned banks created overseas loan programs,[11] and the State Administration of Foreign Exchange simplified procedures and reduced thresholds for Chinese firms to obtain foreign currencies for overseas investments.[12] In the early 2010s, as foreign exchange reserves continued to multiply, the Chinese government replaced the investment approval regime with a reporting system.[13]

As the government policies evolved, so too did the characteristics of China's outbound investment. Due to earlier restrictions and the initial composition of the Chinese economy, state-owned conglomerates had been the dominant players, responsible for 75 percent of the total

[6] *Id.*

[7] Opinions on Strengthening the Management of Overseas Investment Projects (关于加强海外投资项目管理意见 1991).

[8] SHAMBAUGH, *supra* note 5, at 175.

[9] Luo, et al., *supra* note 4, 74–75.

[10] Karl P. Sauvant & Michael D. Nolan, *China's Outward Foreign Direct Investment and International Investment Law*, 18 J. INT'L ECON. L. 893, 933 (2015).

[11] Yuan, et al., *Zhongguo Yinhangye "Zhou Chu Qu" Yinlai Kuaisu Fazhanqi* [*Chinese Banking Industry "Going Global" Entering a Period of Fast Growth*], PEOPLE'S DAILY 3 (August 4, 2016), http://finance.people.com.cn/n1/2016/0804/c1004-28609135.html.

[12] Guo Song, *"Zou Chu Qu" Waihui Zhengce Zhichi Tixi* [*"Going Global" Foreign Exchange Policy Support System*], ZHONG GUO JIN RONG [CHINA FINANCE] 31 (2015).

[13] Section 6, Chapter 2, Jingwai Touzi Guanli Banta [Overseas Investment Management Measures], Order of the Ministry of Commerce No. 3 (2014), www.mofcom.gov.cn/article/b/c/201409/20140900723361.shtml.

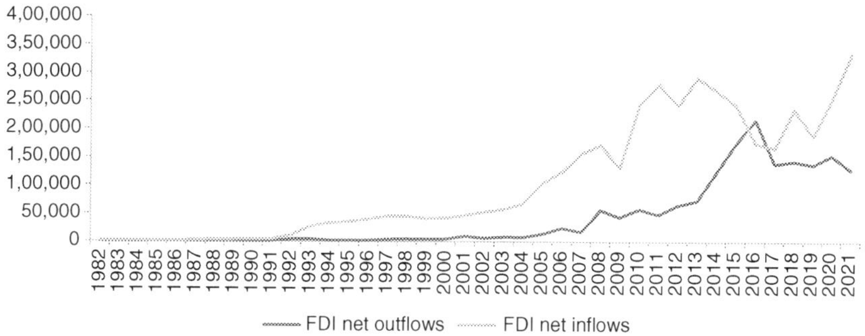

Figure 1.1 FDI inflows and outflows, China 1982–2021 (millions of US dollars)
Source: World Bank: World Development Indicators, https://databank.worldbank.org/source/world-development-indicators (most recent is 2021 data, last checked on March 31, 2023).

amount of Chinese outbound investment until 2010.[14] The majority of these investments were concentrated in a few strategic sectors such as energy and transportation.[15] In the following decade, however, private Chinese investors from various industries significantly increased their acquisitions of foreign assets and surpassed the SOEs as the primary driving force behind China's investment outflow.[16]

However, the growth of China's outward FDI reached its peak around 2016 (see Figure 1.1), as the central government, alarmed by a precipitous drop in its foreign exchange reserves and concerned about capital flight, reinstalled certain approval requirements for major outbound investment deals.[17] Meanwhile, an abrupt deterioration of US–China relations following the election of Donald Trump dimmed the prospects for the Chinese economy and alerted Chinese investors to geopolitical risks and uncertainties associated with overseas investments, causing a sharp drop in China's outbound FDI.

Chinese FDI in the United States follows a similar trajectory (see Figure 1.2). Before the trade war began, the United States had been

[14] SHAMBAUGH, *supra* note 5, at 178.

[15] Shannon Tiezzi, *China Urges Companies to "Go Global,"* THE DIPLOMAT (December 25, 2014), http://thediplomat.com/2014/12/china-urges-companies-to-go-global/.

[16] Zhang Xiaohe, *Minying Qiye Duiwai Touzi Chaoyue Guoqi Zhuanjia Zhizhao Bi Xianjing* [*Private Enterprises Invest More Overseas Than State-Owned Enterprises; Experts Offer Tips to Avoid Pitfalls*], REN MIN WANG (June 20, 2016), http://finance.people.com.cn/n1/2016/0620/c1004-28463387.html.

[17] Gabriel Wildau, et al., *China to Clamp Down on Outbound M&A in War on Capital Flight*, FINANCIAL TIMES (November 29, 2016), www.ft.com/content/2511fa56-b5f8-11e6-ba85-95d1533d9a62.

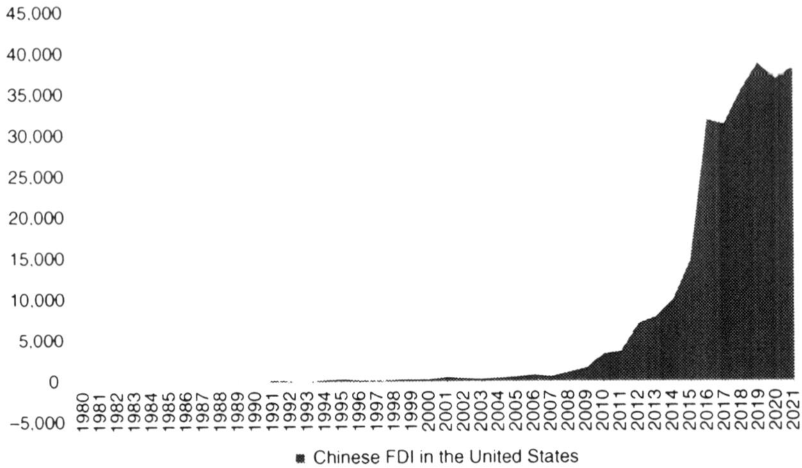

Figure 1.2 Chinese FDI in the United States 1980–2021 (direct investment position on a historical-cost basis; millions of US dollars)
Source: Bureau of Economic Analysis, US Department of Commerce, www.bea.gov/data/intl-trade-investment/direct-investment-country-and-industry.

the largest national recipient of China's outward investment.[18] In contrast to those in resource-rich developing countries, Chinese investments in the United States span various sectors, including real estate, automotive, biotech, and entertainment.[19] Initially, the vast majority of the Chinese investors had embraced long-term business plans and intended to reinvest most or all of their US profits.[20] However, Trump's anti-China policies and the ensuing bipartisan consensus on China as the "most consequential strategic threat" aggravated the already challenging legal and regulatory environment for Chinese investors.[21] New FDI from China dropped significantly, and some investors opted to downsize or even shut down their US operations. Nonetheless, most Chinese investors with substantial US businesses have been reluctant to exit this large, strategically important market.[22]

[18] Cassie Gao & Thilo Hanemann, *Chinese FDI in the US: Tripling Down on America* Rhodium Group (July 22, 2016), http://rhg.com/notes/chinese-fdi-in-the-us-tripling-down-on-america.

[19] *Id.*

[20] Li, *supra* note 3, at 40.

[21] National Security Strategy 11 (October 2022), www.whitehouse.gov/wp-content/uploads/2022/10/Biden-Harris-Administrations-National-Security-Strategy-10.2022.pdf.

[22] *2022 Annual Business Survey Report on Chinese Enterprises in the United States* 22 (June 2022), www.cgccusa.org/wp-content/uploads/2022/07/%E3%80%90FINAL%E3%80%91CGCC-2022-Annual-Report-interactive.pdf.

TikTok's experience in the United States serves as a fitting example. ByteDance, the Chinese owner of TikTok, was founded in 2012 by a twenty-nine-year-old Chinese entrepreneur with an engineering background. After establishing a successful business model in China, ByteDance entered the US market by acquiring Musical.ly in November 2017 and rebranding it as TikTok, a platform for sharing user-generated shortform videos through multifunctional mobile apps.[23] Its proprietary algorithm proved highly effective at retaining users, and in March 2023, TikTok reported as many as 150 million monthly active users in the United States.[24]

With US investment comes litigation. Between the acquisition of Musical.ly and December 2020, TikTok was involved in forty-three lawsuits. Initially, the company had minimal interactions with the US legal system, with only one suit filed against TikTok in 2017 and no litigation in 2018. In 2019, just four lawsuits involved TikTok, a negligible number considering its rapidly growing US operations. However, in 2020, the company participated in thirty-eight US lawsuits. TikTok dealt with a wide variety of cases, not uncommon for a company of its size. Of the total forty-three cases, thirty-nine were filed against TikTok, and among the four lawsuits initiated by TikTok, three named the US government as the defendant.[25] These three high-profile lawsuits warrant detailed analysis, which readers will find in Chapter 6.

The US legal experiences of TikTok are not unique. From Huawei to Bank of China, Chinese companies with operations in the United States increasingly appear in court, often as defendants. But from time to time, Chinese companies take the initiative and "raise the legal weapon" to protect their US interests. However, given the vast institutional differences between China and the United States, the ways in which Chinese companies navigate the US legal system remain an important yet unexplored question.

[23] Musical.ly is a Shanghai-based company with a substantial user base in the United States. See, Liza Lin & Rolfe Winkler, *Social-Media App Musical.Ly Is Acquired for as Much as $1 Billion*, WALL STREET J. (November 9, 2017), www.wsj.com/articles/lip-syncing-app-musical-ly-is-acquired-for-as-much-as-1-billion-1510278123?mod=article_inline.

[24] David Shepardson, *TikTok Hits 150 Mln U.S. Monthly Users, up from 100 Million in 2020*, REUTERS (March 20, 2023), www.reuters.com/technology/tiktok-tell-congress-it-has-150-million-monthly-active-us-users-2023-03-20/.

[25] All the data for this paragraph were collected from Bloomberg Law, www.bloomberglaw.com.

1.2 LITERATURE ON MNCs' INTERACTIONS WITH THE US LEGAL SYSTEM

While Chinese companies may not have received as much attention from socio-legal scholars, the broader debate about how MNCs negotiate US legal risks and opportunities has generated several streams of insightful literature. One stream focuses on the idea of American legal exceptionalism. This theme stems from a comparison of the US approach to legal ordering, termed "adversarial legalism," and the systems found in other economically advanced democracies. The distinct "American way of law," characterized by "formal legal contestation" and "litigation activism,"[26] builds on a network of interconnected institutions:

> An adversarial, lawyer-driven system of litigation shaped by the right to trial by jury; politically-selected, policy-minded judiciaries; a large, entrepreneurial and creative legal profession, armed with powerful tools of pretrial discovery; and a legal culture still pervaded by the idea that law and courts are or should be instruments for effectively protecting individual rights, improving governance, and controlling the exercise of political and economic power.[27]

To substantiate the notion of American legal exceptionalism, researchers have examined the legal and regulatory experiences of MNCs in the United States.[28] The empirical findings suggest that MNCs operating in the US market face additional burdens in the form of onerous legal service expenses and considerable opportunity and compliance costs, which, "while difficult to quantify," are "both salient and troublesome."[29] Without denying some benefits of lawyer-dominated contestation in dispute resolution and government regulation,[30] Kagan and colleagues argue that the US system has "demonstrable, counterproductive consequences," as it pushes foreign investors "toward a more defensive, legalistic relationship with American regulatory officials, consumers, and employees than with their counterparts in other countries."[31] The insightful research, however, focuses only on MNCs headquartered in

[26] Robert A. Kagan, Adversarial Legalism: The American Way of Law 11 (2019).

[27] *Id.*, at 263–64.

[28] Lee Axelrad & Robert A. Kagan, Regulatory Encounters: Multinational Corporations and American Adversarial Legalism 17 (2000).

[29] *Id.*, at 23.

[30] *Id.*

[31] *Id.*

Japan, Canada, Germany, and other post-industrial nations considered to be US allies,[32] and includes only a few case studies from each country, raising questions about the generalizability of the findings.[33]

Another branch of literature, primarily developed by international business scholars, examines the "liability of foreignness" that non-US based MNCs bear when navigating the US legal system. A notable empirical study in this area discovered that foreign-headquartered MNCs are sued more often in the United States than their US counterparts.[34] Once again, the study only considered MNCs from developed countries, likely due to the historical absence of MNCs from developing countries in cross-border investment. Moreover, the existing research has overlooked important topics pertinent to US litigation, such as foreign MNCs' interactions with US lawyers and their development of internal US legal capacity.

Two additional research streams have indirectly explored foreign-based MNCs within the US legal context. First, scholars have debated potential biases against foreign parties in US courts, with one side contending that foreigners and domestic parties receive equal judicial treatment,[35] and the other presenting empirical evidence of systematic bias.[36] Despite these opposing viewpoints, a recent study has found indirect evidence of fair treatment – most Chinese companies with US investments have expressed a positive view of the host-country judiciary.[37] Second, some legal scholars have studied "forum shopping" by foreign parties seeking access to the US judiciary.[38] Although much of this research concentrates on individual rightholders attempting to sue foreign firms in US courts,[39]

[32] Kagan, *supra* note 26, at 9.

[33] Axelrad & Kagan, *supra* note 28, at 17.

[34] John M. Mezias, *Identifying Liabilities of Foreignness and Strategies to Minimize Their Effects: The Case of Labor Lawsuit Judgments in the United States*, 23 Strategic Mgmt J. 229, 241 (2002).

[35] Kevin M. Clermont & Theodore Eisenberg, *Xenophilia in American Courts*, 109 Harv. L. Rev. 1120 (1996); Kevin M. Clermont & Theodore Eisenberg, *Xenophilia or Xenophobia in US Courts? Before and after 9/11*, 4 J. Empirical Legal Stud. 441 (2007).

[36] Kimberly A. Moore, *Xenophobia in American Courts*, 97 Nw. U. L. Rev. 1497 (2002).

[37] Li, *supra* note 3.

[38] Christopher A. Whytock, *The Evolving Forum Shopping System*, 96 Cornell L. Rev. 481 (2010); Donald Earl Childress III, *Escaping Federal Law in Transnational Cases: The Brave New World of Transnational Litigation*, 93 N.C. L. Rev. 995 (2014); Pamela K. Bookman, *The Unsung Virtues of Global Forum Shopping*, 92 Notre Dame L. Rev. 579 (2016).

[39] Donald Earl Childress III, *The Alien Tort Statute, Federalism, and the Next Wave of Transnational Litigation*, 100 Geo. L. J. 709 (2011); Randall S. Thomas & Robert B. Thompson, *A Theory of Representative Shareholder Suits and Its Application to Multijurisdictional Litigation*, 106 Nw. U. L. Rev. 1753 (2012).

and the evolution of relevant US jurisprudence and its policy implications,[40] the literature underscores the agency of transnational litigants (particularly their US lawyers) and the complexity of the US legal institutions, both of which are common themes in the chapters that follow.

In summary, while multiple lines of research have delved into the experiences of MNCs within the US legal system, there remains a conspicuous absence of systematic investigation into how MNCs from developing countries, particularly China, negotiate US legal risks. This book endeavors to address this gap by examining a series of interrelated topics, from the internal legal capacity of Chinese companies in the United States to their preferences and behavior regarding litigation. Besides the literature surveyed in this section, subsequent chapters will leverage insights from research in relevant subject areas. For example, although few scholars have studied the in-house legal capacities of Chinese MNCs – a central theme in Chapter 2 – a sizable body of theoretical and empirical research exists on a closely related topic – the global "in-house counsel movement."[41] Chapter 2 will engage with this scholarship. Likewise, while scant research exists on Chinese companies' litigation in US courts, prior research on trial selection,[42] dispute

[40] Donald Earl Childress III, *When Erie Goes International*, 105 Nw. U. L. Rev. 1531 (2011); Pamela K. Bookman, *Litigation Isolationism*, 67 Stan. L. Rev. 1081 (2015).

[41] Steven L. Schwarcz, *To Make or to Buy: In-House Lawyering and Value Creation*, 33 J. Corp. L. 497 (2007); Omari Scott Simmons & James D. Dinnage, *Innkeepers: A Unifying Theory of the In-House Counsel Role*, 41 Seton Hall L. Rev. 77 (2011); Jonathan C. Lipson, *Who's in the House? The Changing Role and Nature of In-House and General Counsel*, 2012 Wis. L. Rev. 237; Sida Liu, *Palace Wars over Professional Regulation: In-House Counsel in Chinese State-Owned Enterprises*, 2012 Wis. L. Rev. 549; David B. Wilkins, *Is the In-House Counsel Movement Going Global – A Preliminary Assessment of the Role of Internal Counsel in Emerging Economies*, 2012 Wis. L. Rev. 251; David B. Wilkins & Vikramaditya S. Khanna, *Globalization and the Rise of the In-House Counsel Movement in India*, in The Indian Legal Profession in the Age of Globalization: The Rise of the Corporate Legal Sector and its Impact on Lawyers and Society (David B. Wilkins et al. eds., 2017); Fabiana Luci de Oliveira & Luciana Ramos, *In-House Counsels in Brazil*, in The Brazilian Legal Profession in the Age of Globalization: The Rise of the Corporate Legal Sector and its Impact on Lawyers and Society (Luciana Gross Cunha ed., 2018).

[42] George L. Priest & Benjamin Klein, *The Selection of Disputes for Litigation*, 13 J. Legal Stud. 1 (1984); Keith N. Hylton, *Asymmetric Information and the Selection of Disputes for Litigation*, 22 J. Legal Stud. 187 (1993); Peter Siegelman & John J. Donohue III, *The Selection of Employment Discrimination Disputes for Litigation: Using Business Cycle Effects to Test the Priest-Klein Hypothesis*, 24 J. Legal Stud. 427 (1995); Daniel Kessler, et al., *Explaining Deviations from the Fifty-Percent Rule: A Multimodal Approach to the Selection of Cases for Litigation*, 25 J. Legal Stud. 233 (1996); Leandra Lederman, *Which Cases Go to Trial?* 49 Case W. Res. L. Rev. 315 (1999).

resolution,[43] and other relevant topics provide invaluable analytical building blocks for Chapters 4–6. As will be demonstrated throughout this book, examining Chinese companies' experiences within the US legal system both contributes to, and benefits from, these diverse bodies of literature. Despite the seemingly eclectic theoretical mix, this book consistently applies a unifying theoretical framework of institutional duality, effectively linking all subsequent topical analyses in the remaining chapters.

1.3 THEORETICAL FRAMEWORK OF INSTITUTIONAL DUALITY

This book employs a unified framework of institutional duality to dissect the multifaceted interactions between Chinese companies and the complex, rigorous US legal system. An abundance of research on MNCs has explored the influence of institutional environments on crossborder investments, management, and transactions. Despite its subject matter diversity, this body of research draws its intellectual lineage from two theoretical branches, rational choice institutionalism and sociological institutionalism. As these two strains of neoinstitutionalism have already been extensively reviewed and critiqued, and their overlaps and differences well documented elsewhere,[44] a succinct overview of each will suffice for the purposes of this book.

Research grounded in rational choice institutionalism implicitly or explicitly portrays human actors as solving optimization problems,[45] with their choices and preferences constrained by exogenous, behavior-regulating institutions defined variably to suit specific research objectives.[46] In an analytical review of the literature, Williamson aptly

[43] Carrie Menkel-Meadow, *The Trouble with the Adversary System in a Postmodern, Multicultural World*, 38 Wm. & Mary L. Rev. 5 (1996); Carrie Menkel-Meadow, *Mediation, Arbitration, and Alternative Dispute Resolution (ADR)*, International Encyclopedia of the Social and Behavioral Sciences 70 (James D. Wright ed., 2nd ed. 2015).

[44] *See, e.g.*, Thomas A. Koelble, *The New Institutionalism in Political Science and Sociology*, 27 Compar. Pol. 231 (1995); Peter A. Hall & Rosemary C. R. Taylor, *Political Science and the Three New Institutionalisms*, 44 Pol. Stud. 936 (1996); Junko Kato, *Institutions and Rationality in Politics – Three Varieties of Neo-Institutionalists*, 26 Brit. J. Pol. Sci. 553 (1996).

[45] Dani Rodrik, *When Ideas Trump Interests: Preferences, Worldviews, and Policy Innovations*, 28 J. Econ. Persp. 190 (2014).

[46] Douglass C. North, Institutions, Institutional Change, and Economic Performance 3 (1990).

categorizes institutions into four levels, with higher-level institutions "imposing restraints on the level immediately below."[47] At the top of this hierarchy are "institutions of embeddedness," which refers to "norms, customs, mores, and traditions."[48] Although leading rational choice scholars acknowledge the significance of high-level informal institutions in shaping individual preferences and behavior,[49] much of the research in this area is focused on the two levels below – formal institutions safeguarding property rights and governance institutions regulating broadly defined contractual relations – and how these institutions address agency and transaction cost problems.[50]

The collective overlooking of the higher level "institutions of embeddedness" may be attributable to their relative stability.[51] In much of the research adopting this theoretical perspective, informal institutions like social norms tend to remain static, which justifies their analytical exclusion. However, to explore the topics of this book, informal institutions must be taken into account, as they significantly vary between the world's two largest economies, and the ensuing institutional tensions and conflicts characterize the transnational organizational environment for Chinese companies operating in the United States.[52]

In contrast, sociological institutionalism places greater emphasis on "institutions of embeddedness" and accentuates the role of institutions as both conferring meaning to human actions and defining their boundaries. Institutions are not merely restrictive; they also engender agency.[53] Sociological institutionalists, rather than treating "tastes"

[47] Oliver E. Williamson, *The New Institutional Economics: Taking Stock, Looking Ahead*, 38 J. ECON. LIT. 595, 596 (2000).

[48] *Id.*, at 597.

[49] NORTH, *supra* note 46; John Groenewegen, et al., *On Integrating New and Old Institutionalism: Douglass North Building Bridges*, 29 J.ECON. ISSUES, 467 (1995).

[50] Williamson, *supra* note 47, at 599.

[51] *Id.*

[52] While this book adopts the dichotomy of institutions as formal and informal institutions to be consistent with how the questions of interest herein are approached in major socio-legal debates, scholars in other fields such as organizational behavior have divided them into regulative, normative, and cognitive (or cultural-cognitive). *See, e.g.*, Jennifer Palthe, *Regulative, Normative, and Cognitive Elements of Organizations: Implications for Managing Change*, 1 MGMT. & ORG. STUD. 59 (2014). Different typologies, however, should not affect the analytical validity or power of the framework.

[53] Martha Finnemore, *Norms, Culture, and World Politics: Insights from Sociology's Institutionalism*, 50 INT'L ORG. 325, 343 (1996).

or "preferences" as exogenous or static,[54] investigate how institutions enable human actors to "construct" their interests and define the set of choices available for "rational" selection. Moreover, they highlight actions that are spurred by concerns for legitimacy or social appropriateness,[55] or actions that are simply taken for granted,[56] rather than deliberative, utility-maximizing calculations. Empirically, sociological institutionalists underscore corporate isomorphism in their organizational fields, as opposed to the behavioral and preferential heterogeneity often predicted by rational choice institutionalists.[57] Additionally, sociological institutionalism often "over-socialize[s]" human actions, downplaying the role of agency as an exogeneous variable.[58] Under this framework, MNCs tend to be seen as "institutional dopes blindly following the institutionalized scripts and cues around them."[59] However, given the multitude and complexity of "institutional pressures from the metaglobal field, the MNC internally, and the idiosyncratic institutional environment of each particular MNC unit,"[60] as well as the ample space for agency resulting from myriad institutional voids, ambiguities, tensions, and contradictions,[61] the analytical approach

54 Rational choice institutionalists also recognize that preferences are not entirely exogenous, but in their studies preference formation tends to be secondary or assumed away. Groenewegen, et al., *supra* note 49, at 470–71.

55 As noted by Powell and DiMaggio, this emphasis on legitimacy and social appropriateness does not necessary conflict with the rational choice theory as actors may pursue those ends for their functional values: THE NEW INSTITUTIONALISM IN ORGANIZATIONAL ANALYSIS, 33 (Walter W. Powell & Paul J. DiMaggio eds., 2012). *See* Victor Nee & Richard Swedberg, *Economic Sociology and New Institutional Economics*, *in* HANDBOOK OF NEW INSTITUTIONAL ECONOMICS 798 (Claude Ménard & Mary M. Shirley eds., 2005).

56 W. Richard Scott, *Unpacking Institutional Arguments*, THE NEW INSTITUTIONALISM IN ORGANIZATIONAL ANALYSIS, *supra* note 55, at, 179.

57 Paul J. DiMaggio & Walter W. Powell, *The Iron Cage Revisited: Institutional Isomorphism and Collective Rationality in Organizational Fields*, 1983 AM. SOCIO. REV. 147, 148–49; Tatiana Kostova, et al., *Institutional Theory in the Study of Multinational Corporations: A Critique and New Directions*, 33 ACAD. MGMT. REV. 1001 (2008).

58 Mark Granovetter, *Economic Action and Social Structure: The Problem of Embeddedness*, 91 AM. J. SOCIO. 481 (1985).

59 John L. Campbell, *Institutional Analysis and the Role of Ideas in Political Economy*, 27 THEORY AND SOCIETY 377, 382 (1998).

60 Kostova, et al., *supra* note 57, at 999.

61 Kostova, et al., *supra* note 57, at 1001. Because of the heterogeneity of their institutional environment, MNCs exhibit greater diversity and complexity than domestic

of sociological institutionalists falls short in explaining MNCs' preferences and behavior in their transnational field.

Incorporating insights from both theoretical approaches,[62] I devise a dual institutional framework to examine how Chinese companies operating in the United States engage with key components of the host-state legal system. As transnational entities "exposed to two or more cultures, social structures, or sets of routines, one in the home country, and one or more in the host countries in which they operate,"[63] MNCs constantly face disparate and sometimes conflicting institutional pressures[64] that influence their strategies and preferences.[65] Likewise, any national subsidiary of an MNC encounters "dual institutional pressures originating from its home and host countries."[66] When these institutions diverge significantly, as is the case between China and the United States, "competing institutional forces provide different cognitive knowledge, social norms, and regulative policies, which prescribe diverse role models and scripts" for MNC subsidiaries.[67] Hence, inquiries into how Chinese companies navigate the US legal system must account for the institutional differences and possibly diverging "isomorphic pulls"[68] from both the home and the host states.[69] This dual institutional framework extends the rational choice

firms. Martin Kilduff, *The Reproduction of Inertia in Multinational Corporations*, *in* ORGANIZATION THEORY AND THE MULTINATIONAL CORPORATION 259 (Sumantra Ghoshal & D. Eleanor Westney eds., 1993).

[62] Koelble, *supra* note 44, at 235.

[63] Mauro F. Guillén & Sandra L. Suárez, *The Institutional Context of Multinational Activity*, *in* ORGANIZATION THEORY AND THE MULTINATIONAL CORPORATION 124–25 (Sumantra Ghoshal & D. Eleanor Westney eds., 2nd ed., 2005).

[64] Tatiana Kostova & Kendall Roth, *Adoption of an Organizational Practice by Subsidiaries of Multinational Corporations: Institutional and Relational Effects*, 45 ACAD. MGMT. J., 215 (2002).

[65] Gerhard Schnyder & Dorottya Sallai, *Between a Rock and a Hard Place: Internal-and External Institutional Fit of MNE Subsidiary Political Strategy in Contexts of Institutional Upheaval*, 26 J. INT'L MGMT 1, 2 (2020).

[66] Yanlong Zhang, et al., *Institutional Duality and Political Strategies of Foreign-Invested Firms in an Emerging Economy*, 51 J. WORLD BUS. 451, 453 (2016).

[67] *Id.*

[68] D. Eleanor Westney, *Institutionalization Theory and the Multinational Corporation*, 53 ORGANIZATION THEORY AND THE MULTINATIONAL CORPORATION *supra* note 63.

[69] Kostova, et al., *supra* note 57, at 999; Anne Ngoc Vo & Chris Rowley, *The Internationalization of Industrial Relations? Japanese and US Multinational Companies in Vietnam*, 16 ASIA PACIFIC BUS. REV., 222 (2010); Lin Cui & Fuming Jiang, *State Ownership Effect on Firms' FDI Ownership Decisions Under Institutional Pressure: A Study of Chinese Outward-Investing Firms*, 43 J. INT'L BUS. STUD. 264, 266–67 (2012).

institutionalist approach by emphasizing the effects of heterogeneous *informal* institutions and, by underscoring the agency of MNCs and the institutional tensions they face, sets itself apart from sociological institutionalism. Further details of the framework are provided in the sections that follow.[70]

1.3.1 Host-State Institutions of Chinese Companies in the United States

At the risk of stating the obvious, the US institutional contexts in which Chinese companies operate directly modify their managerial behavior and preferences.[71] First, these Chinese companies, now domiciled in the United States, are obligated to comply with US laws and regulations and subject to the general jurisdiction of US courts. In this environment, Chinese companies may adapt individually to an extent that rational choice scholars deem optimal (where the marginal investment in mitigating US legal risks equals the marginal return) or collectively display what sociological institutionalists term "coercive isomorphism."[72] Second, Chinese companies operating in the United States engage continually with local nonstate actors such as customers and suppliers. Steeped in this network of US cultural and normative carriers, these companies are subject to pervasive influence of US "institutions of embeddedness." US norms and values may alter their behavior either by adjusting the payoffs of their strategies, as rational choice institutionalists suggest, or by reformulating their views on the appropriateness or legitimacy of available strategies, as sociological institutionalists propose. Despite the diverging views regarding the causal mechanism, both theoretical approaches predict conforming behavior – Chinese companies behaving similarly to their local counterparts. In summary, to understand how Chinese companies navigate the US legal system, it is essential to consider their host-state institutional environment and its impact on their preferences and behavior. Although this part of the dual institutional framework might seem trivial, its importance should not be understated.

[70] There is also a sizable literature of legal pluralism, which examines "overlapping normative orders within societies": Ralf Michaels, *Global Legal Pluralism*, 5 ANN. REV. L. & SOC. SCI. 245 (2009). While the broad concept of legal pluralism overlaps with the dual institutional framework, the bulk of the existing research has been conducted by legal anthropologists and sociologists, which is mainly ethnographic and descriptive. For a summary of the literature, see Paul Schiff Berman, *The New Legal Pluralism*, 5 ANN. REV. L. & SOC. SCI. 225 (2009).

[71] Cui & Jiang, *supra* note 69, at 266–67.

[72] DiMaggio & Powell, *supra* note 57.

1.3.2 Home-State Institutions of Chinese Companies in the United States

While it is well documented that MNCs often carry features of their home-state institutions "with them when expanding abroad,"[73] few studies have explored their impacts on MNCs' adaptation, or lack thereof, to host-state *legal* environments. Filling that gap, the dual institutional framework developed here pays special attention to the influence of home-state formal institutions, such as laws and regulations, and informal institutions, such as social and cultural norms governing compliance and litigation.[74] To simplify, I classify the home-state institutional influence into direct and indirect effects.

Both formal and informal home-state institutions can directly influence Chinese companies operating in the United States.[75] Certain Chinese laws and regulations apply extraterritorially to Chinese businesses overseas. The long arm of Chinese laws has been extending as a result of China's growing economy and sprawling worldwide interests,[76] and, in certain instances, as countermeasures to the extraterritorial application of US laws.[77] Moreover, most senior executives at Chinese companies in the United States, especially those of state ownership, remain Chinese citizens.[78] These expatriates, most of whom reasonably

[73] Guillén & Suárez, *supra* note 63, at 123.

[74] *See, e.g.*, Schon Beechler & Zhuang Yang John, *The Transfer of Japanese-Style Management to American Subsidiaries: Contingencies, Constraints, and Competencies*, 25 J. INT'L BUS. STUD. 467 (1994); Anthony Ferner, *Country of Origin Effects and HRM in Multinational Companies*, 7 HUMAN RES. MGMT. J. 19 (1997); Raymond Fisman & Edward Miguel, *Corruption, Norms, and Legal Enforcement: Evidence from Diplomatic Parking Tickets*, 115 J. POL. ECON. 1020 (2007); Saul Estrin, et al., *Home Country Institutions and the Internationalization of State Owned Enterprises: A Cross-Country Analysis*, 51 J. WORLD BUS. 294 (2016).

[75] Sociological and organizational research about the home-state institutional influence uses the term "imprinting" to describe the continuous effects of the institutional features reflected in the corporate routines and habits at the founding of MNCs: Guillén & Suárez, *supra* 124–25. For the purposes of this book, however, the concept is too vague and narrow. For instance, formal Chinese institutions impose extraterritorial restraints over Chinese MNCs' foreign subunits, which is specific to and beyond the typically defined institutional "imprinting effects."

[76] Guillén & Suárez, *supra* note 63, 124–25; Zhengxin Huo & Man Yip, *Extraterritoriality of Chinese Law: Myths, Realities and the Future*, 2021 CHINESE J. COMPAR. L. 328.

[77] *See, e.g*, Huo & Yip, *supra* note 76, at 352; Ji Li, *Superpower Legal Rivalry and the Global Compliance Dilemma*, 45 U. PA. J. INT'L L. (forthcoming, 2024).

[78] LI, *supra* note 3.

anticipate returning to China, are theoretically subject to the jurisdiction of Chinese laws based on their citizenship.

Meanwhile, informal Chinese institutions (i.e., "institutions of embeddedness" such as social norms and cultural values) can also directly affect Chinese companies in the United States.[79] These institutions,[80] often regarded as preserving stability amid fluctuations in domestic settings,[81] exert two distinct influences on transnational actors' behavior and preferences: cognitive effects and normative effects.[82] Cognitive components of an informal institution, often taken for granted and "virtually invisible to the actors themselves,"[83] provide descriptions, theories, schemata, and scripts that "specify cause-and-effect relationships"[84] and "influence the way a particular phenomenon is categorized and interpreted."[85] On the other hand, normative components relate to values and attitudes toward objectives, choices, and actions.[86] These cognitive and normative influences shape the perspectives, values, and interpretations of top managers at Chinese companies operating in the United States, who are often expatriates and "carriers of institutions,"[87] as they navigate the US legal landscape.[88] Confronted

[79] Christopher Marquis & András Tilcsik, *Imprinting: Toward a Multilevel Theory*, 7 Acad. Mgmt. Annals 204 (2013).

[80] Culture is notoriously difficult to define and has been assigned a wide range of meanings such as the "underlying codes of meaning and conduct." John Van Maanen, *Mickey on the Move: Observations on the Flow of Culture in the Multinational Corporation*, *in* Organizational Theory and the Multinational Corporation (2005), *supra note* 63, at 255; and "collective programming of the mind," or "norms, values, shared meanings, and cognitive structures." Guillén & Suárez, *supra* note 63, at 131. This book adopts the broad enumerative definition of culture but breaks it down into two parts based on its effects on the preferences and behavior of MNC actors.

[81] Williamson, *supra* note 47, at, 597; Guillén & Suárez, *supra* note 63, at, 123–24.

[82] Campbell, *supra* note 59, at, 378.

[83] *Id.*, at 381; Westney, *supra* note 69, at 49–50.

[84] Campbell, *supra* note 59, at 378–384.

[85] Kostova & Roth, *supra* note 65, at, 217.

[86] Campbell, *supra* note 59, at 384.

[87] Kostova & Roth, *supra* note 65, 218.

[88] Guy L. F. Holburn & Bennet A. Zelner, *Political Capabilities, Policy Risk, and International Investment Strategy: Evidence from the Global Electric Power Generation Industry*, 31 Strategic Mgmt J. 1290, 1292–93 (2010); Klaus E. Meyer & Htwe Htwe Thein, *Business Under Adverse Home Country Institutions: The Case of International Sanctions Against Myanmar*, 49 J. World Bus. 156, 158 (2014).

with normative and cognitive discrepancies in a heterogenous environment, middle-aged Chinese executives naturally resist significant changes that "threaten individuals' sense of security, increase the cost of information processing, and disrupt routines."[89] Additionally, rapid technological progress since the 2010s has made cross-country socialization more accessible and virtually cost-free, reinforcing the norms and scripts internalized by expatriates before their overseas assignments and influencing their law-related preferences and behaviors in the United States.[90] In summary, both formal laws and informal norms may directly affect the US operations of Chinese MNCs.

Home-state institutions can also indirectly influence Chinese companies operating in the United States through their headquarters.[91] As legal entities based in China, the parent companies must, at least in theory, ensure that their overseas operations comply with relevant Chinese laws. For instance, as will be detailed shortly, Chinese regulations governing SOEs mandate timely reporting of material foreign legal risks, which may alter the way state-owned Chinese companies approach US litigation. Moreover, informal home-state institutions may also indirectly affect foreign operations through their headquarters, as the norms and values shape how executives at the helm of a global business empire interact with staff at foreign subsidiaries by interpreting or evaluating the behavior of local managers.

Additionally, MNCs' internal organizational structures often facilitate the transmission of home-state institutional pressure to foreign affiliates.[92] To reduce agency problems and transaction costs,[93] headquarters typically design and disseminate corporate rules and practices to subsidiaries.[94] Even without deliberate top-down diffusion of corporate routines, rules, and structures, local managers may engage in internal mimetic isomorphism, copying the actions and organizational structures of the headquarters when dealing with unfamiliar

[89] Powell, *Expanding the Scope of Institutional Analysis*, The New Institutionalism in Organizational Analysis, *supra* note 55, 194.

[90] Sumantra Ghoshal & Christopher A. Bartlett, *The Multinational Corporation as an Interorganizational Network*, 15 Acad. Mgmt. Rev. 606 (1990).

[91] Kostova, et al., *supra* note 57, at 998; Kostova & Roth, *supra* note 65, at, 218–19.

[92] Kostova, et al., *supra* note 57, at 999.

[93] Such measures are compelled by the strong demand for efficiency within MNEs as profit-driven business associations competing for survival in a globalized economy. Ghoshal & Bartlett, *supra* note 90, at 612.

[94] Kostova & Roth, *supra* note 65, at 218.

complex situations in the host country.[95] Moreover, the internal organizational dynamics both mediate and reflect the institutional effects, rendering them less deterministic.[96] Thus, the relationship between a Chinese MNC's headquarters and its US operations, previously studied under the framework of agency theory or transaction cost theory,[97] remains an important variable to consider, especially in research about intra-organizational personnel arrangement such as the appointment of in-house legal managers in the United States.[98]

1.3.3 Dual Institutional Influences

The two preceding subsections have succinctly highlighted the dual institutional influence that Chinese companies endure while traversing the US legal environment. The ensuing chapters will empirically explore the manifestation of the influence. Topics include the development of internal legal capacities, the selection of US lawyers and consumption of legal services, and their litigation experiences within US courts. Yet, this book does more than merely presenting a special case of transnational legal pluralism.[99] It takes a major step further by theorizing and investigating how the dual institutional influence varies across firms and its effects on these companies' interactions with and impacts on the US legal system.

The starting point of the theoretical construction is an inquiry about institutional difference. As alluded to earlier, when an MNC's home and host-state institutional contexts align, the force of inertia is likely to dominate,[100] leading the MNC to organize and manage its foreign affiliate akin to a domestic subsidiary.[101] The inertia will meet little

95 *See, e.g.*, Westney, *supra* note 69, *at* 58; Philip M. Rosenzweig & Jitendra V. Singh, *Organizational Environments and the Multinational Enterprise*, 16 ACAD. MGMT. REV. 340 (1991).

96 Kostova, et al., *supra* note 57, at 999.

97 The principal-agent structure characterizes the headquarters-subsidiary relationship in MNCs. Yaping Gong, *Subsidiary Staffing in Multinational Enterprises: Agency, Resources, and Performance*, 46 ACAD. MGMT. J. 729.

98 Kostova & Roth, *supra* note 65, at, 218.

99 For a review of the literature on legal pluralism in the global context, see Michaels, *supra* note 70.

100 Jacques Delacroix, *Ecological Analysis of MNCs*, *in* ORGANIZATION THEORY AND THE MULTINATIONAL CORPORATION, *supra* note 57, at 95.

101 Michael T. Hannan & John Freeman, *Structural Inertia and Organizational Change*, 49 AM. SOCIO. REV. 149 (1984). By comparison, some argue that organizational inertia at MNCs is "achieved only at great effort and cost." Kilduff, *supra* note 61, at 241.

resistance. Canadian companies, for instance, can probably transpose their management preferences and practices onto their US subsidiaries, which likely dovetail with local expectations. However, when the institutional environments diverge significantly, host-state institutional pressure can disrupt and modify the inertial structures, preferences, and behaviors.[102] The wider the institutional chasm, the more substantial the hurdles and costs the MNC confronts in adapting to the host-state environment.

Notably, the institutional gaps vary at the firm level, reflecting differences in both formal and informal institutional contexts for Chinese companies operating in the United States. Regarding the formal dual institutional context, Chinese companies differ systematically based on their ownership type. As will be elaborated shortly, state-owned Chinese companies must navigate a unique set of formal rules and regulatory mechanism designed to incentivize their staff toward achieving multiple, fluid, and often ambiguous goals.[103] This unique, ownership-specific institutional environment can exacerbate agency problems and increase transaction costs significantly as these companies engage with market players and regulatory bodies in the United States.[104] And the distinct institutional effect may surface in various legal dimensions. For instance, to address enhanced agency and transaction costs, state-owned Chinese investors may lean toward expatriating home-state managers, who are trusted, well acquainted with the home-state institutions, and privy to firm-specific information, to oversee US legal matters. The same institutional influence may also modify the way in which state-owned Chinese companies select US lawyers or litigate US disputes.

In addition to formal institutional disparities, Chinese companies must grapple with variable informal institutional gaps between their home and host states. The variations are determined by numerous factors such as a firm's embeddedness in the home-state environment, corporate decision-makers' education, age, and exposure to diverse

[102] Kildutt, *supra* note 61, at 241.

[103] For a summary of the research on the agency costs plaguing SOEs, see Alvaro Cuervo-Cazurra & Cheng Li, *State Ownership and Internationalization: The Advantage and Disadvantage of Stateness*, 56 J. WORLD BUS. 1, 10 (2021).

[104] Meanwhile, certain US institutions also differentiate foreign SOEs, especially those owned by a non-allied governments, for enhanced scrutiny or restriction. Such institutions (e.g., national security review of foreign investment), however, are limited in number, and will be discussed when necessary in the following chapters.

cultures, and intra-enterprise decision-making dynamics.[105] Broad disparities in norms and values can result in miscommunication, mistrust, and conflicting beliefs and expectations, which generally give rise to high transaction costs and disputes. The gaps may also impact how Chinese companies navigate the US legal landscape. Those facing significant cultural hurdles in the United States, for instance, may prefer local lawyers with Chinese backgrounds, who can more effectively bridge these gaps. Moreover, companies facing large normative discrepancies may struggle to defuse disputes, consequently becoming more susceptible to US lawsuits.

The manner in which Chinese companies respond to differences in the dual institutional environment, formal as well as informal, also hinges on the equilibrium of the divergent and competing institutional pulls. Specifically, the preferences and behaviors of a Chinese company operating in the United States may vary according to the balance of the institutional pressures – "which side of these institutional pressures (often channeled through organizational linkages with the environments) is more potent and exerts a stronger impact."[106] At the same time, the companies, while pulled away from their habitual systems of cognition, internalized norms, routines and actions, may resist or strategically implement nonconforming responses.[107] These interactions determine not only the manner, velocity and extent of the companies' host-state adaptation, but also their impacts on the host-state institutional environment. Scholars have long recognized that "multinational practices influence local environment,"[108] and the extent of the influence depends largely on their relationships with the constituents of the organizational field, such as suppliers, customers, and US regulatory agencies.[109] If the companies have more leverage over these local actors, part of the host-state institutional pressure may be diminished

[105] Martin Owusu Ansah & Lynette Louw, *The Influence of National Culture on Organizational Culture of Multinational Companies*, 5 COGENT SOC. SCI. 1 (2019); Susan C. Schneider, *National vs. Corporate Culture: Implications for Human Resource Management*, 27 HUMAN RES. MGMT. 231 (1988).

[106] Zhang, et al., *supra* note 66, at 453.

[107] Patrick Regnér & Jesper Edman, *MNE Institutional Advantage: How Subunits Shape, Transpose and Evade Host Country Institutions*, 45 J. INT'L BUS. STUD. 275.

[108] Jean-François Hennart, *Control in Multinational Firms: The Role of Price and Hierarchy*, *in* ORGANIZATION THEORY AND THE MULTINATIONAL CORPORATION, *supra* note 63, at 119.

[109] Westney, *supra* note 61, at 49–50; Hennart, *supra* note 108, at 119.

or offset.[110] Otherwise, we shall observe adaptation and assimilation,[111] with the host-state institutional influence eclipsing that of the company's home state.[112]

To illustrate the point, consider the impacts of Western MNCs on Chinese institutions. Up until quite recently, foreign-invested firms in China wielded considerable leverage over their local suppliers, customers, and even regulators.[113] Consequently, investors from the United States and other developed countries, while adjusting to the Chinese environment in myriad ways, managed to maintain many of their home-state practices, and by doing so significantly transformed their organizational fields in China. For instance, recent empirical research suggests that Chinese regions with concentrated direct investments from the United States and Europe developed better courts.[114] In stark contrast, the remainder of this book will show that Chinese MNCs, typically lacking leverage over key US market and state actors, have made no more than marginal impacts on the host-state legal institutions.

Figure 1.3 illustrates the different sets of home and host-state institutions that will guide the analysis of the interconnected topics in Chapters 2–6: the internal legal capacity of Chinese companies in the United States; their selection of US lawyers and consumption of US legal services; and their dispute resolution and litigation in US courts. Note that the dual institutional environment varies across these different subject areas.[115] For instance, the dual institutions governing the production and purchase of legal services are related to, yet distinct from, those regulating dispute resolution. Therefore, within the dual institutional framework, the analysis of each subject will commence with a detailed issue-specific institutional comparison.

In summary, this book constructs an analytical model of dual institutional influence and employs it to explore how Chinese companies navigate the complex US legal system. It investigates formal and informal

[110] An actor has more leverage if it possesses more resources, defined as "activity, service, or commodity" valued by the other parties in the field. Ghoshal & Bartlett, *supra* note 90, at, 607.

[111] Westney, *supra* note 61, at 51.

[112] *Id.*, at 49.

[113] For the purposes of this book, leverage is regarded as a manifestation of power, which correlates with resource dependence. For a thorough review of the concept and the resource dependence theory, see Amy J. Hillman, et al., *Resource Dependence Theory: A Review*, 35 J. MGMT. 1404 (2009).

[114] YUHUA WANG, TYING THE AUTOCRAT'S HANDS 15 (2015).

[115] Kostova & Roth, *supra* note 65, at, 217.

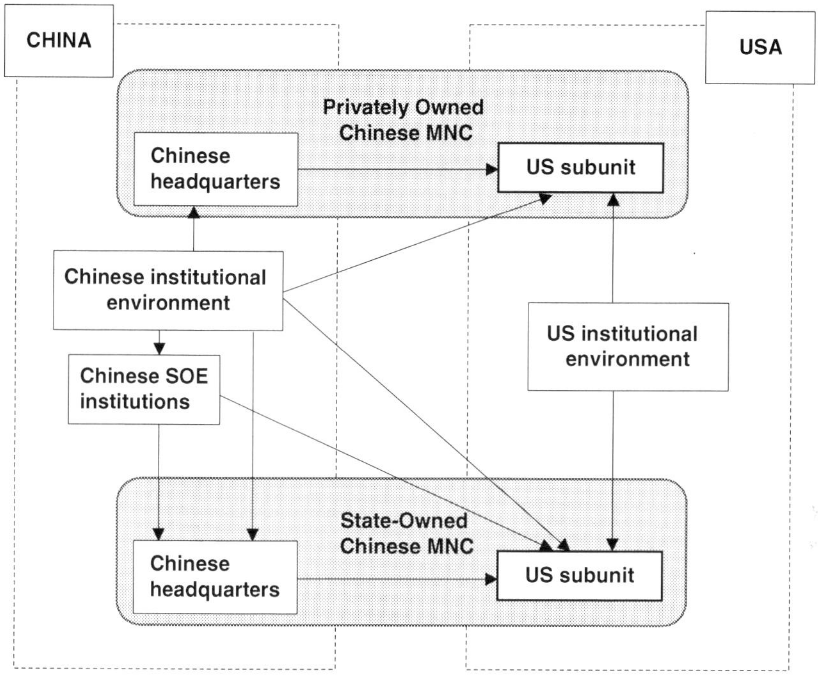

Figure 1.3 Dual institutional influence on Chinese companies operating in the United States

institutions of both the home and the host states while accounting for inter-company variations.[116] Among the multiple factors that differentiate the Chinese institutional environment from that of the United States, this book pays particular attention to a unique institutional feature: the state ownership of certain Chinese investors. Before proceeding, Section 1.4 below sketches the main characteristics of the broad institutional environment of China, particularly the SOE institutions, to provide readers with the necessary background knowledge and avoid repetition in subsequent topical analyses.

1.4 HOME-STATE INSTITUTIONAL ENVIRONMENT AND INSTITUTIONS FOR SOEs

The post-Cultural Revolution era witnessed the metamorphosis of China from an impoverished hermit state to the world's second-largest

[116] Mainstream studies of FDI have rarely applied a comparative approach. Hennart *supra* note 108, at 111.

economy with a relatively open and dynamic market. In this transformative process, business organizations evolved in sync with their legal and regulatory environments. Prior to the economic liberalization, the Chinese government owned and micro-managed most business enterprises,[117] which suffered inefficiency and incurred continuous losses.[118] The government experimented with various performance enhancement schemes, yet almost all of them failed.[119] At the same time, businesses with alternative ownership structures sprouted and, without the organizational weaknesses of the SOEs, proved highly competitive.[120] Their success enabled the reformers to make the case for a radical reform.[121]

In the mid-1990s, the reformers began the massive privatization of the SOEs,[122] with the goal of establishing a "socialist market economy."[123] A policy of "grabbing the big and letting go [of] the small" was implemented, resulting in the privatization of most small and medium-sized SOEs. The government, however, retained ownership over large SOEs in key strategic sectors.[124] When the dust settled, a sui generis economic system took shape. A defining feature of the system is a cohort of "modernized" SOEs,[125] which underwent corporatization and adopted organizational structures resembling contemporary Western firms.[126]

117 Sujian Guo, *The Ownership Reform in China: What Direction and How Far?*, 12 JOURNAL OF CONTEMPORARY CHINA 553, 556 (2003).

118 Xiaobo Hu, *The State, Enterprises, and Society in Post-Deng China: Impact of the New Round of SOE Reform*, 40 ASIAN SURVEY 641 (2000); Yongnian Zheng & Minjia Chen, *China's State-Owned Enterprise Reform and Its Discontents*, 56 PROBLEMS OF POST-COMMUNISM 36 (2009).

119 Guo, *supra* note 117, at 556–57.

120 Barry Naughton, *Chinese Institutional Innovation and Privatization from Below*, 84 AM. ECON. REV. 266, 268 (1994).

121 Hongbin Cai & Daniel Treisman, *Did Government Decentralization Cause China's Economic Miracle?* 58 WORLD POLIT. 505 (2006); YUEN YUEN ANG, HOW CHINA ESCAPED THE POVERTY TRAP (2016).

122 Ross Garnaut, et al., *Impact and Significance of State-Owned Enterprise Restructuring in China*, 2006 CHINA J. 37.

123 Gary Sigley, *Chinese Governmentalities: Government, Governance and the Socialist Market Economy*, 35 ECON. & SOC'Y 487 (2006).

124 Zheng & Chen, *supra* note 118, at, 37.

125 Chi-Wen Jevons Lee, *Financial Restructuring of State Owned Enterprises in China: The Case of Shanghai Sunve Pharmaceutical Corporation*, 26 ACCOUNTING, ORG. & SOC'Y 673, 681 (2001).

126 Scott Waldron, et al., *State Sector Reform and Agriculture in China*, 186 CHINA Q. 290 (2006). Formally, the corporate governance structure of Chinese corporations bears more resemblance to German companies than US companies.

Over time, many of the SOEs have listed their stocks on major securities exchanges in China and abroad.[127]

The Chinese government also adjusted its mode of control over these "modernized" SOEs. First, it consolidated the supervision of the largest national SOEs and delegated it to a newly established agency under the State Council – the State-Owned Assets Supervision and Administration Commission (SASAC). The SASAC functions as both the nominal controlling shareholder and the primary regulator of the national SOEs. Instead of engaging in micro-management,[128] the SASAC periodically reviews important corporate matters, evaluates senior corporate officers, and makes long-term strategic business plans for the SOEs under its supervision.[129] The agency is also responsible for implementing rules and regulations concerning the preservation of state assets.[130] Modeled after the national agency, the provincial and municipal SASACs supervise Chinese SOEs of their corresponding levels in all business sectors.[131]

127 Laixiang Sun & Damian Tobin, *International Listing as a Mechanism of Commitment to More Credible Corporate Governance Practices: The Case of the Bank of China (Hong Kong)*, 13 Corp. Governance 81, 82 (2005).

128 Jonathan G. S. Koppell, *Political Control for China's State-Owned Enterprises: Lessons from America's Experience with Hybrid Organizations*, 20 Governance 255, 265–66 (2007).

129 Li-Wen Lin & Curtis J. Milhaupt, *We Are the (National) Champions: Understanding the Mechanism of State Capitalism in China*, 65 Stan. L. Rev. 697, 738–43 (2013).

130 While the SOEs under the nominal management of the SASAC are clearly among the largest in China, there are many sizable centrally controlled SOEs that, for historical reasons, remain outside SASAC's jurisdiction. Currently about 6,000 such SOEs exist and are controlled by approximately 80 central government agencies. Unirule Institute of Economics, *The Nature, Performance, and Reform of the State-Owned Enterprises* (April 12, 2011), 34, at www.unirule.org.cn/xiazai/2011/20110412.pdf. For these SOEs, the Ministry of Finance exercises "ownership rights" on behalf of the central government. Moreover, state agencies traditionally in charge of propaganda still hold control over assets such as most television stations, mass media publishers, and movie producers.

131 The government of Beijing, for instance, supervises SOEs in areas such as real estate, utilities, public transportation, steel making, pharmaceuticals, construction, insurance, and commercial retailing. *See* official webpage of the SASAC of Beijing Municipal Government, accessed February 25, 2014, www.bjgzw.gov.cn/QtCommonAction.do?method=xxcx&type=0000006010&flag_qt=6.

A sophisticated nomenklatura system enables the state to realize its effective control over the SOEs,[132] with the central government making personnel decisions over officials of the vice-ministerial or vice-provincial level and above.[133] Promotion of SOE staff to positions at this level is overseen by the Central Organization Department of the CCP, with the Political Bureau having the final say.[134] In this process, the SASAC, as the regulating government agency, plays an extensive role.[135] Apart from the SASAC, other party and state agencies may also assert control over Chinese SOEs either directly pursuant to special rules,[136] or indirectly through their supervision over SOE employees who are CCP members.[137]

Though transformational in myriad ways,[138] the SOE reform and the contraction of the state sector are by no means a linear process. The global financial crisis and its aftermath greatly empowered Chinese SOEs,[139] and the central government has been sending contradictory signals ever since about the intended role of SOEs in the economy. While some top officials insisted on further deepening the market reform,[140] others charged the SOEs to grow "larger and stronger."[141]

[132] Wendy Leutert, *The Political Mobility of China's Central State-Owned Enterprise Leaders*, 233 CHINA Q. 1–2 (2018).

[133] PIERRE F. LANDRY, DECENTRALIZED AUTHORITARIANISM IN CHINA: THE COMMUNIST PARTY'S CONTROL OF LOCAL ELITES IN THE POST-MAO ERA (2008).

[134] Chen Li, *Holding "China Inc." Together: The CCP and the Rise of China's Yangqi*, 228 CHINA Q. 927, 937 (2016).

[135] Ruilong Yang, et al., *Zhunguanyuan Jinsheng Jizhi: Laizi Zhongguo Yangqi de Zhengju ("Promotion Mechanism for Quasi-officials: Evidence from Chinese Centrally-Controlled Enterprises")*, MGMT. WORLD, 4 (2013).

[136] For instance, state-owned banks in China are under direct control of the Ministry of Finance, not the SASAC.

[137] Chen Li, *supra* note 134, at, 939.

[138] EDWARD S. STEINFELD, PLAYING OUR GAME: WHY CHINA'S RISE DOESN'T THREATEN THE WEST (2010).

[139] By the end of 2011 there were totally 144,715 Chinese SOEs in total. *See* WEIBING QIAO, CHINA'S STATE-OWNED ASSETS SUPERVISION AND ADMINISTRATION YEARBOOK 735 (2012).

[140] Cary Huang, *Party's Third Plenum Pledges "Decisive Role" for Markets in China's Economy*, SOUTH CHINA MORNING POST (November 12, 2013), at www.scmp.com/news/china/article/1354411/chinas-leadership-approves-key-reform-package-close-third-plenum.

[141] Xiaoyi Shao & Matthew Miller, *China Aims to Make State-owned Firms "Stronger, Better, Larger,"* REUTERS (September 13, 2015), at www.reuters.com/article/china-soe-reform-idUSB9N11D01920150914.

Meanwhile, the CCP has reasserted its absolute reign over SOEs,[142] marking a sharp reversal of the previous policy to "separate management from politics"[143] and further blurring the boundary of the state.[144]

As the Chinese market expanded, non-state-owned business enterprises also grew in number and scale. Though they initially lacked state support and institutional legitimacy, the market reform improved their macro-environment, and some have since managed to achieve global competitiveness, especially in sectors traditionally unoccupied by powerful central level SOEs. Also, an increasing number of privately owned Chinese firms have gone public, enabling state investors to purchase significant equity interest in such firms.[145]

In brief, the market reform of the last few decades gave rise to a distinct economic system, often labeled as state capitalism with Chinese characteristics.[146] It features government dominance over strategic and important industries with direct ownership control over corporatized SOEs or through policy and regulatory intervention, and an expanding, dynamic market highly integrated in the global economy.[147]

To facilitate the "socialist market economy," the central government enacted a comprehensive set of new laws and regulations that borrowed extensively from the existing laws and legal principles of the United States and other developed countries.[148] Despite the convergence in formal laws and legal principles, the laws in action are vastly different between China and the United States. Since the end of the Cultural Revolution, Chinese courts have been undergoing rapid changes. Historically designated as a state instrument for class oppression, the Chinese judiciary had been staffed by loyal veterans without any formal

142 John Zhuang Liu & Angela Huyue Zhang, *Ownership and Political Control: Evidence from Charter Amendments*, 60 Int'l Rev. L. & Econ. 1, 3 (2019).

143 Emily Feng, *Xi Jinping Reminds China's State Companies of Who's the Boss*, NY Times (October 13, 2016), at www.nytimes.com/2016/10/14/world/asia/china-soe-state-owned-enterprises.html.

144 Cui & Jiang, *supra* note 69, at 265.

145 Curtis Milhaupt & Wentong Zheng, *Beyond Ownership: State Capitalism and the Chinese Firm*, 103 Geo. L.J. 665, 672 (2015).

146 Barry Naughton & Kellee S. Tsai, State Capitalism, Institutional Adaptation, and the Chinese Miracle (2015).

147 *Id.*

148 Gao Hongjun, *The Globalization of American Law: Typical Examples and Jurisprudential Reflections*, 1 China Legal Sci. 003 (2011).

legal education until 1998, when the *Law on Judges* took effect, requiring candidates for the judiciary to obtain a college degree and pass the national judicial examination.[149] Concurrent with the professionalization of the judiciary, the number of first instance cases rose dramatically from 906,051 in 1981 to 30,805,000 in 2020.[150] Meanwhile, the Chinese bar expanded from near non-existence toward the end of the Cultural Revolution to an association of 574,800 practicing lawyers in 2021.[151] Legal education also bloomed, with tens of thousands of students graduating each year from more than six hundred law programs.[152] The remarkable progress notwithstanding, the Chinese judiciary remains subordinated to the CCP, and personal connections or the power distribution of litigants, rather than relevant statutes, often determine how lawsuits of political, social, and economic significance transpire.[153]

For much of the reform period, Chinese laws and regulations lagged behind the fast-changing economy and society. To a certain extent, the Chinese experience exemplifies an institutional version of Schumpeterian creative destruction. Risk-taking entrepreneurs pushed porous institutional boundaries with unsolicited and implicit support from the reformers among the ruling elites, who then selectively legitimated and formalized the incremental changes, which motivated further grassroots entrepreneurial experiments. The incessant recursive process gave rise to more market friendly institutions that gradually replaced the rigid Soviet-style planned economy.[154] However, among the downsides of this institutional creative destruction is an entrenched culture of disrespect for formal rules and procedures and legal uncertainties for social and economic transactions. Embedded in such an institutional

[149] Benjamin L. Liebman, *China's Courts: Restricted Reform*, 21 COLUM. J. ASIAN L. 1, 13 (2007).

[150] 2020 Report of Supreme People's Court (March 15, 2021), at www.gov.cn/xinwen/2021-03/15/content_5593012.htm.

[151] Statistical Analysis of Lawyers and Grassroots Legal Services in 2021, Ministry of Justice Government website, www.moj.gov.cn/pub/sfbgw/zwxxgk/fdzdgknr/fdzdgknrtjxx/202208/t20220815_461680.html2.

[152] Carl F. Minzner, *The Rise and Fall of Chinese Legal Education*, 36 FORDHAM INT'L L.J. 334, 349 (2013).

[153] Ji Li, *The Power Logic of Justice in China*, 65 AM. J. COMPAR. L. 95 (2017); Xin He & Kwai Hang Ng, *"It Must Be Rock Strong!" Guanxi's Impact on Judicial Decision Making in China*, 65 AM. J. COMPAR. L. 841 (2017); Yuen Yuen Ang & Nan Jia, *Perverse Complementarity: Political Connections and the Use of Courts among Private Firms in China*, 76 J. POL. 318 (2014).

[154] Naughton, *supra* note 120, at 266; ANG, *supra* note 121.

environment, Chinese managers often under-appreciate legal and regulatory risks or deal with them in a highly opportunistic manner.[155]

Within this transitional Chinese social setting, actions invoking the application of formal law (e.g., litigation) have acquired ingrained and contextualized extra-judicial meanings. For instance, as just noted, the judiciary's subordination to political power and the incremental legal reform marginalized the role of Chinese courts in private ordering. Long regarded as an ineffective means of resolving high-stakes disputes, litigation in such an institutional context can be viewed as a sign of incompetence or lack of political resources.[156] Firms striving to avoid sending such a signal would be reluctant to litigate. Additionally, due to the relatively peripheral role of law, many business transactions in China have relied on relational contracts impervious to formalistic judicial intervention.[157] In short, depending on the specific context, litigation or the threat thereof contains a variety of socially constructed meanings such as incompetence, hostility, desperation, vindication, or an intent to end a cooperative relationship.

How do firms interact with such a legal system? First, Chinese SOEs may differ from privately owned enterprises (POEs) in this regard. As the Chinese party-state continues to rely on SOEs to implement its policies, raise revenues, and maintain social control,[158] profit maximization is rarely the primary, or even a prioritized, goal for SOE managers.[159] The multitasking of Chinese SOEs complicates their management of risks, including legal risks. Moreover, government ownership spawns an acute multiagency problem.[160] While the separation of ownership and control

[155] Li, *supra* note 3, at 66.

[156] Alena V. Ledeneva, Can Russia Modernise?: Sistema, Power Networks and Informal Governance 161 (2013).

[157] For an explanation of the concept, *see, e.g.*, Stewart Macaulay, *Non-Contractual Relations in Business: A Preliminary Study*, 1963 Am. Socio. Rev. 55; Lisa Bernstein, *Opting out of the Legal System: Extralegal Contractual Relations in the Diamond Industry*, 21 J. Legal Stud. 359 (1992).

[158] Naughton & Tsai, *supra* note 146, at 9–10 (2015).

[159] *See, e.g.*, Chong-En Bai, et al., *The Multitask Theory of State Enterprise Reform: Empirical Evidence from China*, 96 Am. Econ. Rev. 353 (2006); Estrin, et al., *supra* note 74.

[160] *See, e.g.*, Zhou Mi & Xiaoming Wang, *Agency Cost and the Crisis of China's SOE*, 11 China Econ. Rev. 297 (2001); Garry D. Bruton, et al., *State-Owned Enterprises around the World as Hybrid Organizations*, 29 Acad. Mgmt. Persp. 92 (2015); Mike W. Peng, et al., *Theories of the (State-Owned) Firm*, 33 Asia Pacific J. Mgmt. 293 (2016).

has long been the hallmark of modern corporations, the misalignment of interests is more severe in Chinese SOEs, as their managers answer to multiple layers of supervising bodies, and none possesses a genuine ownership interest.[161] The complex agency problem begets suboptimal responses to corporate legal risks. On the one hand, SOE managers heavily discount losses from the companies' illegal acts and therefore may under-invest in diagnostic and preventive measures such as employing competent in-house counsel. On the other hand, SOE managers may over-invest in mitigating legal risks as cost savings generate no immediate personal benefits, whereas conspicuous breaches of law may reach the public domain and jeopardize their careers. Despite the predictive ambivalence, Chinese SOEs historically under-invested in the management of legal risks,[162] as their political influence begets favorable adjudicatory bias, providing a layer of protection for the directors and managers.[163] However, as will be detailed in Chapter 2, the SASAC has taken the management of overseas legal risks more seriously, so how state-owned Chinese MNCs navigates the US legal system remains an open empirical question.

Unlike SOEs, private Chinese companies must maintain a delicate relationship with the state.[164] Without the political status of SOEs, private companies approach legal risks with an eye on minimizing state intervention and the expenditure of precious social capital. Sizable private firms in China cultivate personal connections with powerful officials, in exchange for protection and favors.[165] The system builds

[161] Bruton, et al., *supra* note 160.

[162] Wilkins, *supra* note 41, at 286; Liu, *supra* note 41, at 565.

[163] *See, e.g.*, Xin He & Yang Su, *Do the "Haves" Come Out Ahead in Shanghai Courts?*, 10 J. Empirical Legal Stud. 120 (2013); Ning Jia, et al., *Political Connections and Directors' and Officers' Liability Insurance–Evidence from China*, J. Corp. Fin. 353 (2019); Li, *supra* note 153.

[164] Yue Hou, The Private Sector in Public Office (2019); K. S. Tsai, *Capitalists without a Class: Political Diversity among Private Entrepreneurs in China*, 38 Compar. Pol. Stud. 1130 (2005); Bruce J. Dickson, Wealth into Power: The Communist Party's Embrace of China's Private Sector (2008).

[165] Seung Ho Park & Yadong Luo, *Guanxi and Organizational Dynamics: Organizational Dynamics: Organizational Networking in Chinese Firms*, 22 Strategic Mgmt. J. 455 (2001); John A. Pearce II & Richard B. Robinson Jr, *Cultivating Guanxi as a Foreign Investor Strategy*, 43 Bus. Horizons 223 (2000); Peng Wang, *Extra-Legal Protection in China: How Guanxi Distorts China's Legal System and Facilitates the Rise of Unlawful Protectors*, 54 Brit. J. Criminology 809 (2014); Katherine R. Xin & Jone L. Pearce, *Guanxi: Connections as Substitutes for Formal Institutional Support*, 39 Acad. Mgmt. J. 1641 (1996).

on the fundamental social principle of reciprocity, so once a favor has been returned, additional investment must be made to replenish the *guanxi* capital. Thus, savvy business owners would refrain from seeking the intervention of powerful officials in routine legal matters.[166] Investing in legal risk management enables a business owner to avoid drawing on precious *guanxi* capital. Hence, demand for legal services has increased, though "know who" ultimately trumps "know how."[167] Moreover, managers of privately owned Chinese companies, whose interests are better aligned with corporate profits, take a more pragmatic and efficient approach toward litigation. The efficiency, however, must be understood in the firms' normative context. Without state ownership, private businesses often need to signal to the market about their adequate resources, status, credibility, and trustworthiness. In a society where informal institutions have assigned complex meanings to litigation, managers of POEs would typically avoid it unless certain socially constructed interpretations are intended, or the costs associated with the interpretations are clearly outweighed by the expected benefits.[168]

To summarize, the institutional environment for Chinese firms has undergone a profound transformation in the past four decades, giving rise to a sui generis model of state capitalism.[169] In the process, Chinese courts have become relatively more professional, the legal profession has expanded, and the number of lawsuits has surged. Nonetheless, the judiciary remains subordinate to powerful state actors and their affiliates; formal law continues to play a secondary role in business transactions, therefore quality legal services are generally undervalued. All these, coupled with circumscribed authority of the courts, reinforce the culture of legal pragmatism and opportunism, and entrench the social norms attaching complex non-legal meanings to litigation.

Juxtaposing with this is the legal environment in the United States. Relatively speaking, formal laws in the United States assume a more

[166] Li, *supra* note 3, at 65.

[167] Ang & Jia, *supra* note 153.

[168] Ji Li, *Interactions between Domestic Social Norms and International Law over Trade Dispute Resolution*, *in* The Rule of Law at the National and International Levels: Contestations and Deference (Machiko Kanetake & André Nollkaemper eds., 2015).

[169] Mark Wu, *The "China, Inc." Challenge to Global Trade Governance*, 57 Harv. Int'l L.J. 261 (2016).

important role in corporate management and business transactions.[170] US courts, especially those at the federal level, enjoy considerably more independence and authority than Chinese courts. Kagan characterizes the US legal environment as comprising both the "day-to-day practice of adversarial legal contestation," and "the structures of adversarial legalism," defined as "a complex of legal institutions, mechanisms, rights, and rules that facilitate or encourage adversarial, party-dominated legal contestation."[171] Compared with other economically advanced democracies, not only the "fear of litigation is greater in the United States, but also that litigation really is more common in the United States than in parallel policy areas in the other countries."[172] The institutional hallmarks that are part and parcel of the allegedly "unique" lawyer-driven US adversarial system include "ready access to the courts, contingency fees, class actions, large money damages, broad judicial authority to reverse governmental decisions, a politically appointed judiciary, and relatively higher levels of legal malleability and uncertainty."[173]

The debate has not yet settled on whether adversarial legalism accurately describes the "style" of dispute resolution and regulatory enforcement in the United States, or whether the United States is "exceptional" in that regard.[174] Recent evidence suggests that the "conservative legal movement" might have alleviated litigation risk for US businesses.[175] Meanwhile, some evidence indicates that other countries have Americanized in the sense that participatory formal contestations figure more prominently in policy implementation and dispute resolution.[176] As a matter of fact, one may even consider China as a case in point, where

[170] Scholars have documented some industries and sectors where businesses operate on norms, not formal law. *See, e.g.*, Bernstein, *supra* note 157; Macaulay, *supra* note 157.

[171] Robert A. Kagan, *On Surveying the Whole Legal Forest* 28 Law & Soc. Inquiry 833, 837 (2003).

[172] *Id.*, at 839.

[173] *Id.*

[174] Charles R. Epp, *The Judge over Your Shoulder: Is Adversarial Legalism Exceptionally American?* 28 Law & Soc. Inquiry 744 (2003). Some contend that US "litigiousness" is a myth created by corporations to serve their interests in reforming the adjudicatory system and raising litigation cost. David M. Engel, The Myth of the Litigious Society: Why We Don't Sue (2016).

[175] Kagan, *supra* note 171, at 837.

[176] R. Daniel Kelemen & Eric C. Sibbitt, *The Globalization of American Law*, 58 Int'l Org. 103 (2004); R. Daniel Kelemen & Eric C. Sibbitt, *The Americanization*

many market-enabling laws contain US legal transplants or neoliberal principles, and Chinese citizens litigate significantly more cases than before.[177] Nonetheless, as the major institutions undergirding the US judicial system are absent in China, I believe few scholars would seriously contest the claim that legal encounters in the United States are generally more formalistic, adversarial, complex, costly, and lawyer-driven than those in China.[178] Are Chinese companies able to surmount the vast institutional divide and navigate the complex, unfamiliar host-country legal terrain? The rest of this book will attempt some answers.

1.5 METHODOLOGY

This book employs both quantitative and qualitative methods. The primary quantitative evidence comprises two large datasets: a unique set of multiyear survey data about Chinese companies operating in the United States and a set of hand-collected federal litigation data involving a large sample of Chinese companies. Since 2014, I have been collecting annual survey data from Chinese MNCs' US subunits in collaboration with the China General Chamber of Commerce USA (CGCC), by far the largest association of Chinese-invested businesses in the United States.[179] Its membership moved roughly in proportion with the number of Chinese companies in the United States during the surveyed period, so did the size of the survey sample. In 2017, for example, the questionnaires were sent to about 600 CGCC members, and 213 responded (a response rate of approximately 35.5 percent).

of Japanese Law, 23 U. Pa. J. Int'l Econ. L. 269 (2002); Rosa Kim, *The Americanization of Legal Education in South Korea: Challenges and Opportunities*, 38 Brook. J. Int'l L. 49 (2012); Frans Van Waarden, *Power to the Legal Professionals: Is There an Americanization of European Law?*, 3 Regul. & Governance 197 (2009); Wolfgang Wiegand, *The Reception of American Law in Europe*, 39 Am. J. Compar. L. 229 (1991).

177 Ji Li, *The Evolving "Rule of Law with Chinese Characteristics" and Its Impacts on the International Legal Order*, 8 UC Irvine J. Int'l, Transnat'l & Compar. L. 151, 156 (2023).

178 Notably, empirical evidence affirms the comparative differences. Based on a 2016 survey, 74 percent of Chinese MNC managers considered US legal and compliance costs to be higher than the costs they incur at home.

179 Besides Chinese-invested companies, the membership also includes fee-paying US companies. that do not have the right to vote. The US firms are excluded from the survey sampling.

From 2014 to 2019, the survey response rate remained relatively stable. Due to COVID-19 and the deterioration of US–China relations, the response rates dropped to about 27 percent for the 2022 survey. The sample size also shrank as some Chinese companies have chosen to exit the US market. Comparisons between the responding and non-responding companies revealed no significant differences in major aspects of the firms such as business size and ownership structure. Meanwhile, a comparison with US-investing Chinese firms registered with the Ministry of Commerce of China suggests that large businesses and SOEs are over-represented in the CGCC sample.[180] This serves well the purposes of this book, as state ownership is a key variable of interest and some of the topics such as in-house legal capacity are pertinent only to sizable Chinese investors. The job titles of the respondents vary, with the vast majority being CEOs, CFOs, general managers, presidents, and representatives.

Each of the survey questionnaires contained a wide range of questions, a portion of which were repeated every year (e.g., location, year of entry, investment plan) to gauge key aspects of the Chinese companies, others were included in only one or two surveys due to shifting preference and focus of the CGCC and its board members.[181] Hence, most of the in-depth analyses in the following chapters rely on data from selected years. To be more specific, Chapter 2 analyzes the 2019 and 2022 data to

[180] The detailed comparison was conducted by a member of a separate research team working on the CGCC survey and was with the Ministry of Commerce data for 2014. A few more words about the possible issues of bias: first, survival bias, i.e., Chinese companies that have withdrawn from the US market after the realization of certain legal risks are not observed. Chinese companies were all expanding in the United States before the onset of the trade war. A thorough search of public sources has not identified any sizable Chinese corporate members of CGCC that had entirely withdrawn from the US market by 2019. Wherever data from later surveys are used, readers will be cautioned about the effect of biases. Second, common method bias. Though it is a potential methodological issue for survey research, in this paper common method bias is of less concern because most of the variables are simple and specific objective attributes, e.g., employment of full-time legal managers, legal fees, and so on. Also, different questions were asked in each year. Moreover, the questions generating the data were placed far apart in the survey, with no indication of any implicit theories connecting them. Philip M Podsakoff, et al., *Common Method Biases in Behavioral Research: A Critical Review of the Literature and Recommended Remedies*, 88 J. App. Psych. 879, 883–85 (2003). Furthermore, the survey data are supplemented by data derived from the interviews or retested with objective data (e.g., Chapter 5).

[181] The survey subjects were unaware of the hypotheses to be tested using the survey data. Also, the questions are typically dispersed in different sections of the survey questionnaires.

TABLE 1.1 Background of interviewees

Managers	In-house counsel	Lawyers	Consultants	Others	Total
73	21	65	13	4	176

understand the in-house US legal management at the Chinese companies, and statistically tests the 2019 data to investigate the inter-company variations. Chapter 3 examines the 2017 data for lawyer selection preferences, and the 2019 and 2022 data for legal service purchases. Chapter 4 investigates the 2014, 2017, and 2018 survey data for insights about the companies' litigation preferences and their US litigation experiences. Chapter 5 studies the dataset of federal lawsuits involving all Chinese companies that had responded to the 2019 CGCC survey. More details about the hand-collected litigation data can be found in that chapter. Last, Chapter 6 investigates the firms' contemplation of litigating against perceived mistreatment by the US government by analyzing relevant data from the 2014, 2015, 2016, and 2017 surveys, and examines their actual coping measures with data from the most recent 2022 survey.

In addition to the quantitative evidence, this book draws upon a wealth of qualitative data to analyze how Chinese companies navigate legal challenges in the United States. The qualitative evidence includes 176 interviews with knowledgeable informants, such as business executives, in-house counsel, lawyers, and consultants employed by Chinese companies. These interviews were collected using a multisource snowball sampling method, which generated a sizable sample of professionals with diverse backgrounds (see Table 1.1 for more details). Personal acquaintances, who are professionals working for Chinese businesses in the United States, comprised one core group of the interview subjects. They shared valuable insights and introduced more interview candidates. Another cohort consists of CGCC members, some of whom also tapped into their personal and business networks to recruit potential interviewees for this project. In addition, interviews were conducted at various panels, workshops, and conferences on law and foreign investment.[182] Together, the interviews substantiate the varying dual institutional influence as manifested in different subject areas to be explored in this book, assist in

[182] An example of such events is the annual Practicing Law Institute program on Doing Business in and with Emerging Markets, see more details at www.pli.edu/programs/doing-business-in-and-with-emerging-markets.

the generation of testable hypotheses, and make sense of the statistical findings. To supplement the interviews, I also collected and analyzed a large number of legal archives, media reports, corporate filings, publicly available personal profile information, and other secondary materials. In summary, research based on the combined quantitative and qualitative data enables a comprehensive and nuanced understanding of how Chinese companies address legal challenges and navigate the complex legal landscape when operating in the United States.

1.6 CONCLUSION

Numerous Chinese companies have established a significant foothold in the United States, immersing themselves in its complex, rigorous, and adversarial US legal system. The ways in which they negotiate the omnipresent, consequential legal risks, however, remain underexplored. To begin to address this deficiency, this chapter constructed an overarching theoretical framework of dual institutional influence and canvassed the relevant institutional contexts of both China and the United States, underscoring their stark contrasts.

Within the dual institutional framework, the following chapters will sequentially investigate four interrelated topics: (i) the internal legal capacity of Chinese companies in the United States; (ii) their selection of US lawyers and acquisition of US legal services; (iii) their dispute resolution and litigation experiences in US courts; and (iv) their legal reactions to perceived discriminatory practices by US government agencies. Each chapter will begin with an in-depth examination of both the home-state and host-state institutions pertaining to the relevant subject area. Following the institutional comparison, it will analyze the survey and interview data to discern how the dual institutional influence impacts Chinese companies operating in the United States as they navigate the intricate US legal system. Further, each chapter will perform statistical tests to elucidate inter-company variations and to identify potential correlations between key institutional factors (e.g., state ownership and cultural difference) and the preferences and actions of these Chinese companies. As one experienced US lawyer observed about the seemingly irrational legal strategies of his Chinese clients, "these clients are not stupid. They choose what they think is the best solution within the U.S. and the Chinese contexts."[183]

[183] Interview with a partner of a large US law firm (June 8, 2020).

CHAPTER TWO

IN-HOUSE LEGAL MANAGERS OF CHINESE COMPANIES IN THE UNITED STATES

Sophisticated legal risk management in the US requires capable in-house counsel. Chinese companies do not yet have that capability.

—Partner at a prominent US law firm

The US legal system is notoriously complex, encompassing an intricate web of federal and state laws, regulations, and court rulings that often vary across jurisdictions. Navigating this labyrinthine structure requires knowledge of legal precedents, procedures, and rules, along with the ability to anticipate and adapt to shifts in the legal landscape. Businesses, therefore, need the guidance and expertise of US lawyers.

Over the past few decades, US corporations have increasingly turned to in-house lawyers for legal services, leading to their rising prominence in the corporate hierarchy and profound changes in the US legal profession and corporate governance. Today, general counsel of US firms not only manage external lawyers and provide routine legal services, but also partake in key strategic corporate decision-making.[1] Therefore, one cannot fully comprehend how US companies navigate their legal environment without examining their in-house lawyers.[2] This could also be true for Chinese companies operating in the United States, as they share the institutional environment and the

[1] Jonathan C. Lipson, *Who's in the House? The Changing Role and Nature of In-House and General Counsel*, 2012 Wis. L. Rev. 237, 239.

[2] Mary C. Daly, *The Cultural, Ethical, and Legal Challenges in Lawyering for a Global Organization: The Role of the General Counsel*, 46 Emory L.J. 1057, 1067 (1997).

US in-house counsel movement is "going global."[3] Hence, Chapter 2 investigates the Chinese companies' utilization of full-time internal legal managers within the dual institutional context. For those employing such managers, this chapter scrutinizes two key aspects: (1) whether these legal managers are locally hired or are expatriates – defined as "home country nationals (citizens of the country in which the multinational firm is headquartered) who are sent by the headquarters to the foreign positions,"[4] and (2) whether they are licensed lawyers in the United States, which approximates their ability to handle US legal risks and opportunities. The analysis under the dual institutional framework reveals not only effects of both home and host-state institutions, but also substantial inter-company variations. These variations are further examined, with a special focus on the Chinese companies' ownership structure, a defining feature of China's state capitalism and outbound foreign direct investment,[5] as well as other institutional and firm-specific variables of theoretical and policy importance (e.g., cultural difference).

The remainder of this chapter is divided into five parts. Section 2.1 offers a succinct review of the literature on corporate in-house counsel and international human resource management, highlighting their insights and limitations. Applying the dual institutional framework outlined in Chapter 1, Section 2.2 scrutinizes the relevant home- and host-state institutions that shape the legal staffing of Chinese companies in the United States. The comparative institutional analysis will emphasize a unique feature of the in-house legal movement in China – government-mandated corporate legal capacity building for Chinese state-owned enterprises (SOEs). Section 2.3 introduces empirical evidence gleaned from the 2019 and 2022 surveys of Chinese companies and interviews with business and legal professionals, and statistically deciphers the inter-company variations in the presence, identity, and qualification of the in-house legal managers. Section 2.4

[3] *See, e.g.*, David B. Wilkins, et al., *Globalization, Lawyers, and Emerging Economies: The Rise, Transformation, and Significance of the New Corporate Legal Ecosystem in India, Brazil, and China*, 61 HARV. INT'L L.J. 281 (2020); David B. Wilkins, *Is the In-House Counsel Movement Going Global? A Preliminary Assessment of the Role of Internal Counsel in Emerging Economies*, 2012 WIS. L. REV. 251.

[4] Danchi Tan & Joseph T. Mahoney, *Why a Multinational Firm Chooses Expatriates: Integrating Resource-Based, Agency and Transaction Costs Perspectives*, 43 J. MGMT. STUD. 457, 458 (2006).

[5] Hao Liang, et al., *An Anatomy of State Control in the Globalization of State-Owned Enterprises*, 46 J. INT'L BUS. STUD. 223, 224 (2015).

discusses the significance of these findings and their connection to the other chapters of this book. Finally, Section 2.5 concludes the chapter.

2.1 LITERATURE ON CORPORATE COUNSEL AND INTERNATIONAL HUMAN RESOURCE MANAGEMENT

The topic of Chinese companies' internal legal capacity spans two distinct literatures: corporate in-house counsel and international human resource management. Both offer valuable but inadequate insights. As will be demonstrated, current research on corporate counsel has largely overlooked multinational companies (MNCs), especially those from developing countries like China. Meanwhile, the scholarship on international human resource management has neglected the staffing of in-house legal positions. Both areas of research have been mostly silent about state-owned MNCs.

2.1.1 Corporate In-House Counsel

Corporate legal departments have undergone a remarkable expansion in the United States, and the topic has drawn a great deal of academic attention, spawning a sizable literature on its causes and implications (e.g., the ascent of in-house counsel vis-à-vis both outside lawyers and business executives).[6] The accumulated scholarship revolves around three main analytical concepts: legal service cost, agency, and regulatory environment. First, some scholars attribute the process of bringing legal service production in-house to rising costs.[7] Undergirding this argument is the enduring question of corporate "making versus buying."[8] Companies rely on internal production of legal services to mitigate costly opportunism associated with asset specificity and incomplete contracts.[9] Vertical integration is also preferable when transferring knowledge and information is more efficient via directions

[6] *See, e.g.*, Wilkins, *supra* note 3; Omari Scott Simmons & James D. Dinnage, *Innkeepers: A Unifying Theory of the In-House Counsel Role*, 41 SETON HALL L. REV. 77 (2011); Steven L. Schwarcz, *To Make or to Buy: In-House Lawyering and Value Creation*, 33 J. CORP. L. 497 (2007); Lipson, *supra* note 1.

[7] *See, e.g.*, Lipson, *supra* note 1, at 240; Craig B. Glidden, *The Evolution and Influence of Corporate Legal Departments*, 12 FLA. ST. U. BUS. REV. 134 (2013).

[8] Schwarcz, *supra* note 6, at 523.

[9] *See, e.g.*, Oliver E. Williamson, *Transaction-Cost Economics: the Governance of Contractual Relations*, 22 J.L. & ECON. 233 (1979); Benjamin Klein, et al., *Vertical Integration, Appropriable Rents, and the Competitive Contracting Process*, 21 J.L. & ECON. 297 (1978).

to employees (to make) than by instructions to suppliers (to buy).[10] Following this logic, the expansion of in-house legal departments in the United States results from increasingly complex and idiosyncratic corporate information. Second, some scholars attribute the "corporate counsel movement" to the collective actions of in-house counsel to elevate their status and power,[11] which generates upward spiraling effects – the rising status of in-house counsel attracts first-rate lawyers to join their ranks, which consolidates their positions in the corporate hierarchy.[12] Third, some researchers credit the US in-house movement to the shifting regulatory environment that has amplified corporate compliance risks and prompted executives to expand in-house legal capacity as a safety measure.[13]

In summary, the in-house movement in the United States has greatly expanded the duties of corporate counsel. They now manage outside lawyers, deliver routine and firm-specific legal services, counsel top executives on regulatory matters, and create and adjust compliance programs.[14] At some US companies, general counsel even engage proactively in devising key business strategies.[15] Outside the United States, scholars have also uncovered evidence of similar "corporate in-house movements."[16] However, despite the growing interest in the subject, few studies have explored the in-house legal capacity of MNCs, especially those based in China.[17]

[10] Harold Demsetz, *The Theory of the Firm Revisited*, 4 J.L., Econ. & Org. 141 (1988).

[11] *See, generally*, Deborah A. DeMott, *The Discrete Roles of General Counsel*, 74 Fordham L. Rev. 955 (2005); Robert L. Nelson & Laura Beth Nielsen, *Cops, Counsel, and Entrepreneurs: Constructing the Role of Inside Counsel in Large Corporations*, 34 Law & Soc'y Rev. 457 (2000); Schwarcz, *supra* note 6; Robert Eli Rosen, *The Inside Counsel Movement, Professional Judgment and Organizational Representation*, 64 Ind. L.J. 479 (1988); Daly, *supra* note 2, at 1063.

[12] Glidden, *supra* note 7, at 135.

[13] Simmons & Dinnage, *supra* note 6, at 99.

[14] Daly, *supra* note 2, at 1061.

[15] Nelson & Nielsen, *supra* note 11.

[16] Sida Liu, *Palace Wars over Professional Regulation: In-House Counsel in Chinese State-Owned Enterprises*, 2012 Wis. L. Rev. 549; Wilkins, *supra* note 3; David B. Wilkins & Vikramaditya S. Khanna, *Globalization and the Rise of the In-House Counsel Movement in India*, in The Indian Legal Profession in the Age of Globalization: The Rise of the Corporate Legal Sector and its Impact on Lawyers and Society (David B. Wilkins et al. eds., 2017); Wilkins, et al., *supra* note 3.

[17] Ji Li, *"Going Out" and Going In-House: Chinese Multinationals' Internal Legal Capacity in the United States*, Law & Soc. Inquiry 487, 490 (2021).

2.1.2 International Human Resource Management

The appointment of legal managers for US affiliates is ultimately a staffing decision for MNCs, which, though largely neglected by socio-legal scholars,[18] has spurred a sizable international management literature. This literature has documented an inherent tension between, on the one hand, the institutional pressure of host countries conducive to localized staffing, and, on the other, the pressure from within MNCs for organizational integration and from their home-state institutions that compels management expatriation.[19] Variable confluences of the dual institutional pressures shape the MNCs' personnel decisions.[20] To be concrete, MNCs tend to deploy expatriates to achieve "control, coordination, and information processing within the multinational network"[21] or to implement headquarters' strategies.[22] MNCs that value local knowledge and adaptation, however, are more inclined to recruit host-state professionals for management positions at their foreign affiliates.[23]

Another line of international management literature underscores the effect of transaction cost on the staffing decisions. For positions that require a great deal of firm-specific knowledge, MNCs tend to rely on expatriates due to the scarcity of qualified local candidates

[18] For notable exceptions, *see* Toshimitsu Kitagawa & Luke Nottage, *Globalization of Japanese Corporations and the Development of Corporate Legal Departments: Problems and Prospects*, *in* RAISING THE BAR: THE EMERGING LEGAL PROFESSION IN EAST ASIA (William P. Alford, et al. eds., 2007); Setsuo Miyazawa, *Legal Departments of Japanese Corporations in the United States: A Study on Organizational Adaptation to Multiple Environments*, 20 KOBE U. L. REV. 97 (1986).

[19] *See, e.g.*, Yaping Gong, *Toward a Dynamic Process Model of Staffing Composition and Subsidiary Outcomes in Multinational Enterprises*, 29 J. MGMT. 260 (2003); Philip M. Rosenzweig & Nitin Nohria, *Influences on Human Resource Management Practices in Multinational Corporations*, 25 J. INT'L BUS. STUD. 229 (1994); Dean Xu, et al., *The Effect of Regulative and Normative Distances on MNE Ownership and Expatriate Strategies*, MIR: MGMT. INT'L REV. 285 (2004).

[20] Xu, et al., *supra* note 19, 286.

[21] Tan & Mahoney, *supra* note 4, at 458; Anders Edström & Jay R. Galbraith, *Transfer of Managers as a Coordination and Control Strategy in Multinational Organizations*, 22 ADMIN. SCI. Q. 248–49 (1977); Michael Harvey, et al., *A Theory-Based Framework for Strategic Global Human Resource Staffing Policies and Practices*, 12 INT'L J. HUMAN RES. MGMT. 898 (2001).

[22] Tan & Mahoney, *supra* note 4, at 458; Meredith Downes & Anisya S. Thomas, *Knowledge Transfer Through Expatriation: The U-Curve Approach to Overseas Staffing*, J. MANAGERIAL ISSUES 132 (2000).

[23] Tan & Mahoney, *supra* note 4, at 458.

and the relatively low cost of retention.[24] MNCs would also deploy reliable expatriates to perform overseas tasks that are hard to specify in contractual terms.[25] Moreover, large institutional gaps between the home and host states, which inevitably raise intra-firm transaction costs, typically induce management expatriation.[26] The ubiquitous principal-agent problem has also spawned a sizable body of human resource management research.[27] In areas where employees' performance is hard to monitor and evaluate, and where their incentives diverge from those of the headquarters, MNCs often assign expatriates with a proven track record to lead foreign subsidiaries.[28] By contrast, where the agency problem is less severe, MNCs tend to entrust local recruits.[29]

Though insightful, the literature on international human resource management has neglected legal management staffing, which is distinct in several major aspects such as expertise, organizational role, and professional identification.[30] Additionally, prior research has primarily focused on MNCs based in the United States or other developed countries, and largely ignored questions unique to developing country MNCs.[31]

To summarize, the literature on corporate in-house counsel and international human resource management, having neglected developing country MNCs, legal management staffing, and state-owned MNCs, fails to adequately address questions concerning the existence, identity, and qualification of legal managers at Chinese companies in the United States.

[24] *Id.*, at 463–64.

[25] *Id.*, at 463.

[26] Yaping Gong, *Subsidiary Staffing in Multinational Enterprises: Agency, Resources, and Performance*, 46 ACAD. MGMT. J. 728 (2003).

[27] Harvey, et al., *supra* note 21; Tan & Mahoney, *supra* note 4; Gong, *supra* note 26; Fiona Moore, *Strategy, Power and Negotiation: Social Control and Expatriate Managers in a German Multinational Corporation*, 17 INT'L J. HUMAN RES. MGMT. 399 (2006).

[28] Gong, *supra* note 26, at 729.

[29] Tan & Mahoney, *supra* note 4.

[30] Nelson & Nielsen, *supra* note 11.

[31] *See, e.g.*, Can Ouyang, et al., *Overcoming Liabilities of Origin: Human Resource Management Localization of Chinese Multinational Corporations in Developed Markets*, 58 HUMAN RES. MGMT. 543 (2019); Chris Smith & Yu Zheng, *The Management of Labour in Chinese MNCs Operating Outside of China: A Critical Review*, in CHINA AT WORK: A LABOUR PROCESS PERSPECTIVE ON THE TRANSFORMATION OF WORK AND EMPLOYMENT IN CHINA (Mingwei Liu & Chris Smith eds., 2016).

2.2 DUAL INSTITUTIONS AND THE INTERNAL LEGAL CAPACITY OF CHINESE COMPANIES IN THE UNITED STATES

As elaborated in Chapter 1, Chinese companies in the United States find themselves embedded within a dual institutional context. Given their pronounced differences, the home- and the host-state institutions invariably generate tensions and contradictions, which result in varying institutional pressures. These pressures play a significant role in shaping how the Chinese companies structure their internal mechanisms for managing US legal risks. Building on the discussion about the institutional environments in the previous chapter, this section surveys the companies' home- and host-state institutions pertinent to corporate in-house legal capacity building. While the comparison begins with an examination of the US institutions, its primary focus is the less explored home-state institutional pressure on Chinese companies to cultivate their internal legal capacity.

2.2.1 Host-State Institutions for Developing Corporate In-House Legal Capacity

As just noted, the institutional environment of the corporate in-house counsel movement in the United States has been extensively studied. Factors such as high costs of legal services, significant transaction costs, stringent regulations, and the agency of corporate in-house lawyers have collectively driven the trend for internal legal service production.[32] The institutional characteristics that underpin these explanatory factors should exert a similar influence on Chinese companies operating in the United States. The rising costs of legal services should incentivize those with recurring US legal issues to produce the services internally, so should the enormous information asymmetry between the Chinese managers and their US lawyers. Additionally, heightened regulatory scrutiny should motivate the managers to mitigate the legal and regulatory risks by investing in internal legal capacity building. Moreover, corporate in-house lawyers have been growing in number for decades, providing a pool of potential candidates for Chinese companies to select, though, as will be discussed, those requiring a great deal of firm-specific information will have a hard time recruiting US legal managers. In brief, Chinese companies face similar host-state

[32] Li, *supra* note 17.

institutional pressures as their local counterparts to develop internal US legal capacities.

2.2.2 Home-State Institutions for Cultivating Corporate In-House Legal Capacity

How does the home-state institutional context influence the legal capacity building of Chinese companies in the United States? The previous chapter reviewed the transformation of the Chinese political economy in the past few decades, which foreshadowed a hybrid in-house counsel movement in China comprising a top-down state-driven component and a bottom-up market-driven one. The former refers to measures taken by Chinese government agencies to enhance corporate in-house legal capacity, the latter the economic and regulatory factors motivating private market participants to develop internal legal capacity.

2.2.2.1 State-driven In-House Movement

In stark contrast to the United States, the corporate in-house counsel movement in China gained momentum through state-sponsored campaigns to strengthen SOEs' legal departments. As noted in Chapter 1, the Chinese party-state continues to rely heavily on SOEs to implement its policies, raise revenues, and maintain social control.[33] Due to the state control, profit maximization is rarely the primary, or even a prioritized, goal for SOE managers,[34] and this multitasking feature complicates their handling of risks, including legal risks. The state control also engenders an acute multiagency problem,[35] which begets sub-optimal management of corporate legal risks. While Chinese SOEs historically under-invested in internal legal capacity,[36] they began to expand in-house legal departments as soon as the central government clearly signaled its preference. In 2004, the State-Owned Assets Supervision and Administration Commission (SASAC) promulgated

[33] Barry Naughton & Kellee S. Tsai, State Capitalism, Institutional Adaptation, and the Chinese Miracle 9–10 (2015).

[34] Chong-En Bai, et al., *The Multitask Theory of State Enterprise Reform: Empirical Evidence from China*, 96 Am. Econ. Rev. 353 (2006); Saul Estrin, et al., *Home Country Institutions and the Internationalization of State Owned Enterprises: A Cross-Country Analysis*, 51 J. World Bus. 294 (2016).

[35] Zhou Mi & Xiaoming Wang, *Agency Cost and the Crisis of China's SOE*, 11 China Econ. Rev. 297 (2001); Garry D. Bruton, et al., *State-Owned Enterprises Around the World as Hybrid Organizations*, 29 Acad. Mgmt. Persp. 92 (2015); Mike W. Peng, et al., *Theories of the (State-Owned) Firm*, 33 Asia Pacific J. Mgmt. 293 (2016).

[36] Wilkins, *supra* note 3, 286; Liu, *supra* note 16, at 565.

Measures for the Administration of In-House Legal Counsels of State-Owned Enterprises, giving detailed instructions for SOEs to develop internal legal capacity to safeguard state assets.[37] The SASAC also attempted to elevate the status of legal counsel within the corporate hierarchy – the 2004 *Measures* designate the chief legal officer as a member of the senior executive team.[38] Additionally, the SASAC designed metrics to assess progress, and in doing so it repeatedly looked to Western firms for benchmarks.[39] The stated goals of the campaign, for instance, include attaining the average ratio of in-house legal staff to total employees for MNCs from advanced economies and ensuring that one-third of the central SOEs would "become world leaders in this regard."[40]

After the 18th Communist Party Congress initiated a concerted push to "build a rule-of-law China,"[41] the SASAC announced a five-year plan (following consecutive three-year plans) to further expand the internal legal capacity of Chinese SOEs.[42] As a result of these efforts, in-house positions at the SOEs tripled from 7,000 in 2005 to 21,000 in 2016,[43] and all of the 102 central corporate groups under

[37] Order of the State-Owned Assets Supervision and Administration Committee of the State Council (No. 6), effective June 1, 2004, at www.sasac.gov.cn/n2588035/n2588320/n2588335/c4258898/content.html.

[38] Section 16, *The Measures for the Administration of In-House Legal Counsels of State-Owned Enterprises*.

[39] Litao Zhou, *Qiye Falu Guwen de Liangda Fazhan Qushi* [*Two Major Development Trends for Corporate Legal Advisors*], 1 Fa Ren [Legal Person] 19 (2015).

[40] Guanyu Tuidong Luoshi Zhongyang Qiye Fazhi Gongzuo Wunian Guihua Youguan Shixiang de Tongzhi [Notice re Matters Concerning the Implementation of the Five-Year Legal Reform of the Central SOEs], SASAC Directive # 193 (2014), at www.sasac.gov.cn/n2588020/n2588072/n2590860/n2590862/c3718525/content.html.

[41] Lizhi Dong, *Fazhi Zhongguo Shiyuxia de "Fazhi Laigang" Jianshe Fanglue* [*The Construction Strategy of "Laigang under the Rule of Law" from the Perspective of the Rule of Law in China*], Zhongguo Qiye Fawu Guancha [China Corporate Legal Insights] 64 (Xiaozhong Ye, et al. eds., 2014).

[42] Xin Hong, *Luoshi Quanmian Yifa Zhiguo Zhanlue Litui Fazhi Yangqi Jianshe* [*Implementing the Rule of Law Strategy and Promoting Legal Development at Central SOEs*], Legal Daily (September 22, 2017), at www.legaldaily.com.cn/index/content/2017-09/22/content_7326185.htm?node=20908. The plan sets lofty goals. Duties and responsibilities are specified by the SASAC in "Rules re Duties for Primary Managers of Central SOEs in Implementing the Legal Development Plan," SASAC Party Committee Directive #8 (2017), at www.sasac.gov.cn/n2588035/n2588320/n2588335/c7444087/content.html.

[43] SASAC Report on Legal Affairs #10 [Guoziwei Xitong Fazhi Gongzuo Jianbao Dishiqi] (March 29, 2017), at www.sasac.gov.cn/n2588020/n2588072/n2590860/n2590862/c7857000/content.html.

direct SASAC supervision have established the requisite system of chief legal officers.[44]

The remarkable progress on paper and in numbers, however, is a veneer for the many remaining problems with the corporate legal departments of Chinese SOEs. As the top-down approach relies on observable and measurable factors, the unmeasurable aspects of legal risks have been neglected. For instance, the competency of the legal staff, crucial to providing high quality services,[45] has not improved nearly as much as the size of the in-house legal departments would indicate.[46] Although the SASAC permitted open recruitment of chief legal officers, some SOEs either had senior executives retain top in-house legal posts concurrently or assigned unqualified managers to those positions.[47] It is therefore not unusual for non-lawyers to be chief legal officers of Chinese SOEs.[48] Moreover, structural relegation of the legal officer role to low status and poor compensation also contribute to the non-professional staffing of the legal departments.[49] According to one estimate, merely 20 percent of the in-house legal staff at Chinese SOEs have passed the national bar examination.[50] Neither has the top-down movement substantially boosted the authority of in-house counsel at Chinese SOEs. Although the SASAC guidelines require that chief legal advisers be allowed to participate in all major corporate decisions, senior SOE executives do not often take their presence seriously, resulting in a tangential role for the legal departments.[51] As observed

[44] *Id.*

[45] Guanghui Tao, Gongsi Fawubu: Jiekai Gongsi Fawu de Miansha [Corporate Legal Departments: Uncovering the Veil of Corporate Legal Affairs] 45 (2016).

[46] Dong, *supra* note 41.

[47] Rui Zhai, *Qiye Falu Guwen Zhidu de Xianzhuang ji Fazhan Qushi Tantao* [*Discussion on the Current Situation and Development Trend of Corporate Legal Advisor System*], Jingmao Shijian [Economic and Trade Practice] (2017).

[48] *Id.*

[49] *Id.*; Li Ma, *Gongsi Fawuguan Jueqi* [*The Rise of Corporate Legal Officers*], Fa Ren [Legal Person] (2013). The staffing of legal departments by non-lawyers is not unusual outside the United States: Daly, *supra* note 2, at 1099.

[50] Li Ma, *Qiye Falu Guwen yu Gongsi Lushi Ronghe Nanti Daijie* [*The Problem of Integrating Corporate Legal Advisors and Corporate Lawyers Remains to be Solved*], Fa Ren [Legal Person] (2015).

[51] Li Ma, *Guoqi Wenlu Falu Guwen Zhidu Gaige* [*Reform of Legal Advisory System for State-Owned Enterprises*], Fa Ren [Legal Person] (2015); Hao Zhang, *Lun Gongsi Lushi Zhidu de Kunjing yu Goujian* [*On the Dilemma and Construction of the Corporate Lawyer System*], Xingzheng yu Fa [Administration and Law]

by a Chinese lawyer who once served as general counsel at a central level SOE, the position is merely for "staging."[52]

2.2.2.2 *Market-driven In-House Movement*

Extensive as it is, the authority of the SASAC and its regional counterparts is limited to SOEs. So, the top-down in-house campaign does not explain the recent expansion of legal departments at private Chinese companies. As elaborated in Chapter 1, much of China's economic growth in the 1980s and 1990s was made possible by entrepreneurs routinely ignoring, bypassing, bending, or outright disobeying pre-existing rules designed to sustain a Soviet-style planned economy.[53] Widespread grassroots noncompliance created opportunities for reform-minded political elites to nurture a budding market economy.[54] This transformative mentality, however, ossified into a corporate culture of disrespect for formal rules and rampant grassroots noncompliance.[55] The weak judiciary, plus robust informal institutions, further marginalized the role of Chinese law in private business transactions.[56]

It is, therefore, of no surprise that in-house legal staff are often either absent or relegated to a low status in the corporate hierarchy,[57] and the majority of them are not qualified to practice law.[58] Nonetheless, a market-driven in-house movement has gathered some momentum, as the importance of law has increased piecemeal, especially in commercially developed regions and for transactions between parties of political and economic equality.[59]

(2016); Xiaojun Chen, *"Fazhi Guoqi" Zai Shandong de Shijian [The Practice of "State-Owned Enterprises under the Rule of Law" in Shandong]*, *in* ZHONGGUO QIYE FAWU GUANCHA [CHINA CORPORATE LEGAL INSIGHTS] (Xiaozhong Ye ed., 2015).

52 Interview with a partner of the New York office of a Chinese law firm (July 3, 2019).

53 David Daokui Li, et al., *Institutional Entrepreneurs*, 96 AM. ECON. REV. 358, 359–60 (2006).

54 YUEN YUEN ANG, HOW CHINA ESCAPED THE POVERTY TRAP (2016).

55 *See, e.g.*, JI LI, THE CLASH OF CAPITALISMS? CHINESE COMPANIES IN THE UNITED STATES (2018); JUN JIAN, CORPORATE CHIEF LEGAL OFFICER – NIGHT WATCHMAN OF THE COMPANY (2017).

56 Wei Zhang & Ji Li, *Weak Law v. Strong Ties: An Empirical Study of Business Investment, Law and Political Connections in China*, 13 REV. L. & ECON. 1, 36 (2017).

57 JIAN, *supra* note 55, at 277.

58 Ma, *supra* note 50.

59 *See, e.g.*, Ji Li, *The Power Logic of Justice in China*, 65 AM. J. COMPAR. L. 95 (2017); Xin He, *A Tale of Two Chinese Courts: Economic Development and Contract Enforcement*, 39 J.L. & SOC'Y 384 (2012).

In summary, two institutional forces have propelled a nascent in-house counsel movement in China. Top-down pressure from the state has led to the rapid expansion of legal departments in Chinese SOEs, while bottom-up market forces within the socio-political context have incentivized some private Chinese firms to cultivate internal legal capacity. As noted in Chapter 1, the institutional influence may extend beyond China and shape the internal legal capacity building of Chinese companies in the United States. First, the home-state institutions exert normative and cognitive influence on the managers.[60] The relatively low status of in-house counsel in China and the secondary role of law in business transactions may affect how managers running the US operations perceive the value and efficacy of internal legal capacity. Second, the home-state institutions governing Chinese SOEs might directly influence their US operations, as the headquarters in China typically retain the power to make major personnel decisions concerning top-level and sometimes even mid-level managers of the US subunits.[61] Additionally, the SASAC and other state agencies have promulgated increasingly complex rules to curb the discretion of SOE managers, including those expatriated to run the foreign operations. In brief, extensive extraterritorial, hierarchical control modifies the corporate behavior of Chinese firms that have ventured abroad, including internal legal capacity building at their foreign subunits.

To recapitulate, this section has surveyed the dual institutional context for the in-house legal capacity building of Chinese companies in the United States. The host-state institutional environment is characterized by a complex and adversarial legal system and a mature and costly legal service market.[62] In contrast, the Chinese institutional setting features extensive state engineering and nascent commercial incentives for expanding corporate legal capacity. How do these tensions implicate the Chinese companies' internal legal risk management in the United States? The following section offers some preliminary answers.

[60] Klaus E. Meyer & Htwe Htwe Thein, *Business Under Adverse Home Country Institutions: The Case of International Sanctions against Myanmar*, 49 J. World Bus. 156 (2014); Guy L.F. Holburn & Bennet A. Zelner, *Political Capabilities, Policy Risk, and International Investment Strategy: Evidence from the Global Electric Power Generation Industry*, 31 Strategic Mgmt. J. 1290 (2010).

[61] Li, *supra* note 55, at 76.

[62] *See, generally*, Robert A. Kagan, Adversarial Legalism: The American Way of Law (2019); Lee Axelrad & Robert A. Kagan, Regulatory Encounters: Multinational Corporations and American Adversarial Legalism (2000).

2.3 LEGAL MANAGERS OF CHINESE COMPANIES IN THE UNITED STATES

In today's corporate governance landscape in the United States, in-house lawyers are deemed indispensable in managing legal and regulatory risks. However, for Chinese MNCs, which have traditionally operated in a home-state environment lacking the rule of law, the situation may vary. As these companies venture into the US market, it is uncertain whether they modify their conventional practices and develop internal capacity to navigate the intricate host-state legal system. This raises several important questions: Do Chinese companies in the United States establish full-time legal management positions? If so, who occupies these positions that are arguably crucial to negotiating US legal risks and opportunities? Are they filled by expatriates from the headquarters or local recruits? Moreover, are these individuals licensed to practice US law? This section addresses these questions empirically, using the dual institutional framework. As noted in Chapter 1, the empirical analysis of this topic is based primarily on data derived from the 2019 and 2022 CGCC surveys, as well as in-depth interviews.

2.3.1 Establishing a Full-Time Legal Management Position

As shown in Figure 2.1, the majority (56.9 percent) of Chinese companies operating in the United States do not have a full-time in-house legal manager. Cost calculations within the host-country market appear to have a significant effect on this outcome. Many Chinese investors, having recently entered the highly competitive US market, have directed their attention and resources to cultivating a niche clientele, such as businesses with extensive exposure to China.[63] These companies do not generate a regular stream of legal matters, and thus would consider it wasteful to hire a full-time in-house counsel. One interviewee, an executive of a large Chinese SOE, dismissed the idea of hiring an in-house lawyer for the US operations as too expensive and unnecessary, regardless of the company's capacity to afford such hiring, given that its current US businesses do not give rise to many legal problems.[64] Even a gradual increase in legal service demand does not always result in the hiring of full-time in-house counsel, as companies can opt for less costly alternatives, such as a retainer arrangement.

[63] Li, *supra* note 55, at 38.

[64] Interview with the executive of the US operations of a Chinese state-owned company (January 17, 2018).

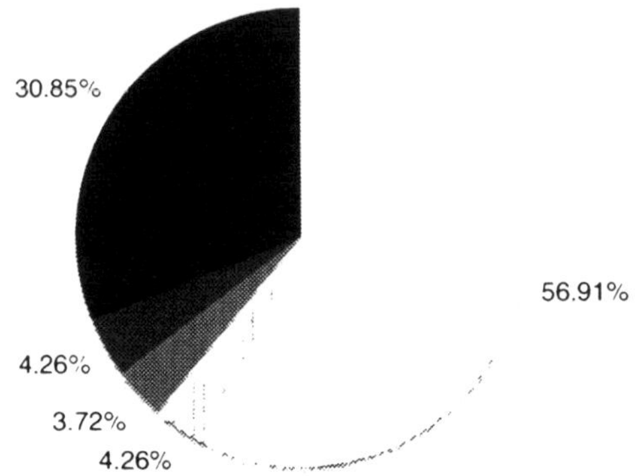

Figure 2.1 Legal managers at Chinese companies in the United States
Source: 2019 CGCC survey data.

By paying a fixed retainer fee, which is typically less than the salary of professional in-house counsel, Chinese companies can ensure timely legal services provided by outside lawyers familiar with their businesses. For example, the CEO of a Chinese-invested business mentioned that his company had a lawyer on retainer because they only had a few lawsuits a year and primarily engaged in standardized transactions.[65]

In addition to the market-driven cost-based calculation, the absence of in-house counsel at some Chinese companies in the United States can be attributed to a shared under-estimation of US legal risks, which is rooted in the cultural neglect of law in China. An experienced lawyer described Chinese investors as "headless flies" with "shocking ignorance of US law."[66] To illustrate, the lawyer shared an example where one of his Chinese clients made a real estate investment in the United States worth hundreds of millions of dollars without hiring any US lawyer to perform due diligence.[67] Another lawyer echoed the observation, noting that "Chinese managers don't respect rules, so they find the US market

[65] Interview with a manager of the US business of a Chinese private company (April 7, 2019).
[66] Interview with a partner at the US office of a Chinese law firm (July 3, 2019).
[67] *Id.*

full of legal landmines."[68] A third lawyer observed that Chinese clients appeared to be much more tolerant of US legal risks, "probably because that's how law works in China."[69] However, the influence of the home-state environment may fade after a US legal risk materializes and causes significant damage. According to an in-house lawyer, Chinese firms will spend more on legal capacity building after having "paid expensive tuition" for not managing US legal risks properly.[70] The in-house lawyer's superior decided to hire a full-time legal manager only after its "naïve" reliance on the US business partner led to substantial liabilities.[71]

Meanwhile, 43.1 percent of Chinese companies have employed full-time legal managers, which, again, can be partly attributed to market-driven cost calculations. For Chinese companies with substantial US investments, the demand for repeated legal services and their high cost justify internal production. One interviewee cited cost saving as the primary reason for the decision to hire an internal legal manager in the United States.[72] Moreover, information asymmetry partly accounts for this finding. Due to the wide institutional gaps between the two countries, US lawyers are typically ignorant about the corporate culture, organizational structure, and management style of Chinese companies. Yet, such knowledge is crucial for providing high quality, tailored legal services. Prior research by institutional economists has shown that this type of company-level "asset specificity" induces mutual dependence, opportunism, and consequently vertical integration.[73] For example, the in-house counsel of a Chinese company with multi-billion-dollar US investments complained that "US lawyers know nothing about Chinese businesses," yet at the same time "Chinese managers, new to the US market, are oblivious about the potential legal and regulatory issues." The company eventually decided to hire an in-house lawyer after experiencing several costly setbacks.[74] Another executive observed that, compared with local peers, Chinese companies encounter more intricate US legal issues and, therefore,

[68] Interview with a lawyer at an international law firm (November 16, 2018).
[69] Interview with a partner at a US law firm (September 17, 2020).
[70] Interview with in-house counsel of the US subsidiary of a large Chinese MNC (May 14, 2017).
[71] *Id.*
[72] Interview with CEO of the US subsidiary of a large state-owned Chinese MNC (May 29, 2019).
[73] *See, e.g.*, Williamson, *supra* note 9; Schwarcz, *supra* note 6; Rosen, *supra* note 11.
[74] Interview with in-house counsel of the US subsidiary of a large Chinese MNC (May 14, 2017).

require special legal advice. Consequently, her company recruited a former outside lawyer, who was a Chinese American licensed to practice in both China and New York, as its general counsel.[75]

One might wonder why US lawyers fail to gain a better understanding of their Chinese clients. Isn't knowing your client the acclaimed winning strategy of US law firms? As the following chapter will demonstrate, the limited legal service budget of most Chinese companies disincentivizes the accumulation of company-specific knowledge. When US lawyers do acquire company-specific knowledge, Chinese corporate clients become highly dependent on their services. One interviewee complained about overbilling by an outside law firm, yet she took no action. "The firm has been working with us for years. We don't want to offend the senior partner [who overbilled], as it's hard for us to switch."[76] Obviously, such costly reliance would further motivate Chinese companies to bring the production of US legal services in-house.[77]

In summary, Chinese companies differ in their approach to establishing full-time legal management positions in the United States. The available qualitative evidence suggests that both home-state normative influence and cost-based calculations play significant roles in this decision. This finding aligns with data from the 2022 survey on the companies' organizational arrangements for coping with US legal and compliance affairs (see Table 2.1 in the Appendix to this chapter), which shows that 46 percent of Chinese companies in the United States have no legal department, compared with 18 percent that have a standalone legal department. About 35 percent have one department overseeing legal and other types of risks such as compliance and audit.

The dual institutional influence is further evidenced in two key attributes of the in-house legal managers: the managers' professional bases (expatriates versus local recruits) and their professional qualification (US lawyers versus lay managers).

2.3.2 Expatriates or Local Hires

It is curious to note that some Chinese companies have appointed expatriates to manage their US legal matters, as shown in Figure 2.1. This should

75 Interview with a senior executive of the US subsidiary of a state-owned Chinese MNC (June 23, 2017).

76 Interview with an in-house lawyer at the US subsidiary of a large Chinese MNC (December 2, 2017).

77 Ronald J. Gilson, *The Devolution of the Legal Profession: A Demand Side Perspective*, 49 Md. L. Rev. 869, 899 (1990).

perplex scholars of the legal profession, because "law is a highly localized practice, and much of lawyers' expertise consists of insider knowledge of the local legal system and social connections with law enforcement officials."[78] Therefore, the question arises: Why would any Chinese company rely on home-state staff to supervise complex and high-stakes US legal matters? A former executive of a Chinese company commented that assigning an expatriate to be the "boss of the local legal department," which has been the practice of his company, is "very inefficient because the Chinese person does not know local law or even the local language."[79] A satisfactory answer is missing in the existing literature on the corporate in-house movement. Assigning a Chinese expatriate is hardly a cost-efficient substitute for purchasing US legal services, nor is it an effective means to navigate the complex US regulatory regime.

However, the staffing "oddity" of some Chinese companies appointing expatriates to manage their US legal matters may be explained by home-state institutional influence, particularly the extraterritorial and hierarchical control by the SASAC. As discussed in Chapter 1, Chinese SOEs are subject to top-down governmental pressure, which can reach abroad and shape their legal capacity building in the United States. The headquarters of the state-owned companies retain the power to make key personnel decisions concerning the US subsidiaries, and the SASAC has recently tightened its leash over SOEs to curb the managerial discretion of their foreign affiliates.[80] The SASAC rules that have driven the top-down corporate in-house movement in China may also motivate SOEs to establish in-house legal management positions in the United States. An informant who oversees the US legal matters of a Chinese SOE candidly acknowledged that the SASAC requirement was one of the main reasons for his appointment.[81] But why would SOEs choose expatriates to fill these positions? As previously discussed, MNCs that incur high transaction and agency costs in managing US subunits tend to assert more direct control. Companies with complex firm-specific information may have difficulty specifying their legal needs, let alone contracting for legal service provision. Moreover, firm-specific information disincentivizes knowledge investment by

[78] Sida Liu, *The Legal Profession as a Social Process: A Theory on Lawyers and Globalization*, 38 Law & Soc. Inquiry 670, 678 (2013).

[79] Interview with a former executive of a large Chinese MNC (March 23, 2020).

[80] Ouyang, et al., *supra* note 31, at 550.

[81] Interview with an executive of the US subsidiary of a Chinese MNC (May 24, 2018).

service providers, which is necessary for supplying tailored services.[82] Both factors can induce in-house legal capacity building. However, given the complexity of US law, the headquarters of Chinese companies may struggle to articulate valid performance standards or effectively monitor and assess the performance of legal managers in the United States. Therefore, much of the management will depend on cultural control via shared understanding.[83] Hence, the expatriation of managers with deep organizational knowledge.

In addition, certain features of the US regulatory regime exacerbate the agency problem and justify the expatriation of legal managers from China. US regulatory agencies have long deputized enforcement to outside and in-house corporate counsel,[84] which fosters and exploits the misalignment of interest between investors and managers. A nightmare scenario from the perspective of Chinese companies is for their legal managers to become whistleblowers and report their corporate employers for reward money from US government agencies. "Anyone trying hard enough will probably find some violations," commented a senior executive of the US subsidiary of a Chinese SOE, "We want the general counsel to help us mitigate legal risks, not to turn around and report us to the US government."[85] The same agency concern is evident in the description by another executive about how they recruit the legal manager for their US operations, "[we are] searching for a candidate only through acquaintances, to ensure the person is reliable. Otherwise, it will take a long time to build trust."[86] In the absence of local recruits that can meet the requirement, expatriating legal managers from China offers a second-best solution. Years of socialization in the home state can cultivate common values and beliefs that "provide the harmony of interests that erase the possibility of opportunistic behavior."[87] A Chinese manager put it bluntly, "Why does the company use expatriates to manage the US business? The headquarters wants to assert control [over the US operations], and it's easy to do so through expatriates."[88] Likewise, the

82 Klein, et al., *supra* note 9; Gilson, *supra* note 77.

83 Gong, *supra* note 26.

84 Daly, *supra* note 2, at 1089.

85 Interview with a senior executive at a US subsidiary of a Chinese state-owned MNC (August 27, 2018).

86 Interview with a manager of the US business of a large Chinese MNC (February 20, 2020).

87 William G. Ouchi, *Markets, Bureaucracies, and Clans*, 25 Admin. Sci. Q. 129, 138 (1980).

88 Interview with a general counsel of the US subsidiary of a large Chinese MNC (July 16, 2019).

executive who considered management expatriation "very inefficient" ascribed it to headquarters control, "The person can report in Chinese what the subsidiary is doing. That's their default system."[89]

The vast institutional gaps between China and the United States also present significant challenges for local hires trying to understand the corporate objectives of Chinese companies, especially those owned by the state.[90] If profit maximization is not the primary KPI (key performance indicator), what is? What role does the Communist Party cell play, and why do routine business decisions require lengthy approval processes? Local professionals based in the United States would have few clues.[91]

To summarize, one can attribute the "abnormal" expatriation of legal managers to several factors in the dual institutional context: the SASAC directive for Chinese SOEs to enhance internal legal capacities, high agency and transaction costs resulting from the substantial institutional gap between China and the United States, and the US regulatory incentivization for whistleblowing. In other words, qualitative evidence suggests that some Chinese companies, particularly those with state ownership, prefer to send expatriates who have internalized the parent company's interests and values and earned the headquarters' trust to manage their US legal affairs.[92]

2.3.3 US Lawyers Versus Non-US Lawyers

Readers may also find it puzzling that 8.5 percent of Chinese companies employ full-time legal managers who are not US lawyers. Again, home-state institutional influence may explain this "odd" finding. Clearly, had Chinese investors responded solely to the US institutional pressure, none would have employed a lay person to supervise US legal risk management. However, as previously discussed, non-lawyers routinely lead corporate legal departments in China, and the practice may be duplicated by the US subunits due to the home-state institution's extraterritorial influence.[93] Chinese executives at the US subunits, susceptible to

[89] Interview with a former executive of a large Chinese MNC (March 23, 2020).

[90] Alvaro Cuervo-Cazurra, et al., *Governments as Owners: State-Owned Multinational Companies*, 45 J. Int'l Bus. Stud. 919 (2014); Ouyang, et al., *supra* note 31.

[91] Chong-En Bai & Lixin Colin Xu, *Incentives for CEOs with Multitasks: Evidence from Chinese State-Owned Enterprises*, 33 J. Compar. Econ. 517 (2005); Lin Cui & Fuming Jiang, *State Ownership Effect on Firms' FDI Ownership Decisions Under Institutional Pressure: A Study of Chinese Outward-Investing Firms*, 43 J. Int'l Bus. Stud. 264 (2012).

[92] Gong, *supra* note 26, at 729; Harvey, et al., *supra* note 21, at 903.

[93] Holburn & Zelner, *supra* note 60, at 1292–93.

the home-state cultural neglect for formal rules, may under-appreciate the importance of professional qualifications for in-house legal managers. Moreover, as just discussed, concerns about high transaction and agency costs motivate Chinese companies with a great deal of company-specific information to appoint trusted colleagues as US legal managers. Yet, given the relatively low status of in-house counsel in their home offices, candidates assigned to senior management positions often lack extensive legal experience, let alone a license to practice law in the United States. The US legal director of a large Chinese company confessed that he had no US legal training and observed that no senior executive in the headquarters had any legal education. He at least had previously worked with US lawyers.[94] Furthermore, state-owned Chinese companies, responding to the regulatory pressure from Beijing, may "stage" in-house legal managers. Since the position is not created for managing actual US legal risks, a lay person will suffice.

In short, the descriptive survey data provides a snapshot of the internal legal capacity of Chinese companies and reveals significant inter-company variations in the presence and identity of in-house legal managers. Interviews with knowledgeable informants suggest that the Chinese institutions, which motivate and constrain the recent corporate in-house movement, as well as the institutional gaps between China and the United States, shed light on the puzzling expatriation of US legal managers and the employment of lay people for these positions. Section 2.4 will further examine these variations under the dual institutional framework.

2.4 VARIATIONS IN THE INTERNAL US LEGAL CAPACITY

Building upon the qualitative data, this section examines closely the significant inter-company variations in the internal legal capacity of Chinese companies in the United States by testing a series of hypotheses formulated under the dual institutional framework. Before delving into the details, let me summarize the main hypotheses. Chinese companies subject to stronger influence from the home-state institutions are expected to be more likely to have expatriates and laypeople managing their US legal matters, while those immersed in the US institutional context tend to recruit local US legal professionals. Conversely,

[94] Interview with an executive of the US subsidiary of a Chinese MNC (May 24, 2018).

Chinese companies with substantial and recurrent US legal service needs are more likely to hire local, professional legal managers. As noted earlier, the analysis pays special attention to the ownership type of the Chinese investors, an under-explored attribute that defines China's state capitalism and distinguishes Chinese MNCs from those of most other countries. This variable also demarcates the boundary of SASAC jurisdiction, a distinct feature of the home-state institution regarding the recent development of corporate in-house legal capacity in China.

2.4.1 Factors Potentially Associated with Varying Attributes of US Legal Managers

As just discussed, a significant minority of Chinese companies have appointed expatriates or laypeople to fill their full-time legal management positions, which contradicts conventional wisdom. I investigate this puzzle by testing three categories of variables. The first category includes variables that measure or approximate the potential influence of relevant home-state and host-state institutions. The second focuses on key attributes of Chinese companies that are theoretically interesting. The third consists of other hitherto unexplored variables that may correlate with the US legal capacity of Chinese companies (see Table 2.2 in Appendix).

State ownership. Chinese companies with state ownership operate within a distinct home-state institutional environment. As discussed earlier, a top-down, state-driven in-house counsel movement has primarily impacted Chinese SOEs. The rules set by the SASAC to execute the campaign may motivate state-owned Chinese companies to establish full-time legal management positions in the United States. Additionally, state-owned Chinese companies feature unique organizational and contextual attributes that are unfamiliar to US lawyers without any Chinese background. And the knowledge deficiency can result in increased transaction and agency costs, which headquarters may attempt to mitigate by relying on expatriates to manage their US operations.[95]

Cultural difference. The diverging influence of informal institutions may impact how Chinese companies develop their internal legal capacity in the United States. As some of the interviewees have observed, Chinese companies facing intense home-state normative pressure may have internalized the cultural disrespect for formal rules and the penchant

[95] To test this hypothesis, I create a dummy variable from the survey data that equals one if a Chinese government entity owns more than 50 percent of the Chinese investors, zero otherwise. I also construct a dummy representing minority state

for opportunistic compliance, leading them to under-appreciate the value of internal legal capacity. Additionally, cultural gaps can increase transaction costs associated with misunderstanding, miscommunication, and distrust, which may cause Chinese investors to rely on expatriates to manage their US legal affairs. In other words, Chinese companies experiencing strong cultural and normative tensions in the United States may be less inclined to recruit local legal managers.[96]

Corporate internationalization. Presumably, Chinese companies with extensive international exposure have typically distanced themselves from the home-state institutional environment and are more likely to "adopt a cosmopolitan attitude" and localize their foreign operations.[97] Lenovo serves as an illustrative example, as the company acquired IBM's personal computer business in 2005 and has since marketed itself as a global business with Chinese heritage, refraining from expatriating home office managers.[98] As will be shown in Chapter 5, Lenovo even appointed a US lawyer as its global general counsel. Additionally, managers at internationalized Chinese companies face fewer barriers in communicating with local recruits. For instance, an interviewee who is an executive at a large Chinese company in the United States commented on the hiring of a former prosecutor as general counsel, stating, "She does not speak any Chinese. But that's not a problem as managers at the headquarters can speak English."[99] Therefore, I hypothesize that Chinese companies with a high degree of internationalization are more likely to recruit local US legal managers.[100]

ownership to account for government influence beyond majority equity ownership. The dummy equals one if a Chinese government entity owns more than 10 percent but less than 50 percent of a Chinese investor. The two dummies jointly account for the three categorical scenarios: private ownership (including state ownership of less than 10 percent, which is the conventional threshold for passive investment), significant minority state ownership, and majority state ownership (including 100 percent state ownership).

96 To test this hypothesis, I codify a survey question that requests the respondents to choose the major challenges they face while doing business in the United States. The variable equals one if a respondent chose "cultural challenge," zero otherwise.

97 Rosenzweig & Nohria, *supra* note 19, at 234.

98 Li, *supra* note 55, at 25.

99 Interview with a senior executive of the US branch of a large state-owned Chinese MNC (January 8, 2020).

100 To measure the internationalization of Chinese MNCs, I create a dummy variable from a survey question that inquired about the competitive edge of the responding firm. Among the multiple choices was "globalized business operation." The dummy equals one if the respondent made this selection, zero otherwise.

Importance of US market. According to previous research on international human resource management, the importance of a foreign market induces tight headquarters control.[101] Interviews have suggested that this connection might also apply to the staffing of US legal management positions. For instance, the legal director of a large Chinese company stated that the company had established US operations years before and regarded the market as strategically important, which is why they have consistently relied on expatriate managers to oversee US legal affairs.[102] According to the interviewee, the current legal director is primarily responsible for coordination and control, regularly reporting to the headquarters on US legal and regulatory risks and conducting internal audits of local managers.[103] Therefore, holding other factors constant, those that view the US market as essential to their global operations may seek greater control over the associated risks, and one way to achieve this is by dispatching trusted home-state managers. In other words, both interviews and descriptive survey data suggest a positive association between the importance of the American market to a Chinese company and the likelihood of expatriating legal managers to the United States.[104]

Listing status. As noted in Chapter 1, major capital markets facilitated China's economic reform by compelling or inducing the "corporatization" and "Westernization" of Chinese business organizations,[105] and many Chinese companies large enough to invest in the United States have listed their stocks on securities exchanges in China and abroad. The listing status of these companies may be related to their US legal capacity, as the extra regulatory oversight may amplify the impact of US legal risks on publicly traded companies. For instance,

[101] Tan & Mahoney, *supra* note 4, at 476; Harvey, et al., *supra* note 21, at 903.

[102] Interview with the legal director of the US subsidiary of a large Chinese state-owned MNC (September 15, 2020).

[103] *Id.*

[104] To test this hypothesis about internal control, I codify the variable using data derived from the survey, which contained a question that ranked the importance of the US market in the Chinese MNC's global business in the following order: (i) the US market is the top one market of the global business; (ii) not the top one market, but among the top three; (iii) one of many investment destinations; and (iv) not an important market. I create a scale measure of market importance commensurate with this ranking. The scale measure is from one to four, with one being the least important and four being the most important.

[105] *See, e.g.*, Edward S. Steinfeld, Playing Our Game: Why China's Rise Doesn't Threaten the West (2010); Gongmeng Chen, et al., *Have China's Enterprise Reforms Led to Improved Efficiency and Profitability?*, 7 Emerging Markets Rev. 82 (2006).

mandatory disclosure of lawsuits with "a material effect" on share price may increase transaction and compliance costs for listed companies and negatively affect their share price.[106] Despite being in a transitional phase, the Chinese capital market is responsive to major legal and regulatory risk disclosures.[107] Therefore, publicly traded Chinese companies may take legal risks more seriously and exercise tighter control over their global management, resulting in the expatriation of US legal managers. However, an alternative argument can be made that the additional institutional pressure from securities regulators may motivate listed Chinese companies to mitigate legal risks by localizing their management. Statistical analysis helps to weigh in on the indeterminate effect.[108]

Size of US operation. Chinese companies with substantial operations in the United States inevitably encounter more local legal issues that require repeated and routine legal services. Research on the in-house counsel movement has shown that companies often handle such matters internally to save costs.[109] An executive at a Chinese company in the financial sector offered an illustrative example, stating, "Initially, we did not have a legal department. The company received several subpoenas each year, and the compliance director handled them through outside lawyers. As the business expanded, we received more subpoenas, and the company decided to hire an in-house counsel."[110] Similarly,

106 Paragraph 1, Section 11, Rules re Listing of Shares on the Shenzhen Stock Exchange; Paragraph 1, Section 11, Rules re Listing of Shares on the Shanghai Stock Exchange; Paul A. Griffin, et al., *Stock Price Response to News of Securities Fraud Litigation: An Analysis of Sequential and Conditional Information*, 40 ABACUS 25 (2004).

107 Min Yu, et al., *Zhida Susong Gonggao Pilu Dui Shangshi Gongsi Gujia de Yingxiang-Jiyu Zhongda Susong Gonggao de Shijian Yanjiu [The Impact of Disclosure of Major Litigation Announcements on the Stock Prices of Listed Companies – An Event Study Based on Major Litigation Announcements]*, SHIDAI JINRONG [TIMES FINANCE] 137, 137–38 (2014).

108 To test the indeterminate effects of listing status, I codify a dummy variable from the survey data that takes the value of one if a Chinese business in the United States is managed by a listed company, zero otherwise. One may reasonably argue that accessing the US securities market differs significantly from having securities traded elsewhere in terms of compliance cost. Sung Hui Kim, *The Banality of Fraud: Re-situating the Inside Counsel as Gatekeeper*, 74 FORDHAM L. REV. 997 (2005). Therefore, I create an alternative listing status dummy that equals one if a Chinese investor is listed in the United States, zero otherwise. I incorporate this alternative variable in robustness tests.

109 Daly, *supra* note 2, at 1960; Gilson, *supra* note 77; Simmons & Dinnage, *supra* note 6.

110 Interview with a general counsel of the US subsidiary of a large Chinese MNC (July 16, 2019).

a US in-house lawyer at another sizable Chinese company described her job as primarily "reviewing draft contracts (e.g., nondisclosure agreements) based on fixed templates."[111] Additionally, Chinese companies with significant US investments are more deeply embedded in the stringent and complex host-country legal and regulatory system, subjecting them to strong isomorphic pressure.[112] These factors should contribute to localized, professional legal risk management.[113]

Sectoral regulation. The degree of formal institutional pressure from the host state varies across different sectors. In highly regulated sectors such as banking and telecommunications, Chinese companies may encounter more firm-specific legal issues, which leads to internal legal service production. Moreover, local knowledge is critical in such sectors for dealing with government agencies, and it is not a trivial task for expatriates to earn the trust of host-state regulators. According to the manager of a Chinese company operating in the financial sector, which is subject to extensive regulation at both the federal and state levels, one-third of the firm's US staff were hired to handle compliance and legal matters,[114] a ratio significantly higher than the average for commercial banks in China. Thus, it is reasonable to speculate that Chinese companies operating in heavily regulated sectors in the United States are more likely to hire full-time *local* legal managers.[115]

[111] Interview with in-house counsel of the US subsidiary of a large Chinese MNC (January 31, 2019).

[112] Daly, *supra* note 2, at 1075; Tan & Mahoney, *supra* note 4, at 474; Rosenzweig & Nohria, *supra* note 19, at 237.

[113] To test this hypothesis, I measure the size of Chinese MNCs' US operations with the US business revenue reported by the surveyed Chinese firms. Each of the respondents chose one of five levels of revenue, with the lowest level being "below one million dollars" and the highest level "above 100 million dollars." This variable also helps to control for a possible correlation with the ownership structure of Chinese investors, as SOEs dominate the list of the largest Chinese firms.

[114] Interview with an executive of the US branch of a Chinese MNC (September 1, 2018).

[115] To evaluate this hypothesis and to control for a possible correlation with the ownership structure of Chinese MNCs, I rely on the regulation intensity index compiled by McLaughlin and colleagues. The survey collected information about the responding firms' primary sector of business, designated by a two-digit NAICS code which corresponds to a regulatory intensity index number. All the respondents report their industries. I checked all their official websites or, when such websites are not available, third-party reports to ascertain their industries. For those operating in multiple industries, I use the one most heavily regulated. As is typical with this type of proxy measures, the index is not perfect. For instance, real estate is a relatively heavily regulated industry, but because it is normally regulated at

Duration of US investment. The length of time that a Chinese company has been conducting business in the United States may also be correlated with their internal US legal capacity building.[116] Pioneer investors may have adapted to the host-country legal context and recognized the importance of professional in-house legal management. "In the beginning, they didn't appreciate the value of legal service," observed a US lawyer with years of experience advising Chinese clients, "until a lawsuit hit, and they suffered a heavy loss. Then they learned not to care about nickels and dimes in buying [US] legal services."[117] Early entrants might also have encountered recurrent legal issues that justified the use of internal legal service production. Additionally, research in international human resource management shows that the longer a company operates in a foreign country, the more likely it is to rely on local recruits, as trust can be forged through repeated interactions with the home office.[118] However, recent empirical research has identified contradictory evidence.[119] To assess the indeterminate effects of investment duration, I propose a working hypothesis that Chinese companies with a longer US investment history are more likely to employ full-time local legal managers.[120]

Mode of US investment. Investment strategies adopted by Chinese companies in the United States may potentially influence their legal management staffing decisions.[121] Specifically, acquiring an operational US company may result in a more localized workforce.[122] One interviewee mentioned that her company took over a US firm and retained the entire workforce, including the in-house legal team. In this case,

the state and local level, the industry appears to be subject to light federal regulation. For more details, see Patrick A. McLaughlin & Oliver Sherouse, RegData US 3.1 Annual (dataset), QuantGov, Mercatus Center at George Mason University, Arlington, VA, 2018, https://quantgov.org/regdata-us/.

116 Downes & Thomas, *supra* note 22, at 132; Gong, *supra* note 26, at 728–29; Rosenzweig & Nohria, *supra* note 19, at 235.

117 Interview with a partner of the US office of a large Chinese law firm (June 8, 2019).

118 Gong, *supra* note 26, at 729; Rosenzweig & Nohria, *supra* note 19.

119 Tan & Mahoney, *supra* note 4, at 475.

120 Adding this variable also controls for its possible correlation with the ownership structure of Chinese investors, as SOEs played a more central role in earlier Chinese outbound investment. Yadong Luo, et al., *How Emerging Market Governments Promote Outward FDI: Experience from China*, 45 J. World Bus. 68 (2010); Li, *supra* note 55. The variable equals the number of years a Chinese investor has operated in the United States.

121 Rosenzweig & Nohria, *supra* note 19, at 234.

122 Tan & Mahoney, *supra* note 4, at 475.

the Chinese headquarters sent only one person, the interviewee herself, to oversee the US operations.[123] The Lenovo example, previously discussed, tells a similar story of management localization through the acquisition of an established US business.[124]

2.4.2 Analysis of Test Results

As shown in Table 2.3, in the Appendix to this chapter,[125] Chinese investors with majority state ownership are more likely to expatriate legal managers to the United States, which affirms the influence of home-state institutions. The Chinese government agencies supervising SOEs have been advocating for their expansion of in-house legal capacity, and this pressure extends beyond China's borders. Moreover, Chinese companies with majority state ownership exhibit acute multitasking and multiagency issues,[126] leading to performance ambiguity for locally recruited managers and incongruent interests with the headquarters. To address these issues, state-owned companies often rely on trusted home office employees to oversee the management of complex host-country legal risks and to coordinate myriad internal matters and transactions. For example, an interviewee who is the US legal director of a state-owned Chinese company described his job as "open-ended."[127] His numerous responsibilities include, among others, compliance training and monitoring, internal auditing, analyzing legal, regulatory, and policy risks, writing reports to the headquarters, and

123 Interview with an executive of the US subsidiary of a Chinese company (June 23, 2017).

124 I use two dummy variables extrapolated from the survey data to evaluate this hypothetical association. The first dummy equals one if a Chinese company entered the US market via a merger or an acquisition or by forming a joint venture, zero otherwise. For some of the Chinese companies, however, the type of entry does not fully account for the investment mode. They may start by setting up a small presence in the United States to test the market and identify potential acquisition targets, and large-scale mergers or acquisitions may occur years later. Thus, I create another dummy variable that equals one if a responding firm has engaged in a merger or acquisition in the past two years, zero otherwise. The working hypotheses corresponding with the two dummies are the following: (i) all else being equal, Chinese companies that entered the US market via a merger, an acquisition, or a joint venture are more likely to employ local legal managers; and (ii) Chinese companies that recently conducted mergers or acquisitions in the United States are more likely to employ local legal managers.

125 Because the dependent variable is categorical (e.g., no US legal manager; expatriated US legal manager; locally recruited US legal manager), I run a series of multinomial logit tests.

126 Cuervo-Cazurra, et al., *supra* note 90.

127 Interview with the legal director at the US subsidiary of a large Chinese state-owned MNC (September 15, 2020).

organizing study sessions on relevant legal and policy changes.[128] It is difficult to imagine a local hire who would be capable of and entrusted with carrying out all these tasks.

In addition, Chinese companies with majority state ownership are more likely to have a non-legal professional supervising US legal risk management (see Table 2.4 in Appendix). This is because the SASAC rules mandate state-owned Chinese companies to establish in-house positions. However, as discussed earlier, due to the nature of the institutional pressure, SOEs may engage in superficial compliance by appointing a layperson as the US legal manager.

The influence of the home-state institutions is further demonstrated by the fact that Chinese companies experiencing stronger cultural tensions in the United States are *less* likely to establish a full-time legal management position and fill it with a local recruit. Stronger pulls from informal institutions in China shape the executives' normative attitudes and views regarding the significance of law for corporate legitimacy and success. In the same vein, culturally handicapped Chinese companies in the United States are less likely to hire professionals to manage their legal risks (see Table 2.4 in Appendix).

Affirming the control hypothesis, the importance of the US market to a Chinese MNC is significantly associated with the expatriation of US legal managers (see Table 2.3 in Appendix). If the US investment is a significant revenue source for a Chinese MNC, poorly managed US legal risks may imperil its entire business, hence the propensity to rely on expatriates. The US market may be important even if it generates an insignificant amount of revenue. Huawei serves as an illustrative example. Though the revenue from its US businesses is trivial, Huawei's chief legal officer, an engineer by training without any US law background, has been overseeing its litigation against the US government, the policies and measure of which pose an existential threat to the Chinese MNC.[129] As will be detailed in Chapter 6, Huawei's headquarters overrode the objections of its US management team on the decision to sue the US government.[130] In brief, Chinese companies

128 *Id.*

129 Phillip Bantz, *Huawei's Chief Legal Officer Takes Center Stage in Conflict with U.S.*, LAW.COM (May 29, 2019), at www.law.com/corpcounsel/2019/05/29/huaweis-chief-legal-officer-takes-center-stage-in-conflict-with-us/.

130 Dan Strumpf, *Huawei Founder Ren Zhengfei Takes Off the Gloves in Fight against U.S.*, WALL STREET J. (June 6, 2020), at www.wsj.com/articles/huawei-founder-ren-zhengfei-takes-off-the-gloves-in-fight-against-u-s-11591416028.

taking the US market seriously exert more control over the US operations by establishing full-time legal management positions and staffing them with trusted expatriates.

Additionally, consistent with the literature on the corporate in-house movement, the size of Chinese companies' US investments, as measured by revenue, is significantly associated with the employment of locals as US legal managers. Larger operations generate repeat legal matters, which can be dealt with more cost-efficiently by full-time in-house counsel.[131] An interviewee commented on his company's recent switch from retaining an outside lawyer as a part-time "corporate counsel" to hiring a full-time in-house legal manager, noting that "having a full-time general counsel may be less expensive."[132] Comparatively low compensation at Chinese companies operating in the United States further enables cost saving. An interviewee reported that his company filled an in-house position with a recent law school graduate instead of a lawyer with more practice experience, mainly because the former was "much cheaper" and "easy to retain."[133] The executive at another Chinese company made similar observations:

> The in-house counsel has a low rank ... The candidate pool was very small. First of all, the person has to be bilingual. Many executives in China don't speak English. If they cannot understand the in-house counsel, it is hard to have trust in him. Also, the in-house must fit in the highly competitive corporate culture, being able to "eat bitterness." Most Americans cannot ... Our pay is about 70% of the [US] market rate.[134]

Moreover, larger US operations are deeply entrenched in the complex US institutional environment, necessitating adaptation and localization. For instance, the manager of a large Chinese company with extensive US business implored his fellow executives to "think like Americans, speak like Americans, and act like Americans" in order to succeed in the US market.[135] Furthermore, due to the

[131] Lipson, *supra* note 1, at 240; Glidden, *supra* note 7, at 134.

[132] Interview with CEO of the US subsidiary of a large state-owned Chinese MNC (May 29, 2019).

[133] Interview with the general counsel of the US subsidiary of a large state-owned Chinese MNC (September 15, 2020).

[134] Interview with a manager at the US subsidiary of a large Chinese MNC (June 12, 2019).

[135] Statement by Peter Wu, vice president of China Construction America, during a panel at "Roads to USA: Greenfield Investment vs Cross-border M&A Forum" (June 20, 2017).

particular characteristics of the US adjudicatory system, companies with deep pockets are more likely to be targeted with lawsuits and legal threats,[136] and foreign investors with significant US business exposure are no exception.[137] Frequent litigation in the United States justifies hiring local legal managers to coordinate with outside lawyers (see Chapter 5 for further discussion). For the same reasons, Chinese investors with larger US operations are more likely to employ legal managers licensed to practice US law (see Table 2.4).

Furthermore, Chinese companies with higher levels of business internationalization are more likely to hire local legal managers. As previously discussed, companies in China often under-invest in legal capacity due to the secondary role of law in their business transactions. In contrast, Chinese companies with extensive international experience are more aware of the importance of legal risk management.[138] Nonetheless, few of these companies have built a reserve of Chinese managers capable of supervising legal service production in host countries with sophisticated legal systems. Neglected or undervalued, in-house counsel positions at most firms within China typically do not attract high caliber lawyers, let alone lawyers with rich international practice experience capable of managing US legal risks. Additionally, internationalized Chinese firms face less institutional difference, which makes adaptation easier. Thus, Chinese companies with greater international exposure are more likely to fund full-time legal management positions in the United States and to staff them with local recruits. For the same reasons, these Chinese companies are also more likely to hire licensed lawyers to manage their US legal matters (see Table 2.4).

Lastly, Chinese companies that have recently acquired established US businesses are more likely to employ local legal managers. This finding is intuitive as Chinese buyers tend to retain the management team of the target US firm, including the in-house counsel. After all, a key motive driving such transactions is to gain quick access to the sophisticated US market, of which local managers constitute a crucial component. None of the other variables are significant.

[136] Kagan, *supra* note 62.

[137] John M. Mezias, *Identifying Liabilities of Foreignness and Strategies to Minimize Their Effects: The Case of Labor Lawsuit Judgments in the United States*, 23 Strategic Mgmt. J. 229 (2002).

[138] Gregory Shaffer & Henry Gao, *China's Rise: How It Took on the US at the WTO*, 2018 U. Ill. L. Rev. 115.

However, due to the limited sample size, definitive inferences from the null results will be left to future empirical research.

In summary, subject to the dual institutional pressure of their home and host-state environments, Chinese companies in the United States cultivate varying levels of internal legal capacity. Empirical evidence revealed connections between the varying attributes of the US legal managers and the SASAC rules regulating Chinese SOEs, cultural differences between the two countries, size of the US investment, business globalization, US market importance, and recent acquisition of US businesses. These factors exert pressure, often in opposite directions, on the Chinese companies, leading some to adapt by hiring local and professional in-house lawyers, while others resist by relying on expatriates or lay managers to supervise US legal matters.

2.5 CONCLUSION

To navigate the complex US legal system, Chinese companies must have basic legal capacity, which can be either developed internally or acquired from outside lawyers. Competent in-house counsel can identify US legal risks, implement preventive measures, produce or purchase legal services, and manage outside lawyers. However, due to cost concerns and cultural neglect of legal risks, the majority of Chinese companies in the United States have not employed full-time legal managers. Among those that have established such in-house positions, some have filled them with expatriates or non-US lawyers. In particular, state-owned Chinese companies tend to assign expatriates and laypeople to oversee the management of their US legal matters due to distinct SASAC rules, and high transaction and agency costs. Similarly, Chinese companies under stronger home-state cultural influence are less likely to rely on locally recruited US lawyers to manage their US legal risks.

These findings shed light on the other topics this book will explore, namely, Chinese companies' consumption of US legal services and their litigation in US courts. But before proceeding, I would like to highlight a few theoretical and practical contributions outside the scope of this book. First, this chapter adds to the literature on the legal profession, particularly the nascent research about the worldwide in-house counsel movement,[139] where the legal capacity of MNCs has made only a passing

[139] Wilkins, *supra* note 3.

appearance.[149] According to the findings of this chapter, future research about the legal capacity of non-Western MNCs would benefit from considering institutional multiplicity and corporate ownership diversity. Moreover, the empirical findings have affirmed some conventional wisdom, such as a positive association between US business size and MNCs' employment of locally recruited legal managers. Additionally, the analysis highlights the expatriation of US legal managers, a hitherto under-explored phenomenon that contradicts conventional wisdom.

Second, this chapter contributes to the scholarship on international human resource management, which has thus far overlooked emerging market MNCs and staffing in the area of law. Consistent with the control and coordination function of management expatriation documented in prior research, Chinese companies with majority government ownership are more likely to send trusted home-state staff to oversee the management of US legal risks. Also, echoing the mainstream literature, Chinese companies taking the US market seriously tend to have expatriates occupy their legal management positions.

APPENDIX

TABLE 2.1 Legal and compliance departments at Chinese multinationals' US subunits (2022 Survey question: What is the structure of the legal and/or compliance department of your company at the US level? [select all that apply])

Answer choices	Response (%)
There is neither a legal department nor a compliance department	45.92
There is a standalone legal department	18.37
There is a standalone compliance department	17.35
There is a department for both legal and compliance work	18.37
There is a department for legal, compliance, and audit work	5.10
There is a department for risk, legal, compliance, and audit work	11.22

Note: Data from 2022 CGCC Survey; 98 subjects answered this question.

[149] Daly, *supra* note 2; David B. Wilkins & Vikramaditya S. Khanna, *South by Southeast*, *in* THE BRAZILIAN LEGAL PROFESSION IN THE AGE OF GLOBALIZATION: THE RISE OF THE CORPORATE LEGAL SECTOR AND ITS IMPACT ON LAWYERS AND SOCIETY 110–58 (2018).

TABLE 2.2 Summary statistics

Variable	Mean	Standard deviation	Min.	Max.	Number of observations
State ownership (50%)	0.304	0.461	0	1	230
State ownership (10%)	0.078	0.269	0	1	230
Years in the US	10.27	8.325	1	38	218
Cultural challenge	0.275	0.447	0	1	193
Listed company	0.398	0.491	0	1	226
Listed company (US)	0.066	0.249	0	1	226
Entry mode	0.214	0.411	0	1	220
Annual US revenue	2.535	1.587	1	5	202
Recent M&A	0.2697	0.445	0	1	178
Sectoral regulation	50,656.02	52,294.36	511.455	214,953.4	230
Internationalization	0.411	0.493	0	1	197
US market importance	2.396	0.98	1	4	187

Note: M&A = mergers and acquisitions. Data from 2019 CGCC Annual Survey.

TABLE 2.3 Test results

	Variable	Model 1	Model 2	Model 3	Model 4	Model 5
Having an expatriated legal manager	State ownership (50%)	3.470*** (0.985)	3.522*** (1.007)	3.418*** (1.021)	3.603*** (1.133)	3.805*** (1.196)
	State ownership (10%)	1.704 (1.397)	1.465 (1.475)	1.369 (1.483)	1.251 (1.595)	1.646 (1.659)
	Years in the US	−0.011 (0.039)	−0.003 (0.040)	−0.003 (0.040)	0.001 (0.042)	−0.001 (0.043)
	US revenue	0.043 (0.231)	0.002 (0.235)	−0.007 (0.236)	0.021 (0.243)	0.004 (0.247)
	US market importance	1.002** (0.442)	1.069** (.462)	1.035** (0.463)	1.242** (0.535)	1.299** (0.557)
	Internationalization	0.825 (0.694)	0.782 (0.708)	0.757 (0.714)	1.080 (0.781)	1.124 (0.790)
	Cultural challenge	0.947 (0.748)	1.059 (0.769)	1.029 (0.772)	1.296 (0.847)	1.292 (0.849)
	Listed company		0.991 (0.712)	0.970 (0.712)	1.293 (0.790)	1.296 (0.802)
	Entry mode			−0.447 (1.151)	−0.166 (1.176)	0.240 (1.266)
	Recent M&A				0.342 (0.848)	0.282 (0.866)
	Sectoral regulation					−7.56e-06 (9.21e-06)
	Constant	−7.369*** (1.863)	−8.088*** (2.061)	−7.800*** (2.120)	−9.348*** (2.607)	−9.293*** (2.696)

Having a locally hired legal manager	State ownership (50%)	0.104	0.091	0.084	0.182	0.276
		(0.462)	(0.465)	(0.471)	(0.479)	(0.493)
	State ownership (10%)	0.354	0.326	0.327	0.497	0.529
		(0.698)	(0.706)	(0.710)	(0.707)	(0.717)
	Years in the US	–0.030	–0.029	–0.027	–0.034	–0.036
		(0.025)	(0.025)	(0.025)	(0.026)	(0.026)
	US revenue	0.346***	0.334**	0.331**	0.309**	0.313**
		(0.135)	(0.137)	(0.137)	(0.139)	(0.142)
	US market importance	0.159	0.159	0.147	0.112	0.160
		(0.203)	(0.204)	(0.205)	(0.210)	(0.215)
	Internationalization	0.876**	0.856**	0.844**	0.830**	0.854**
		(0.386)	(0.387)	(0.388)	(0.393)	(0.398)
	Cultural challenge	–1.331***	–1.337***	–1.340***	–1.469***	–1.480***
		(0.482)	(0.481)	(0.481)	(0.497)	(0.510)
	Listed company		0.218	0.219	0.139	0.148
			(0.390)	(0.389)	(0.396)	(0.401)
	Entry mode			0.077	0.049	0.073
				(0.449)	(0.464)	(0.472)
	Recent M&A				0.839*	0.880*
					(0.445)	(0.452)
	Sectoral regulation					1.90e-06
						(4.00e-06)
	Constant	–1.659**	–1.710**	–1.692**	–1.674	–1.960*
		(0.652)	(0.661)	(0.683)	(0.700)	(0.759)
Having no legal manager	Base outcome					
	N	159	159	158	156	153
	Pseudo R^2	0.177	0.184	0.183	0.203	0.208

Note: Data source: 2019 CGCC Annual Survey; *p<0.1, **p<0.5, ***p<0.01.

TABLE 2.4 Test results

	Variable	Model 1	Model 2	Model 3	Model 4	Model 5
Having a layperson as legal manager	State ownership (50%)	1.878***	1.905***	1.926***	1.983***	2.064***
		(0.686)	(0.693)	(0.711)	(0.718)	(0.734)
	State ownership (10%)	13.465	–12.482	12.181	12.013	13.188
		(1178.007)	(716.892)	(631.029)	(628.343)	(1164.028)
	Years in the US	–0.024	–0.023	–0.021	–0.024	–0.028
		(0.034)	(0.034)	(0.034)	(0.034)	(0.035)
	US revenue	0.310	0.309	0.309	0.276	0.289
		(0.203)	(0.202)	(0.202)	(0.204)	(0.206)
	US market importance	0.425	0.422	0.417	0.377	0.390
		(0.354)	(0.354)	(0.355)	(0.359)	(0.365)
	Internationalization	0.849	0.850	0.829	0.792	0.809
		(0.613)	(0.628)	(0.629)	(0.634)	(0.641)
	Cultural challenge	–0.703	–0.648	–0.636	–0.751	–0.782
		(0.734)	(0.735)	(0.735)	(0.742)	(0.747)
	Listed company		–0.342	–0.302	–0.150	–0.189
			(0.954)	(0.965)	(0.976)	(0.988)
	Entry mode			0.198	0.207	0.279
				(0.777)	(0.785)	(0.800)
	Recent M&A				0.754	0.774
					(0.691)	(0.692)
	Sectoral regulation					–1.29e-06
						(6.88e-06)
	Constant	–4.450***	–4.443***	–4.500***	–4.475***	–4.478***
		(1.286)	(1.286)	(1.340)	(1.353)	(1.416)

Having a US lawyer as legal manager	State ownership (50%)	0.365 (0.452)	0.473 (0.459)	0.438 (0.465)	0.434 (0.481)	0.578 (0.493)
	State ownership (10%)	0.662 (0.657)	0.615 (0.661)	0.577 (0.668)	0.730 (0.668)	0.823 (0.688)
	Years in the US	–0.027 (0.025)	–0.027 (0.026)	–0.027 (0.026)	–0.030 (0.026)	–0.034 (0.027)
	US revenue	0.276** (0.132)	0.287** (0.133)	0.284** (0.134)	0.270** (0.136)	0.278** (0.138)
	US market importance	0.264 (0.201)	0.276 (0.202)	0.267 (0.203)	0.248 (0.207)	0.291 (0.214)
	Internationalization	0.898** (0.382)	0.953** (0.388)	0.950** (0.388)	0.980** (0.396)	1.005** (0.403)
	Cultural challenge	–0.845** (0.440)	–0.810* (0.448)	–0.818* (0.447)	–0.916** (0.459)	–0.879* (0.469)
	Listed company		–1.210 (0.893)	–1.233 (0.897)	–1.040 (0.904)	–1.056 (0.911)
	Entry mode			–0.137 (0.464)	–0.123 (0.479)	–0.107 (0.489)
	Recent M&A				0.689 (0.444)	0.706 (0.453)
	Sectoral regulation					–2.01e-07 (4.08e-06)
	Constant	–1.999*** (0.665)	–2.057*** (0.670)	–1.977*** (0.689)	–2.085*** (0.712)	–2.285*** (0.776)
Having no legal manager	Base outcome					
	N	159	159	158	156	153
	Pseudo R^2	0.120	0.127	0.125	0.138	0.141

Note: Data source: 2019 CGCC Annual Survey; *p<0.1, **p<0.5, ***p<0.01.

CHAPTER THREE

CHINESE COMPANIES AND THEIR US LAWYERS

Lawyers are like salt in the US [essential to doing business]; whereas in China lawyers are merely MSG [simply to add flavor]

—Senior partner of a Chinese international law firm

With or without professional in-house counsel, Chinese companies must rely heavily on outside lawyers to effectively manage legal risks in the United States. Companies operating in the United States must navigate through an intricate web of legal rights and obligations, which cannot be done without adequate legal assistance. While a vast literature has accumulated on the US legal profession and the legal service market, few scholars have studied the interactions between multinational companies (MNCs) and their US lawyers, leaving important questions open. For instance, do Chinese companies bring their lack of appreciation or even contempt for lawyers and legal services to the United States, or do they adapt to the host-state environment and take legal advice seriously? Moreover, how do Chinese companies choose from the 1.3 million US lawyers, many of whom would claim without hesitation to be "leading experts" in their practice areas? And how much do Chinese companies spend on US legal services? Are they becoming a significant revenue source for US law firms, which will give them pricing power in the market and the ability to dictate how legal services are provided? Do their lawyer selection preferences and legal expenditures vary across different Chinese companies, and if so, what institutional and firm-specific factors may explain the variations?

This chapter answers these crucial yet unexplored questions within the dual institutional framework articulated in Chapter 1. It proceeds in four steps. Section 3.1 briefly reviews the literature on corporate consumption of US legal services, which provides insight into the host-state institutional pressures on Chinese companies in the United States. However, as just noted, the literature has overlooked corporate legal service consumers from China or other developing countries. Section 3.2 analyzes the interviews and the descriptive survey data to examine how Chinese companies use US legal services, how they select US lawyers, and their legal budgets. Section 3.3 investigates the inter-company variations in the lawyer selection preferences and corporate legal budgets, with a focus on the institutional factors such as state ownership and cultural differences experienced by Chinese companies in the United States. Finally, Section 3.4 concludes the Chapter.

3.1 LITERATURE ON CORPORATE CONSUMPTION OF LEGAL SERVICES

Research about the legal profession and legal service market has spawned a vast literature in the past few decades that encompasses diverse theoretical perspectives. However, the existing scholarship on corporate consumption of legal services, like that on corporate in-house counsel, has primarily focused on three key questions. The first is information asymmetry. Legal services are generally considered a credence good, defined as a "service whose usefulness or necessity to the buyer is better known to the seller than to the buyer."[1] In other words, average corporate consumers, unable to identify or assess the needs, quality, and price of legal services,[2] must rely heavily on the diagnostic and referral functions of their outside lawyers.[3] The lawyers therefore hold considerable leverage over their clients when setting the price and quantity of services. As discussed in Chapter 2, corporate clients can mitigate this information asymmetry by internalizing legal service production,[4] that is, bringing lawyers in-house. However, companies usually have

[1] Yuk-fai Fong, *When Do Experts Cheat and Whom Do They Target?*, 36 RAND J. ECON. 113, 113 (2005).

[2] Ronald J. Gilson, *The Devolution of the Legal Profession: A Demand Side Perspective*, 49 MD. L. REV. 869, 889 (1990); Larry E. Ribstein, *The Death of Big Law*, 2010 WIS. L. REV. 749, 753.

[3] Gilson, *supra* note 2, at 902–03.

[4] Ribstein, *supra* note 2, at 760; David B. Wilkins, *Team of Rivals? Toward a New Model of the Corporate Attorney-Client Relationship*, 78 FORDHAM L. REV. 2067, 2080 (2009).

"variable and unpredictable" legal needs, making it cost-ineffective to keep enough full-time, in-house lawyers.[5] Law firms, on the other hand, "can pool the variable demand each client may have, lowering overall volatility of demand"[6] and provide legal services more efficiently, provided their interests are well aligned with those of their clients. Numerous professional rules and contractual arrangements aim at aligning the interests and mitigating the agency costs. After decades of mutual adaptation, many US corporations turn to a panel of repeat service providers.[7] This model reduces management cost, encourages healthy competition among outside lawyers, and incentivizes them to invest in acquiring company-specific knowledge.[8]

Another line of research on corporate legal service consumption centers on the value transactional lawyers may add in a market of incomplete information. First, lawyers can serve as reputational intermediaries that allow their clients to acquire credibility for a transaction.[9] For instance, hiring a prestigious US law firm as an issuer's counsel in an initial public offering can provide quality assurance to potential investors.[10] Second, as repeat players in the market, business lawyers can act as "transaction cost engineers" that mitigate various sources of inefficiency in capital asset transfers.[11] They also accumulate a wealth of deal knowledge that helps corporate clients achieve optimal deal structuring and pricing, which is particularly valuable in a volatile market for innovative transactions.[12] Third, deal lawyers may play a crucial part in ensuring corporate compliance with complex laws and regulations, such as those governing market concentration.[13]

Still another stream of the research examines how business globalization drives the internationalization of the legal service market and

5 John C. Coates, et al., *Hiring Teams, Firms, and Lawyers: Evidence of the Evolving Relationships in the Corporate Legal Market*, 36 LAW & SOC. INQUIRY 999, 1001 (2011).
6 *Id.*
7 Wilkins, *supra* note 4, at 2085.
8 Coates, et al., *supra* note 5, at 1002.
9 Karl S. Okamoto, *Reputation and the Value of Lawyers*, 74 OR. L. REV. 15, 22 (1995).
10 *Id.*, at 27.
11 Ronald J. Gilson, *Value Creation by Business Lawyers: Legal Skills and Asset Pricing*, 94 YALE L.J. 239, 255 (1984).
12 Elisabeth de Fontenay, *Law Firm Selection and the Value of Transactional Lawyering*, 41 J. CORP. L. 393, 405–6 (2015).
13 Steven L. Schwarcz, *Explaining the Value of Transactional Lawyering*, 12 STAN. J.L. BUS. & FIN. 486, 500 (2007).

the legal profession.[14] As US companies grow their businesses overseas, they often rely on trusted American law firms to handle complex cross-border and even foreign law issues, motivating these law firms to expand their services globally.[15] Some have even established offices in major emerging markets and begun to serve local clients,[16] although their services are often circumscribed.[17] The presence of Western law firms has produced spillover effects on the corporate legal service market and the legal profession of developing countries.[18]

To summarize, the existing literature sheds light on the purchase and consumption of legal services by US corporations, but it has largely been silent on MNCs, particularly Chinese companies operating in the United States.[19] The rest of this chapter attempts to address this knowledge gap.

3.2 CHINESE COMPANIES AND US LAWYERS

Chinese companies are exposed to dual institutional pressures from their home and host states. As previously discussed, despite years of

[14] *See, e.g.*, James R. Faulconbridge, et al., *Global Law Firms: Globalization and Organizational Spaces of Cross-Border Legal Work*, 28 Nw. J. Int'l L. & Bus. 455 (2007); John Flood, *Institutional Bridging: How Large Law Firms Engage in Globalization*, 36 B.C. Int'l & Comp. L. Rev. 1087 (2013); Ashly H. Pinnington & John T. Gray, *The Global Restructuring of Legal Services Work? A Study of the Internationalisation of Australian Law Firms*, 14 Int'l J. Legal Profession 147 (2007); Carole Silver, *Local Matters: Internationalizing Strategies for US Law Firms*, 14 Ind. J. Glob. Legal Stud. 67 (2007); Carole Silver, et al., *Between Diffusion and Distinctiveness in Globalization: US Law Firms Go Global*, 22 Geo. J. Legal Ethics 1431 (2009); Richard L. Abel, *Transnational Law Practice*, 44 Case W. Res. L. Rev. 737 (1993).

[15] Wilkins, *supra* note 4, at 2090. Of course, demand from existing clients is not the only reason for the global expansion of US law firms. *See* Abel, *supra* note 14, at 739–41.

[16] Rachel E. Stern & Su Li, *The Outpost Office: How International Law Firms Approach the China Market*, 41 Law & Soc. Inquiry 184, 185 (2015).

[17] *Id.*, at 200.

[18] *See, e.g.*, Bryant Garth, *Corporate Lawyers in Emerging Markets*, 12 Annual Rev. L. & Soc. Sci. 441 (2016); Sida Liu, *Globalization as Boundary-Blurring: International and Local Law Firms in China's Corporate Law Market*, 42 Law & Soc'y Rev. 771 (2008); Gregory Shaffer & Henry Gao, *China's Rise: How It Took on the US at the WTO*, 2018 U. Ill. L. Rev. 115; Swethaa S. Ballakrishnen, *Just Like Global Firms: Unintended Gender Parity and Speculative Isomorphism in India's Elite Professions*, 53 Law & Soc'y Rev. 108 (2019).

[19] Note again that, throughout this book, the empirical analysis concentrates on the US subunits of the Chinese MNCs.

exponential growth, China remains a developing country with a relatively weak judiciary and a highly interventionist party-state. Within such an institutional context, savvy businessmen tend to treat law as secondary to social and governmental connections.[20] Hence, legal services in China are generally undervalued, and the role of lawyers is relatively marginalized in corporate governance and business transactions. By comparison, law in the United Sates enjoys an much more elevated status, and the US regulatory and adjudicatory systems are evidently more complex and adversarial.[21] Doing business in such an institutional setting necessitates extensive reliance on legal professionals.[22] The contrast between the two countries is reflected in a recent survey of Chinese immigrant lawyers showing that 76 percent of them agreed with the statement that "lawyers enjoy higher social status in the United States than in China," and 89 percent concurred that "high quality legal services are valued more in the United States than in China."[23]

How does the divergence of the institutional environments shape the Chinese companies' preferences and behavior in the US legal service market? I begin the inquiry by examining the ability of Chinese companies, accustomed to a home-state setting that undervalues legal services, to appreciate the importance of lawyers for running a US business and, more specifically, for litigating disputes in the United States.

Conversations with knowledgeable informants revealed a mixed picture of institutional inertia and full adaptation. Some observed clear evidence of the "old habits." A US lawyer who regularly advises Chinese corporate clients likened them to "headless flies" that "keep bumping into legal issues."[24] Clueless as they are, Chinese managers are reluctant to pay for US legal services. The lawyer ridiculed some Chinese investors: "They would rather risk wasting a ten-million-dollar investment than pay ten thousand dollars to hire a lawyer."[25] On

[20] *See, e.g.*, Wei Zhang & Ji Li, *Weak Law v. Strong Ties: An Empirical Study of Business Investment, Law and Political Connections in China*, 13 Rev. L. & Econ. 1 (2017); Yuen Yuen Ang & Nan Jia, *Perverse Complementarity: Political Connections and the Use of Courts among Private Firms in China*, 76 J. Pol. 318 (2014).

[21] Robert A. Kagan, Adversarial Legalism: The American Way of Law 17–21 (2nd ed., 2019).

[22] Ji Li, The Clash of Capitalisms? Chinese Companies in the United States 56 (2018).

[23] 2022 Survey of Chinese Immigrant Lawyers in the United States (on file with the author).

[24] Interview with a partner at the US office of a large Chinese law firm (July 3, 2019).

[25] *Id.*

some accounts, Chinese firms that hire US lawyers would underrate the services. A lawyer complained that "clients from mainland China are penny-pinching."[26] Another echoed the observation, "It's easier to work with US clients. Once you have done a good job, they care less about the fees. Chinese clients expect you to do a good job at a low cost."[27] Another lawyer offered more details, "Chinese clients are certainly more fee sensitive than US clients. They want fee caps or discounts. They delay paying bills … our firm charges [Chinese clients] about half of the market rate for top US firms."[28] Another lawyer made a similar observation, "Chinese clients don't like the idea of charging by the hour. We have to offer fee caps."[29] An informant concluded that "Chinese companies' attitude toward attorneys are different. They don't value the opinions of attorneys."[30] Similarly, another lawyer noted that "Chinese clients don't listen to lawyers' opinions. Their response is always: 'Do whatever you can to get the deal done.'"[31] Still another seasoned lawyer remarked that Chinese companies "always treat the legal department as merely a cost center, and if they select lawyers via an open bid, whoever proposes the lowest price will win."[32] And lawyers are to be avoided, according to an informant; Chinese clients would not seek professional legal assistance unless they are left with no other choice.[33] A senior partner at a US law firm attributed the attitude to "undervaluation of intangible goods" such as intellectual property, which is in turn "rooted in both China's legal environment and the traditional mindset."[34]

Contrary to these observations, some informants did not find Chinese companies to be significantly different from other corporate clients. One interviewee, a partner at a top New York firm, acknowledged that Chinese clients do pay a lot of attention to cost, but pointed out that this is also true for many US clients.[35] Another informant noted that Chinese clients are fee sensitive, and "they are very strict

[26] Interview with a senior associate of a large US law firm (June 5, 2019).
[27] Interview with a partner of a large US law firm (June 8, 2019).
[28] Interview with a partner of the US office of a large Chinese law firm (April 6, 2019).
[29] Interview with a partner of a US law firm (April 6, 2019).
[30] Interview with a US lawyer (March 31, 2015).
[31] *Id.*
[32] Comments by a partner at the US office of a Chinese international law firm (May 7, 2021).
[33] Interview with a US lawyer (June 11, 2012).
[34] Comments by a senior partner at a US law firm (May 7, 2021).
[35] Interview with a partner of a large US law firm (November 10, 2018).

about billing. They do not allow us to do legal research for more than two hours or bill on conferences. They do not think those are necessary … But this may not be unique to Chinese clients. [Company X] (a large Korea-based MNC) is the same."[36] A Chinese executive reported that her employer spends more on US legal matters than the local competitors.[37] Moreover, a senior manager working for a Chinese company in the financial sector revealed that his company would sacrifice profits to avoid violating any US laws, with about one-third of their US workforce dedicated to legal and compliance matters.[38]

Still others provided a nuanced perspective on how Chinese companies consume legal services in the United States, indicating that their approach varies depending on the circumstances. "When in trouble, find a lawyer; when in big trouble, find a more expensive lawyer," commented a Chinese executive on how he navigates the complex US business environment.[39] Another lawyer noted that "for routine matters, Chinese companies tend to hire cheap lawyers. But when FBI knocks on the door, they go hire the best lawyer in town."[40] Both accounts illustrate that Chinese companies are adaptive and discerning consumers of US legal services.

Some of the informants noted a significant shift over time in the attitude of Chinese companies toward US legal services. One emphasized that "Chinese companies are changing. They are becoming more aware of the value of professional service and are willing to pay for it."[41] Another observed a pattern where "at the beginning, they didn't appreciate the value of legal service, and would consider [the legal fee of] a hundred dollars an hour to be expensive. Until a lawsuit hits, and they suffer a heavy loss. Then they learn not to care about nickels and dimes in buying [US] legal services … legal troubles make Chinese clients appreciate the importance of US legal services."[42] A different lawyer echoed the sentiment, noting that Chinese clients tend to make the right choice when they are fully aware of the potential consequences.

[36] Interview with a partner of a large US law firm (May 18, 2019).

[37] Interview with an executive of the US subsidiary of a large Chinese MNC (June 23, 2017).

[38] Interview with an executive of the US branch of a Chinese MNC (September 1, 2018).

[39] Li, *supra* note 22, at 106.

[40] Interview with a US lawyer (April 16, 2020).

[41] Interview with a partner of the US office of a large Chinese law firm (April 6, 2019).

[42] Interview with a partner of the US office of a large Chinese law firm (June 8, 2019).

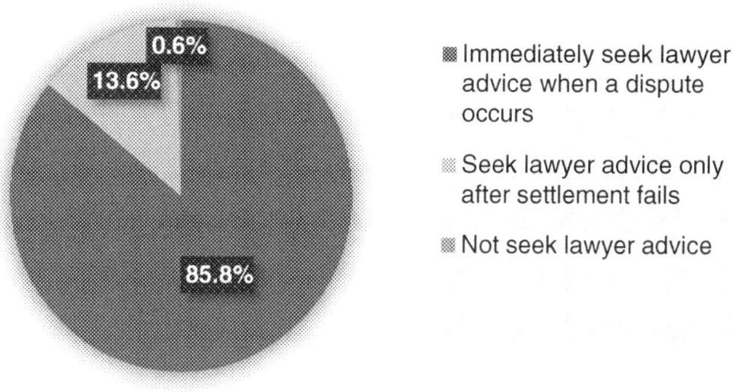

Figure 3.1 Use of US legal services in dispute resolution
Note: 2017 CGCC survey data (213 responded to the survey questionnaire, and 176 to this question); survey question: *What would your company normally do when legal disputes occur?*

"I would describe different scenarios to the CEO: What will happen if they spend $50,000 versus $100,000 or $200,000 on legal services."[43] Another lawyer shared her time-tested response to fee complaints from Chinese clients: "If you think compliance is costly in the United States, try noncompliance."[44]

To summarize, interviews with practitioners and executives have revealed considerable variations across Chinese companies regarding their attitudes toward US lawyers and the value of legal services. The balance of the qualitative evidence suggests that most Chinese investors entered the US market with a normative and cognitive mindset shaped in their home-state setting. As law plays a secondary role in China, business managers reasonably under-appreciate professional legal services. The mindset, however, may vary across different companies and shift over time as managers encounter legal challenges in the United States. For example, costly lawsuits can compel Chinese managers to recognize the importance of high quality legal services and recalibrate their approach to the US legal system.

This mixed picture of inertia and adaptation finds support in the survey data of Chinese companies in the United States. According to Figure 3.1, when a legal dispute arises in the United States, the vast majority (85.8 percent) of Chinese companies immediately consult a US lawyer, while 13.6 percent do so after settlement efforts have

[43] Comments by a senior partner of a US law firm (May 7, 2021).
[44] Comments made by a Chinese lawyer practicing law in the United States (May 7, 2021).

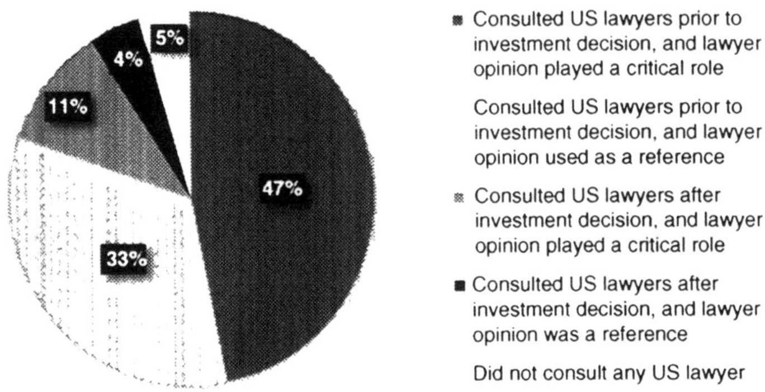

Figure 3.2 US legal services and investment decisions
Note: 2014 CGCC survey data (106 responded to the survey questionnaire, and 66 responded to this question); survey question: *Which of the following best describes your company's use of US legal services in making investment decisions?*

failed. When deciding to litigate disputes in US courts, 79.9 percent of Chinese companies take legal opinions seriously.[45] Resonating with the feedback from the interviewees, the reliance on US lawyers intensifies with the gravity of the matter. In responding to a dispute with a government body in the United States, 87.9 percent of Chinese companies would consult US lawyers and follow their advice. To put that into perspective, only 48.6 percent and 42.2 percent would seek assistance from business associations and the Chinese government respectively.[46]

Additionally, almost all Chinese companies engage US lawyers to aid their business transactions. However, the Chinese home-state institutional influence is evident in the timing of lawyer participation, with 21 percent of Chinese companies bringing lawyers onboard only after an investment decision has been made or not consulting a US lawyer at all (see Figure 3.2). This practice mirrors the common home-state practice of excluding lawyers from active participation in business negotiations.[47] According to an experienced practitioner, it is not uncommon for Chinese clients to seek US legal advice "only after having signed a binding MOU [memorandum of understanding] on a deal."[48]

[45] Data from 2017 CGCC Survey. There were 213 responses to the survey questionnaire, and 144 responses to the survey question.
[46] See Chapter 6 for more details.
[47] Mary C. Daly, *The Cultural, Ethical, and Legal Challenges in Lawyering for a Global Organization: The Role of the General Counsel*, 46 EMORY L.J. 1057, 1080 (1997).
[48] Interview with a US lawyer (June 11, 2012).

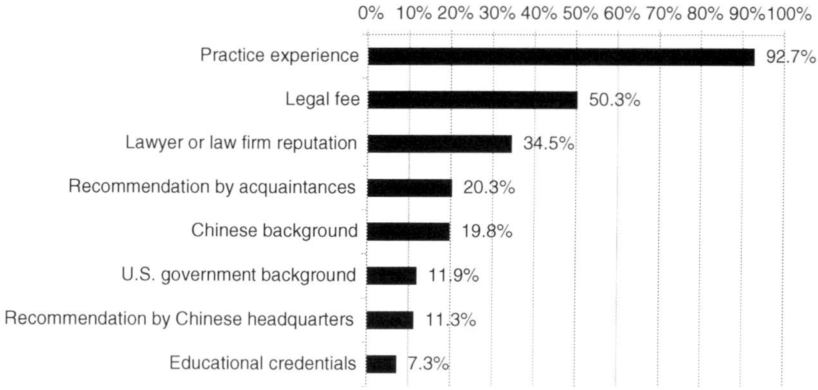

Figure 3.3 Major factors considered in selecting lawyers in the United States
Data source: CGCC 2017 survey (177 responded to this multiple-choice question).

Briefly, the survey data suggests that Chinese companies in the United States face conflicting institutional influence from their home and host states, leading to a wide range of attitudes toward US lawyers and legal services. Despite this, the majority of Chinese companies still rely on US lawyers to navigate the complex host-country legal landscape. However, with over 1.3 million registered US lawyers, many of whom are "leading experts" in their respective practice areas, how do Chinese companies select the right lawyer for their needs? Specifically, what factors do Chinese executives prioritize when selecting US lawyers, and how do these preferences reflect the dual institutional context?

The interviews suggest that cost is a top concern. As one lawyer observed, Chinese clients always choose the law firm that offers the lowest rate.[49] However, the descriptive survey data (see Figure 3.3) indicate that practice experience of a US lawyer is more important than cost. While prioritizing experience over cost may seem like common sense for US companies,[50] Chinese executives may discount the value of premium legal services due to the perception of law as peripheral in their home state.[51] Nonetheless, the survey data make a strong case that the Chinese managers are aware of the complexity of the

[49] Comments by a partner at the US office of a Chinese international law firm (May 7, 2021).

[50] *See, e.g.*, Coates, et al., *supra* note 5, at 999; C.N.V. Krishnan & Ronald W. Masulis, *Law Firm Expertise and Merger and Acquisition Outcomes*, 56 J.L. & ECON. 189 (2013).

[51] Ang & Jia, *supra* note 20, at 318; Zhang & Li, *supra* note 20; Tom Brennan, *What It Takes to Win – And Keep – Clients in Asia*, ASIAN LAWYER (2015), at www.law.com/home/id=1202736565435/?slreturn=20180715144826.

US legal system and understand the importance of practice experience when selecting US lawyers.

But cost still remains an important factor for about half of Chinese companies when selecting US lawyers. Price plays a crucial role in any service market, and the US legal service market is no exception.[52] After the 2008 financial crisis, US "clients began pushing harder to cut their legal costs, continued to pressure firms to discount their rates and provide alternative fee arrangements, and refused to pay 'premium fees for routine work', including the work of young associates."[53] Nonetheless, law is highly consequential in US business transactions, hence the enduring attention to the quality of legal services. By contrast, law's often marginal role in China and the non-differentiated legal services have contributed to "ruthless cost pressure" on Chinese lawyers.[54] To acquire business in the Chinese market, law firms, including the Chinese offices of many elite international firms, must cap their fees or adopt flexible billing methods.[55] Used to such a home-state environment, Chinese companies in the United States inevitably view US legal services as exorbitant.

About 20 percent of the survey respondents pay special attention to US lawyers' Chinese background, indicating clear institutional influence from their home state. Many senior Chinese executives, who rarely speak fluent English, naturally prefer US lawyers capable of explaining key legal issues in Chinese so that they can assess the risk properly. Furthermore, words used in everyday life may carry intricate connotations in the legal context. Thus, even those Chinese executives who speak fluent English may prefer to communicate in their mother tongue. In China, clients of international law firms "increasingly demand that all communications, spoken and written, be in Mandarin."[56] Why not demand the same in the United States? Apart from language, cultural differences can also complicate relationships

[52] *See, e.g.*, Coates, et al., *supra* note 5, at 999; Elisabeth de Fontenay, *Agency Costs in Law-Firm Selection: Are Companies Under-Spending on Counsel?*, 11 CAP. MARKETS L.J. 486 (2016); Stern & Li, *supra* note 16.

[53] Ronit Dinovitzer, et al., *Corporate Lawyers and Their Clients: Walking the Line Between Law and Business*, 21 INT'L J. LEGAL PROFESSION 3, 5 (2014).

[54] David B. Wilkins, *Is the In-House Counsel Movement Going Global – A Preliminary Assessment of the Role of Internal Counsel in Emerging Economies*, 2012 WIS. L. REV. 251, 293.

[55] *See, e.g.*, Brennan, *supra* note 51; Sida Liu, *Client Influence and the Contingency of Professionalism: The Work of Elite Corporate Lawyers in China*, 40 LAW & SOC'Y REV. 751, 762–63 (2006).

[56] Brennan, *supra* note 51.

between US lawyers and foreign clients.[57] A US lawyer's Chinese background should help bridge the gaps.[58] As noted by a US lawyer who grew up in China, his comparative advantage in serving Chinese clients is "being able to understand them and communicate with them at the soul level."[59] Another US lawyer with extensive Chinese background described his firm's advantage as "being a bridge between East and West; we always try to understand clients' Chinese legal and policy contexts before giving them any US legal advice."[60]

As previously noted, legal services are credence goods, making it challenging for managers of Chinese companies to assess their quality even after consumption.[61] To overcome the enormous information asymmetry, Chinese managers must seek credible signals of US lawyers' competence and the quality of their services. Educational credentials have traditionally been considered a signal of desirable employee attributes such as intelligence and diligence.[62] US law firms, mindful of the critical signaling value, have meticulously scrutinized job candidates' pedigrees.[63] Presumably, Chinese managers, hailing from a culture that treasures education credentials, would care a great deal about where a US lawyer earned his or her law degree. However, the survey data suggest the opposite. Only about 7 percent of the respondents consider this factor important when selecting US lawyers. It is possible that the signaling value of a US legal education is weak for Chinese executives. After all, how many Chinese managers could recognize the quality difference, if any, between a top-twenty and a top-fifty US law school? An interviewee who received a Juris Doctor (JD) degree from a top-fourteen US law school and a bachelor's degree from a top Chinese university noted that he would only mention the latter to impress his Chinese clients.[64] The managers' lack of applicable host-state institutional knowledge discounts the signaling value of US educational credentials. Additionally, Chinese executives may believe that, for lawyering, "practice makes perfect." A manager of

[57] Liu, *supra* note 55, at 777.

[58] Joshua Karton, *International Arbitration as Comparative Law in Action*, 2020 J. Dispute Resol. 305.

[59] Interview with a partner of a Chinese international law firm (May 13, 2022).

[60] Interview with a partner of a US law firm (May 13, 2023).

[61] Gilson, *supra* note 2, at 889–90.

[62] For a formal illustration of education as costly signal in the labor market, see Michael Spence, *Job Market Signaling*, 87 Q. J. Econ. 355 (1973).

[63] William D. Henderson, *The Bursting of the Pedigree Bubble*, 21 NALP Bull. 1 (July 2009).

[64] Interview with a partner of a Chinese international law firm (April 8, 2021).

a large Chinese company made the analogy to selecting doctors, "Before surgery, does the patient care about the doctor's skills or where he got his degree?"[65] In other words, the uniform attention to US lawyers' practice experience probably explains the neglect of their credentials.

Another signal of lawyering skills and reliable client service is prestige.[66] According to the survey data, 35 percent of the survey respondents take professional reputation seriously. As noted by an experienced lawyer, "If the goal of a Chinese client is to win a case, it will hire one of the top US law firms. They have the necessary resources."[67] The implicit message is that Chinese clients equate law firm prestige to lawyering capacity. Moreover, prestige can "offer a type of informal insurance to a potential client. If an important and complex transaction or litigation does not go well, directors, the CEO, and others in a corporation will be less likely to second-guess the decision of the general counsel to retain a charmed circle firm."[68] Since "nobody ever got fired for hiring Skadden,"[69] Chinese managers or their in-house counsels naturally prefer US legal professionals with a stellar reputation. Furthermore, Chinese companies with a limited track record may use prestigious law firms as "reputational intermediaries" to impress potential US business partners.[70] For instance, engaging an elite law firm headquartered in New York in a takeover bid signals to relevant US parties the sincerity, capacity, and authenticity of the Chinese party.

Moreover, the survey revealed that 20 percent of Chinese companies would consider the recommendations of acquaintances when selecting US lawyers. Trusted third-party recommendations are essential in remedying the significant information gaps that exist. Prior studies have demonstrated the role of informal networks and influential intermediaries in providing information about legal services.[71] To many,

[65] Interview with an executive of a Chinese company's US subsidiary (March 30, 2016).

[66] William D. Henderson, *From Big Law to Lean Law*, 38 INT'L REV. L. & ECON. 7 (2014).

[67] Interview with Clay Zhu (July 21, 2021).

[68] Daniel D. Sokol, *Globalization of Law Firms: A Survey of the Literature and a Research Agenda for Further Study*, 14 IND. J. GLOB. LEGAL STUD. 5 (2007).

[69] Henderson, *supra* note 66, at 16.

[70] *See, e.g.*, Okamoto, *supra* note 9; Ronald J. Gilson & Reinier H. Kraakman, *The Mechanisms of Market Efficiency*, 70 VA. L. REV. 549 (1984); Reinier H. Kraakman, *Gatekeepers: The Anatomy of a Third-Party Enforcement Strategy*, 2 J.L., ECON., & ORG. 53 (1986).

[71] Jack Ladinsky, *The Traffic in Legal Services: Lawyer-Seeking Behavior and the Channeling of Clients*, 11 LAW & SOC'Y REV. 207, 213 (1976); Erin York Cornwell, et al., *Networking in the Shadow of the Law: Informal Access to Legal Expertise Through Personal Network Ties*, 51 LAW & SOC'Y REV. 635 (2017).

informal referral offers reliable, inexpensive, and tailored information not easily available through formal channels.[72] From the perspective of Chinese companies, endorsements from parties in long-term cooperative relationships also serve as quality assurance, as reference to inferior lawyers may reflect negatively on the credibility and intention of the attestants.[73] The category of acquaintances includes a diverse range of groups, such as lawyers who have established cordial personal relationships with Chinese managers and are willing to provide referrals.

About 11 percent of the surveyed Chinese companies pay close attention to lawyer recommendations from their Chinese headquarters. A prior study found that Chinese state-owned firms frequently use outside legal counsel recommended by their superiors.[74] The rationale behind the preference, that is, hierarchical control within the business organization, remains intact when the companies expand abroad.[75] This control also offers a means for home-state institutions to directly influence the selection of US lawyers by their US subunits.

Interestingly, approximately 12 percent of the survey respondents would consider US lawyers' government background important. Back in China, connections with government officials may be more effective in resolving thorny legal problems than legal knowledge and skills. "Know who" trumps "know how."[76] Here the causal direction is two sided, as inadequate legal services also prompt managers to cultivate political ties to "government actors in regulatory and legal arenas."[77] Chinese managers may apply this mindset to resolving legal issues and selecting lawyers in the United States. One informant noted that his company used a big US law firm as it has many lawyers with government connections; "DC also speaks *guanxi*."[78] Moreover, Chinese companies, especially those with state ownership, suffer from grave a deep-seated mistrust in the United States.[79]

[72] Ladinsky, *supra* note 71, at 218.

[73] Gilson, *supra* note 2, at 896, discussing how reference to inferior lawyers may destroy a long-term attorney-client relationship.

[74] Sida Liu, *Palace Wars over Professional Regulation: In-house Counsel in Chinese State-owned Enterprises*, 2012 Wis. L. Rev. 549, 564.

[75] Li, *supra* note 22.

[76] Ang & Jia, *supra* note 20.

[77] George O. White III, et al., *Does Context Really Matter? The Influence of Deficient Legal Services on the Intensity of Political Ties in the Regulatory and Legal Arenas*, 28 Multinational Bus. Rev. 277 (2020).

[78] Interview with the manager of the US subsidiary of a large Chinese MNC (June 30, 2022).

[79] Klaus Meyer, et al., *Overcoming Distrust: How State-Owned Enterprises Adapt Their Foreign Entries to Institutional Pressures Abroad*, 45 J. Int'l Bus. Stud. (2014).

Hence, the managers may prefer lawyers with some US government background to allay this trust deficiency. Alternatively, this preference may simply reflect a general desire to manage compliance risks and regulatory costs.[80] After all, "much of lawyers' expertise consists of insider knowledge of the local legal system and social connections with law enforcement officials,"[81] and knowledge of regulatory decision-making and access to decision-making agents are especially valuable to foreign investors from a vastly different institutional environment.[82]

To summarize, Chinese companies consider a variety of factors when selecting US lawyers, including legal fees, professional reputation, academic credentials, practice experience, Chinese background, US government background, and recommendations from acquaintances and Chinese headquarters. Interviews and the survey data suggest both inertia and adaptation, reflecting the varied influence of the companies' dual institutional environment.

How much do Chinese companies spend on US legal services? MNCs operating in the United States often incur higher legal and compliance costs due to the unique features of its legal system.[83] The same should hold for Chinese companies operating in the United States as they are accustomed to a home-state business environment where law is less essential.[84] However, empirical research about their US legal budgets is nonexistent. The topic is important as their legal expenses implicate their relationships with US lawyers. A larger budget could give a Chinese

[80] Schwarcz, *supra* note 13.

[81] Sida Liu, *The Legal Profession as a Social Process: A Theory on Lawyers and Globalization*, 38 LAW & SOC. INQUIRY 670 (2013).

[82] Though few scholars have systematically explored this type of preference, several prior studies have made such findings. For instance, the "revolving door" literature about lobbyists demonstrates that the "brokers" between politics and money tend to have substantial government experience. JOHN P. HEINZ, THE HOLLOW CORE: PRIVATE INTERESTS IN NATIONAL POLICY MAKING (1993). Also, lawyers with government background dominate the fast growing practice of white-collar crime. Charles D. Weisselberg & Su Li, *Big Law's Sixth Amendment: The Rise of Corporate White-Collar Practices in Large US Law Firms*, 53 ARIZ. L. REV. 1221 (2011). In addition, the group of professionals that specializes in advising foreign investors about the national security review process (also known as CFIUS review) consists primarily of practitioners who are former staff of participating federal agencies. Diane Bartz & Greg Roumeliotis, *The Washington Insiders Who Work to Get Chinese Deals Approved*, REUTERS (February 24, 2016).

[83] REGULATORY ENCOUNTERS: MULTINATIONAL CORPORATIONS AND AMERICAN ADVERSARIAL LEGALISM 23 (Robert A. Kagan & Lee Axelrad eds., 2000).

[84] LI, *supra* note 22, at 67.

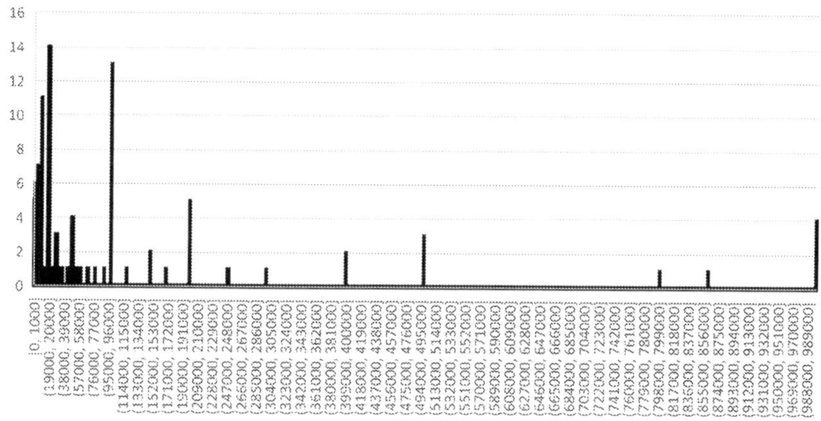

Figure 3.4 Chinese companies' legal fees in the United States
Note: 2019 CGCC survey (one outlier excluded) (247 responded to the questionnaire, and 117 to the survey question); survey question: *What was the approximate fee your company paid to the following third-party professional services organizations in 2018? Please fill in the specific amount in the column, such as $200,000.*

company more leverage and pricing power over US law firms, making them more responsive to the Chinese companies' lawyer selection preferences. This could impact the US legal service market. As discussed in Chapter 1, larger legal budgets would enable Chinese companies to resist the isomorphic pressure from the host-state legal service market and continue their home-state practices. Conversely, if Chinese companies purchase insignificant amounts of US legal services, they would be mere followers of the host-state rules and norms governing the legal market.

As Figure 3.4 illustrates, Chinese companies' average US legal fees fell far below the market average for US companies.[85] Though the distribution is skewed, the vast majority of the Chinese companies paid less than $400,000 in 2018 to US lawyers. The finding is consistent with the data from the 2022 survey that phrased and formatted the question slightly differently. A significant minority of the Chinese companies reported an annual US legal budget of less than $100,000, and the median is less than half a million US dollars (see Figure 3.5).

The survey also inquired about the ratios of Chinese companies' legal costs to operating expenses. This was measured by the percentage

[85] According to the ACC 2018 Survey, in which US respondents were overrepresented, the mean and median for outside legal spending are $9,710,316 and $845,000 respectively. *2019 Global Legal Department Benchmarking Report*, at 9, www.acc.com/sites/default/files/2019-06/ACC_Benchmark_062019.pdf.

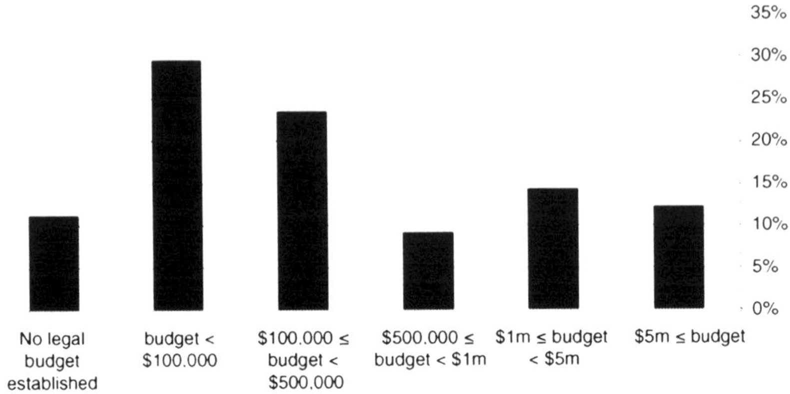

Figure 3.5 Annual US legal budget of Chinese companies
Note: 2022 CGCC survey (135 responded to the questionnaire, and 95 to the survey question); survey question: *What is the approximate annual legal budget of your company?*

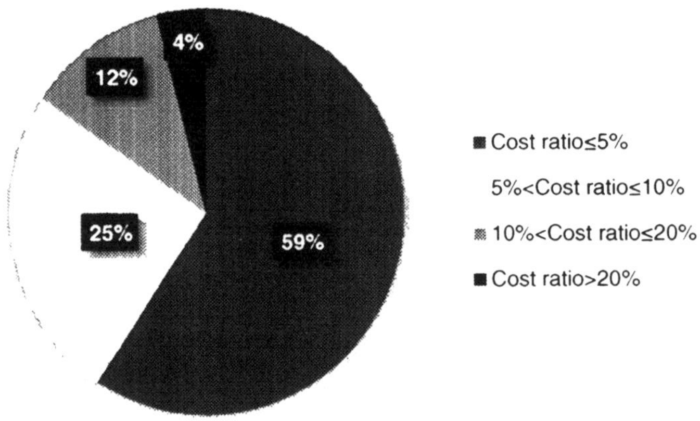

Figure 3.6 Ratio of legal fees to selling, general, and administrative expenses
Note: 2019 CGCC survey (247 responded to the questionnaire, and 155 to the survey question); survey question: *What was the ratio of fees paid to outside law firms to sales and administrative expenses (SG&A) in 2018?*

of US legal fees versus SG&A (selling, general, and administrative expenses), a major category of nonproduction costs often used to present a snapshot of a company's financial condition. This measure takes into account the size of a Chinese company's US operation and the stage of its expansion. As shown in Figure 3.6, the distribution largely mirrors that of the legal expenses in dollar amount, with 59.4 percent of the responding firms reporting a ratio below 5 percent, and only 3.87 percent reporting a ratio higher than 20 percent.

The descriptive survey data indicate that Chinese companies are relatively lightweight consumers in the US legal market. The finding has significant implications. Chinese companies face heightened legal and regulatory risks in the United States due to their special attributes, such as state ownership, and the escalating US–China rivalry. Yet they often lack the diagnostic capacity to identify their US legal service needs. Such a function is typically performed either by trusted lawyers possessing rich company-specific knowledge, or by competent in-house counsel. However, modest fees expected from Chinese companies disincentivize US lawyers from acquiring company-specific knowledge. According to a Chinese in-house counsel, "US lawyers often don't understand our business, nor our legal issues."[86] With so little to contribute to the revenue of large US firms, Chinese companies are treated as "low-quality clients."[87] One lawyer with experience advising China-based corporate clients noted:

> The concept of paying for professional consultation does not exist in China, so [Chinese clients] may keep seeking advice for free; also, the concept of Jiafang (Party A, symbolizing a transactional position of superiority) is prevalent in China, and the Chinese clients expect to be "Chief something," or even "Lord something." I usually avoid or reject such clients. You would not make any money from such engagement. [It's] a waste of time. They will take you as a free consultant, so better end it as soon as you can.[88]

Another lawyer concurred, "Many Chinese clients are like this; they would consult for free every lawyer they can possibly find, and then they would hire the cheapest one."[89] The rational response is "to do absolutely nothing without the payment of a retainer fee, except for giving very vague and ambivalent answers to the client's questions at the consultation stage."[90] Another lawyer commented that he would be upfront with Chinese clients about his fee structure, "If they don't like it, I would simply tell them to find other US lawyers; and they will find that other lawyers also bill by the hour."[91] While in China corporate

[86] Interview with an in-house counsel of the US subsidiary of a large Chinese MNC (May 14, 2017).
[87] Interview with a partner at a US law firm (June 7, 2020).
[88] Comment by a partner of a US law firm (July 12, 2021).
[89] Comment by a partner of a US office of a large Chinese international law firm (July 12, 2021).
[90] Comment by a Chinese American lawyer specializing in tax and litigation (July 12, 2021).
[91] Interview with a partner of a US law firm (July 20, 2021).

clients require law firms to engage in brutal bidding wars, US lawyers often refuse to participate.[92] Still another lawyer recognized the differences but emphasized the importance of client education, "For serious Chinese clients, I would explain to them that in the United States attorney-client relationship is not the Jiafang/Yifang (master/servant) relationship in China. But it's never easy to get it through."[93]

In short, with minimal leverage, Chinese corporate clients must adapt to the US legal service market and the norms governing attorney-client relationships in order to obtain competent legal counsel. A lawyer at a top US firm noted that his firm often loses potential Chinese clients for refusing to lower its fee rate, but "that's OK. We have plenty of work from US clients."[94] The balance of power between Chinese companies and US law firms is vividly illustrated by another lawyer's comment:

> We worked on a deal assisting one of the largest Chinese multinationals in acquiring a US business. The client treated us with disrespect and kept delaying paying the fee … that's how they do things back in China. At one point, the partner on the deal simply told us to "pencil down." We warned the client that we would stop working on the deal. The client paid immediately … The client made other ridiculous demands such as immediate responses to their emails on weekends. We either pushed back or just ignored them.[95]

The lack of leverage implies that the attitudes of Chinese companies toward legal service providers and their preferences for selecting lawyers, which may differ from those socially accepted in the United States, have no significant impact on the US legal market. Instead, Chinese clients must conform to the mature host-state market and the norms that regulate client-lawyer relationships to obtain high quality services.

In summary, this section examined, within the dual institutional framework, the qualitative and descriptive survey data on Chinese companies' attitude toward US lawyers and their services, as well as their managers' preferences for selecting lawyers. The data presented a mixed picture of institutional inertia and isomorphism. Furthermore, Chinese companies spend insignificant amounts on US legal services, making them followers rather than changers of the host-state institutions that regulate as well as constitute the mature US legal market.

[92] *Id.*
[93] Comment by a partner of a US law firm (July 12, 2021).
[94] Interview with a partner of a US law firm (March 11, 2016).
[95] Interview with an associate of a top US law firm (June 27, 2019).

However, these broad observations gloss over significant inter-company variations. Chinese companies differ widely in their lawyer selection preferences and US legal expenses, which the following section will further investigate.

3.3 VARIATIONS IN LAWYER SELECTION PREFERENCES AND US LEGAL EXPENSES

To a certain extent, idiosyncrasies at the firm level are inevitable. Except for those serving solely as corporate shells, holding entities, or some other special transactional purposes, no two companies with substantive operations are identical, regardless of their legal and management bases. So, some of the inter-company variations may be attributable to theoretically trivial, firm-specific factors. However, the dual institutional theory, the various existing theories on the legal profession and the legal market, and the qualitative empirical evidence presented in the preceding section all evince patterned effects of interesting albeit unexplored institutional and organizational variables. This section further investigates such variables, with a focus on the ownership structure of Chinese companies and other institutional factors that may shape the companies' lawyer selection preferences and US legal service expenditures.

3.3.1 US Lawyer Selection Preferences

As mentioned in Section 3.2, the interviews and the survey data presented evidence of both institutional inertia and isomorphism in the attitudes and views of Chinese managers regarding US lawyers. These attitudes seem to reflect both their home-state and host-state institutional environments. However, the inter-company variations require more rigorous analysis. For instance, why do only half of the Chinese companies consider legal fees important when selecting US lawyers? Additionally, why do 80 percent of them downplay a US lawyer's Chinese background? This subsection will test a series of hypotheses.[96]

3.3.1.1 Possible Factors Influencing Lawyer Selection Preferences

State ownership. State ownership is one of the key variables of interest. Recall that Chinese state-owned enterprises (SOEs) are regulated by a distinct set of home-state institutions, including rules of the

[96] I exclude two considerations (i.e., lawyers' practice experience and educational credentials) from the tests for lack of variation – almost all Chinese companies emphasize US lawyers' practice experience, and very few care about their law school credentials.

State-Owned Assets Supervision and Administration Commission (SASAC), and feature more centralized and hierarchical management, governance complexity, and, relatedly, a great deal of firm-specific information. Moreover, government ownership renders them easy targets for suspicion and criticism in their host countries, especially those valorizing free market capitalism. Do these ownership-related characteristics modify the Chinese companies' lawyer selection preferences? If so, how?

To start with legal fee consideration. As previously explained, the interests of SOE managers are severely misaligned with those of the state or their nominal owners.[97] Consequently, managers of state-owned companies may heavily discount corporate cost savings. And fee rates, largely unhinged to the remuneration of SOE managers, may not catch their attention in the selection of US lawyers. However, the same agency problem may lead to an opposite hypothesis. Resembling government bureaucracies in terms of operations and organizational form, Chinese SOEs rely heavily on measurable metrics for corporate control.[98] Given the close attention to performance indicators,[99] managers of state-owned companies may prefer fee-based lawyer selection to selection using more subtle criteria, such as service quality or long-term corporate benefits.[100] As a seasoned US lawyer noted, "State-owned Chinese clients always use bidding to choose outside counsel, whereas privately owned are much more flexible."[101] Anecdotal insider accounts echo this observation. An in-house lawyer of a large state-owned Chinese company observed that, to avoid trouble or suspicion, her department normally selects US lawyers through cost comparison. She once nominated an elite firm in New York where she had spent a year as a visiting lawyer, and for that, she had to "write a detailed report to justify the deviation from the set practice."[102]

For the same reasons, state ownership of Chinese companies may influence management attention to the prestige factor. As discussed earlier, professional reputation serves two major functions: signaling service quality and certifying a client's credibility. Affirming the

97 Alvaro Cuervo-Cazurra, et al., *Governments as Owners: State-Owned Multinational Companies*, 45 J. Int'l Bus. Stud. 919 (2014).

98 Gordon Tullock, The Politics of Bureaucracy (1965).

99 Wei Zhang, *Managing Judges Mathematically: An Empirical Study of the Medical Malpractice Litigations in Shanghai*, 28 Const. Pol. Econ. 373 (2017).

100 de Fontenay, *supra* note 52.

101 Interview with a partner of an international law firm (December 19, 2018).

102 Interview with an in-house counsel of a Chinese state-owned MNC (May 3, 2017).

certification function, a recent study found that Chinese "SOEs want to be seen as engaging top firms … to cast off the image of a developing country SOE and be seen as a global corporation."[103] According to an informant, state-owned Chinese companies like to hire top US firms as they have abundant resources to handle complex matters.[104] Moreover, due to the multiagency problem, managers of state-owned Chinese companies may be more inclined to shift legal risks to outside lawyers. As the chief US counsel of a state-owned Chinese multinational commented, "If anything goes wrong, I won't take the blame, as I have used the best lawyer in town."[105] Such risk avoidance necessitates the engagement of legal professionals with stellar reputations.[106]

Additionally, state ownership may be associated with the company's attitude toward lawyer recommendations by acquaintances. As previously discussed, SOEs feature complex incentive structures and peculiar decision-making mechanisms, which may give rise to distinct legal needs. Acquaintances familiar with these needs may be better situated to recommend suitable US lawyers. Endorsement of a US lawyer's trustworthiness could also be a plus in the host-country context, where Chinese state-owned investors are viewed with strong suspicion.

Regarding the preference for US lawyers with a Chinese background, opposing hypotheses seem to coexist. On the one hand, as elaborated in the preceding chapter, US lawyers without any Chinese background may find it hard to understand Chinese SOEs' organizational structure and governance.[107] To avoid misunderstandings and reduce transaction costs, managers of state-owned Chinese companies may prefer to work with US lawyers who have spent some time in China and speak the language. On the other hand, even privately owned Chinese companies may prefer US lawyers with some Chinese background who can assist in overcoming institutional gaps between their home and host countries.

State ownership may also be related to the preference for US lawyers with government backgrounds. Compared with private companies, state-owned Chinese companies face more coercive pressure

[103] Stern & Li, *supra* note 16.

[104] Interview with a partner of a US office of a Chinese international law firm (June 21, 2021).

[105] Interview with a general counsel of a Chinese state-owned MNC (August 3, 2013).

[106] The desire to shift responsibility should also exist in privately owned companies, so the question is about the degree of risk avoidance.

[107] Liu, *supra* note 55, at 770.

due to trust deficiency in host countries.[108] The heightened need for legitimacy may increase the preference for lawyers with US government backgrounds, which, at least in the eyes of Chinese managers, could mitigate the suspicion. For instance, a US in-house counsel for a state-owned Chinese company commented that her company would choose American attorneys because "the management is worried that the counterparty or the government would see us as government agent, making a fuss about it (xiao ti da zuo)."[109] Moreover, large SOEs enjoy various privileges in their home state, where government agencies are often viewed as facilitating peers rather than impartial regulators.[110] This mindset, cultivated at home and transported to the United States by the Chinese managers and other normative carriers, could also modify the lawyer selection preference of state-owned Chinese companies.

In addition, state-owned Chinese companies may prefer US lawyers recommended by headquarters due to tight hierarchical control, which should incentivize local managers to heed the preferences of their superiors.[111] Also, given the heightened legal and regulatory risks for Chinese SOEs,[112] the agency theory would predict that SOE managers prefer to engage US lawyers recommended by their headquarters to circumscribe their liability.[113]

108 *See, e.g.*, Lin Cui & Fuming Jiang, *State Ownership Effect on Firms' FDI Ownership Decisions Under Institutional Pressure: A Study of Chinese Outward-Investing Firms*, 43 J. Int'l Bus. Stud. 264 (2012); Angela Huyue Zhang, *Foreign Direct Investment from China: Sense and Sensibility*, 34 Nw J. Int'l L. & Bus. 395 (2014).

109 Interview with an in-house counsel at the US subsidiary of a Chinese state-owned MNC (May 11, 2023).

110 Liu, *supra* note 55, at 769.

111 Li, *supra* note 22, at 104.

112 For instance, the national security review of foreign investment in the United States discriminates against the acquisitions of US assets by investors controlled by a foreign state. For more about the system and how Chinese state-owned investors react to it, *see, e.g.*, Ji Li, *Investing Near the National Security Black Hole*, 14 Berkeley Bus. L.J. 1 (2017).

113 To test all these hypothetical ties between state ownership and the various lawyer selection considerations, I use the same dummy as described in Chapter 2, which equals one if a Chinese government entity owns more than 50 percent of a Chinese investor's equity interest and zero otherwise. Majority equity interest in theory enables corporate control over the investor's actions in the United States, yet it may not be a *sine qua non* for the home-state government to exert influence. Thus, I coded an alternative dummy variable to capture more extensive and subtle state control, which equals one if the Chinese government owns more than 10 percent of the investor and zero otherwise. For the 2017 survey data, however, the samples associated with the two dummy variables overlap extensively, so

Cultural difference. Chinese companies experience variable cultural tensions when operating in the United States. Those subject to greater influence from informal home-state institutions may express US lawyer selection preferences akin to what we expect from domestic Chinese companies. For instance, such companies might be more sensitive to legal fees. They may also prefer US lawyers with qualities and skills deemed necessary to ameliorate institutional frictions. Therefore, one might hypothesize that Chinese companies facing greater cultural differences would be more cost-sensitive and attentive to the prestige factor, endorsement from acquaintances and the headquarters, and a US lawyer's Chinese background and government background, as these factors either reflect inertial institutional influence or reduce information and transaction costs arising from wide cultural gaps.[114]

Sectoral regulation. The formal institutional pressure on Chinese companies may vary across different sectors. Take legal fee sensitivity as an example. Previous studies have documented that companies are less cost-conscious when purchasing legal services for "betting the company" matters.[115] In heavily regulated sectors such as banking, companies tend to face numerous high-stakes legal matters and therefore view legal fee as a necessary operational expense. By comparison, companies in less regulated sectors tend to have routine and standardized legal matters that can be handled by average lawyers, and thus may be more inclined to select US lawyers based on fee differences.

Sectoral regulation can also impact the consideration of prestige. Prior research has shown that US corporations' need for regulatory compliance drives their demand for legal services.[116] In sectors governed by complex, high-stakes laws and regulations, Chinese companies might seek out premium legal services to ensure regulatory compliance.

tests employing the two alternative dummies returned similar results. Therefore, I present only those using the 50 percent state ownership dummy. For discussion about the control of the state without majority equity ownership, see, *e.g.*, Curtis J. Milhaupt & Wentong Zheng, *Beyond Ownership: State Capitalism and the Chinese Firm*, 103 GEO. L.J. 665 (2014); Ji Li, *State-Owned Enterprises in the Current Regime of Investor-State Arbitration*, *in* THE ROLE OF THE STATE IN INVESTOR-STATE ARBITRATION (2014).

114 I measure the cultural difference variable using a proxy derived from the 2017 survey data. One question therein asked whether a responding Chinese firm had retention problems in the United States due to cultural differences. If the answer is positive, the dummy is assigned the value of one, and zero if otherwise.

115 Coates, et al., *supra* note 5, at 999.

116 Schwarcz, *supra* note 13.

Prestigious law firms can provide this additional assurance. For similar reasons, one may find a connection between regulatory intensity and the preference for lawyers with US government background or lawyers recommended by the headquarters.[117]

Size of US investment. When it comes to lawyer selection, Chinese companies with extensive US operations presumably differ from those merely testing the market. For instance, Chinese companies with substantial US investments can afford the services of prestigious law firms, and they may also view hiring lawyers from elite firms as a form of status signal.[118] In addition, as the stakes are higher for companies with greater investments in the US market, they may be more concerned with the long-term effects of legal services and therefore, take professional reputation – a proxy for high quality services – more seriously. Furthermore, given that corporate legal risk tends to move in tandem with business size, companies with larger US investments are more likely to opt for premium services from elite firms.[119] Finally, Chinese companies with substantial US business may be less concerned with legal fees, as they account for a smaller fraction of their operating expenses.[120]

117 To test these hypothetical effects, I create a dummy variable that equals one if a Chinese firm invests in a heavily regulated sector in the United States, and zero otherwise. Of the nineteen sectors listed in the 2017 survey questionnaire, I categorize the following eight as heavily regulated at the federal level, at the state and local level, or both: mining, utilities, construction, information technology, finance and insurance, real estate and rental, health care, and public administration. Some may not consider the real estate and rental industry as heavily regulated. I create an alternative dummy that excludes that sector and rerun all the tests using the alternative dummy. All the regression results remain largely the same.

118 Stern & Li, *supra* note 16.

119 Of course, the causality arrow may point in the opposite direction – Chinese companies that have chosen prestigious US law firms are more likely to mitigate their legal risks and, consequently, thrive in the US market. However, given that most Chinese multinationals only recently entered the US market, such a long-term effect of compliance, even if it exists, should remain latent. Also, this study, as the first one on this topic, aims mainly at identifying association, rather than causation.

120 For tests of the 2017 survey data, this variable is measured using a five-level scale of the US revenue of a Chinese MNC. In earlier surveys we asked for exact revenue amounts of the Chinese companies, yet the response rate for the question was very low. The respondents were reluctant to disclose the figure. To address that issue, I made it a scale question. That raised the response rate significantly. Survey respondents choose one of five levels of revenue. The lowest level is "below one million dollars" and the highest level is "above 100 million dollars."

US investment duration. The qualitative evidence has suggested adaptation over time. For instance, new entrants might pay more attention to fees in selecting US lawyers due to the undervaluation of legal services in China. Also, Chinese companies that have been in the United States for a long time may have learned to ignore or discount headquarters' recommendations. Moreover, recent Chinese investors may prefer bicultural lawyers who can help them overcome the enormous institutional barriers.[121]

In-house counsel. Does the in-house legal capacity of Chinese companies have any effect on their US lawyer selection preference? As discussed in the preceding chapter, having internal counsel narrows the informational asymmetry between companies and their outside lawyers and tilts the balance of power toward the former. It is plausible that Chinese companies with full-time professional legal managers might pay less attention to the prestige factor or lawyer recommendations by acquaintances. Moreover, the presence of full-time in-house counsel may signal adaptive managerial attitudes. Chinese companies with in-house legal managers might take legal and compliance matters more seriously than those without. Such an attitude might be reflected in less attention to legal fees or a US lawyer's Chinese background. Furthermore, in-house counsel who are US lawyers likely have internalized the norms of the US legal market, which may manifest in the lawyer selection preferences.[122]

Listing status. The listing status of a Chinese company can serve as a good proxy for its overall size. It also reflects heightened institutional pressure, as companies regulated by securities agencies and securities exchanges bear heightened compliance obligations and amplified legal risks. Therefore, all else being equal, listed Chinese companies may prefer prestigious US law firms and care less about legal fees. With greater transparency, listed companies may also be less attentive to recommendations from acquaintances. The variable may also correlate with the ownership structure of Chinese companies, making it a necessary control (see Table 3.1 in the Appendix to this chapter for summary statistics).

[121] To test all the possible hypotheses, I include the variable, i.e., the number of years of investing in the United States, in the tests.

[122] To test these hypothetical connections, I create a dummy variable that equals one if a responding Chinese MNC has full-time in-house counsel licensed to practice US law, and zero otherwise.

3.3.1.2 Analysis of Test Results

As shown in Table 3.2 in the Appendix,[123] state ownership is significant in three of the six models, with varying odds ratios. First, Chinese investors with majority state ownership are more likely to consider legal cost important when selecting US lawyers. As previously discussed, due to their unique home-state institutional pressure, state-owned Chinese companies tend to centralize decision-making authority and impose tight vertical control over their US operations.[124] Like their US counterparts, sizable Chinese companies usually set a budget for each year's legal expenses. Due to the rigidity of bureaucratic management typically found in SOEs, exceeding the budget spells trouble.[125] To avoid that, local managers strive to keep their actual legal expenses close to the planned budget cap, even though doing so may affect the quality of the legal services and have long-term negative impacts. Of course, fee sensitivity may not always lead to cost-saving behavior, as under-spending could result in a cut of future budgets. As noted by one lawyer, "SOEs sometimes would pick an expensive international firm for a deal in order to exhaust the account and set a high bar for the legal budget of the next year."[126] Such behavior exemplifies the multiple-agency problems that plague Chinese SOEs.

Moreover, state-owned Chinese companies are more likely to select US lawyers recommended by their headquarters because of the centralized and hierarchical management style. Additionally, state-owned Chinese firms face more host-state institutional pressure in the form of heightened legal, regulatory, and political risks.[127] For self-protection, risk-averse local managers prefer to work with lawyers endorsed by their companies' Chinese headquarters. State ownership is also associated with the preference for US lawyers with prior government experience, which likely reflects the intent to rely on such lawyers to remedy the lack of trust in the host state.[128]

123 Because the dependent variables are all binary, I run a series of logistic regression tests.

124 Li, *supra* note 22, at 103.

125 Henderson, *supra* note 66, at 16.

126 Interview with a US lawyer having more than ten years of experience serving US and Chinese corporate clients (January 12, 2018).

127 Ji Li, *In Pursuit of Fairness: How Chinese Multinational Companies React to U.S. Government Bias*, 62 HARV. INT'L L.J. 375 (2021).

128 State ownership, however, is not significantly tied to the other three considerations: recommendation by acquaintances, Chinese background, and prestige. While one cannot draw a definitive inference due to the limited sample size, the

Meanwhile, cultural difference correlates with three considerations: lawyers' Chinese background, headquarters recommendation, and prestige. Intuitively, Chinese companies confronting cultural barriers in the United States prefer local lawyers with some Chinese background, to help overcome potential miscommunication and reduce transaction costs. Moreover, Chinese companies experiencing cultural challenges prefer US lawyers recommended by the headquarters. Here the causality may cut both ways. Tight hierarchical control ensures that local managers heed US lawyer recommendations by the headquarters, which may result in more cultural challenges. Furthermore, Chinese companies less adaptive to the US cultural context pay more attention to the prestige of US lawyers or law firms. Two reasons may explain this association. First, Chinese managers more closely tied to the home-state normative environment may carry their high prestige-consciousness to the selection of US lawyers. Second, those facing cultural challenges lack knowledge about the quality of US legal services and therefore must rely on signals such as professional reputation.

Sectoral regulation also matters when it comes to the selection of US lawyers. Chinese companies in heavily regulated sectors are less likely to prioritize legal fees and more likely to consider prestige and headquarters' recommendations. First, legal costs are of less concern for Chinese companies in sectors where compliance necessitates a steady supply of sophisticated legal services. For instance, dealing with state and federal banking regulators requires frequent assistance from banking law specialists with extensive practice experience, which only sizable law firms can deliver, and these services are invariably expensive. Thus, banks operating in the United States, regardless the national location of their headquarters, are accustomed to costly US legal services. Additionally, as noted earlier, heavy regulations generate coercive pressure for corporate isomorphism, leading to a negative association between regulatory intensity and legal fee sensitivity. Second, Chinese companies in heavily regulated US sectors prefer prestigious firms for the implicit guarantee of high quality service and for conforming with host-country market practices. The third finding, the positive correlation between sectoral regulation and likelihood to consider headquarters recommendation in hiring US lawyers, is more puzzling. One would expect Chinese companies in heavily

findings are suggestive of a nuanced and complex relationship between the ownership structure of Chinese MNCs and their lawyer selection preferences in the United States.

regulated sectors to engage in host-state adaptation due to the coercive isomorphic pressure. However, sectors such as banking are usually subject to heavy regulation in both the home and host states. Coping with the compliance complexity associated with the dual and often conflictual sectoral regulations requires close intra-organizational coordination, hence the preference for US lawyers recommended by the headquarters.

The listing status of Chinese companies correlates with three lawyer selection considerations. First, Chinese companies listed on a major securities exchange are more likely to consider legal fee rates when selecting US lawyers. Publicly traded companies tend to have more refined corporate governance practices that stresses procedural due care. As such, mechanisms for selecting outside counsel may have been put in place, and managers are more attentive to fee rates in US lawyer selection. Second, publicly traded Chinese companies favor US lawyers with Chinese background, as their institutional complexity can benefit from tailored services. Finally, publicly traded Chinese companies do not rely as heavily on prestigious law firms to signal credibility due to their enhanced transparency.[129]

US investment size is positively associated with headquarters' recommendation and the reputational consideration. The former finding is surprising as one would expect substantial US operations to boost local management autonomy. It is possible that Chinese companies without a substantial US presence have little experience working with US lawyers, so the headquarters cannot make recommendations in the first place. Or it could simply reflect more centralized control for the importance of the US market. The other finding, the positive association between business size and the penchant for prestige, is quite intuitive.

The variable of in-house legal capacity is insignificant,[130] which merits some discussion. As noted in Chapter 1, almost all the survey respondents are business executives, whose preferences likely differ from those of in-house legal managers. In addition, although the tests failed to identify robust evidence,[131] the variable exhibits

[129] The significance level is rather low (10 percent), so the preliminary interpretation awaits further investigation.

[130] The data for lawyer selection preferences are subjective, so I add a key demographic control variable (i.e., length of time the survey subject has worked in the United States) to test the robustness of the results. All the key results remain unchanged.

[131] The variable is weakly significant in several models, indicating that Chinese multinationals that have employed full-time US legal managers are less likely to consider recommendations by acquaintances or headquarters recommendations. The finding, however, is not robust.

a close-to-significant negative association with acquaintances' recommendations. This implies that Chinese companies with full-time in-house lawyers are less likely to consider acquaintances' recommendations in selecting outside legal counsel. In-house lawyers are better placed than unaffiliated third parties to evaluate the quality of outside counsel and corporate legal service needs. Therefore, Chinese companies with professional in-house legal managers can ignore US lawyer recommendations from acquaintances.[132]

To summarize, the statistical analyses confirmed the dual institutional influence, especially the influence of home-state factors such as state ownership and cultural differences, on Chinese companies' lawyer selection preferences in the United States. However, it remains unclear whether this home-state institutional influence extends to the companies' US legal expenditures, which would otherwise reflect supply and demand in the US legal service market. Put another way, do the institutional pulls between the companies' home-state institutions and the US legal service market manifest empirically in the companies' varying legal expenses? The descriptive survey data and the interviews presented earlier suggest a negative answer, as Chinese companies with limited legal budgets have little leverage over US lawyers and law firms. The following subsection further explores this question.

3.3.2 Variations in US Legal Expenses

Chinese companies operating in the United States have reported varying legal expenses as measured by dollar amounts and ratios of legal costs to operating costs.[133] This subsection investigates these variations through a series of factors that can be grouped roughly into three categories. First, institutional and organizational factors of interest, such as state ownership of Chinese companies, the normative tensions they face in the United States, and the availability of full-time professional in-house legal managers. Second, several variables, such as the amount

[132] Note that the finding does not rule out the possibility that in-house lawyers will rely on recommendations from their acquaintances for lawyer information. Anecdotal evidence suggests that is indeed the case.

[133] Because the measure of dollar amounts is skewed, I use the log-transformed numbers for the ordinary least square (OLS) tests. Two responding companies reported zero legal expenses. These two values were dropped from the natural log transformation. The costs ratios are scale data, on which I run both OLS and ordered logit tests. The sample of the 2022 survey data is small in size and lacks information about several key business and institutional variables for meaningful statistical analysis, so I left it out of this subsection.

of litigation and business reorganization, that can generate temporary, oscillating legal service demand, which correlate with corporate legal expenses. Third, a few other factors, such as the scale of the company, may give rise to high and stable demand for legal services.

3.3.2.1 Possible Factors Impacting US Legal Expenses

State ownership. The ownership structure of Chinese companies may bear on their US legal expenses, yet the causal relationship is indeterminate. On the one hand, due to the acute multiagency problem, SOE managers may not prioritize corporate cost savings. As one informant noted, "State-owned Chinese companies tend to do better than the privately owned ones in following the rules. It's not their money; they (the managers) don't want to take any risk."[134] On the other hand, tight hierarchical control by headquarters and their supervisory agencies through measurable metrics results in close attention to legal fees rather than service quality or long-term corporate benefits. Indeed, as shown in Section 3.3.1, state-owned Chinese companies are more attentive to fee rates when selecting US lawyers. However, whether their fee sensitivity results in a systematic reduction of US legal expenses is unclear.[135]

Cultural difference. Tensions between informal institutions of China and the United States could also impact Chinese companies' legal expenses in the United States. On the one hand, due to the secondary role of law in business transactions in China, Chinese companies under strong influence of the home-state normative institutions may heavily discount the value of premium legal services and curb legal expenditures. On the other hand, greater cultural differences engender misunderstanding, conflicts, and disputes, and may subsequently inflate US legal cost.[136]

In-house counsel. The availability of corporate counsel at Chinese companies in the United States may be associated with their legal expenses in two opposing ways. On the one hand, in-house counsel

[134] Interview with a US lawyer (March 31, 2015).

[135] To test the hypotheses, I use the same two dummy variables created from the 2019 survey data, with one representing majority state ownership, the other significant minority state ownership. The baseline scenario is private ownership.

[136] To test the conflicting hypotheses, I use the managers' perceived cultural challenges in the United States. As described in Chapter 2, the variable equals one if respondents to the 2019 survey listed "cultural differences between China and the United States" as a major risk for their US operations, zero otherwise.

may serve as a proxy for the amount and complexity of repeat legal issues for a Chinese company, and those encountering frequent and complex legal issues presumably incur higher legal costs. Additionally, in-house counsel could identify company-specific legal needs, resulting in higher fees paid to outside lawyers. Both hypotheses support a positive relationship between in-house capacity and US legal service costs. On the other hand, the literature on the corporate in-house movement highlights cost-saving as a primary driver,[137] suggesting that having internal legal capacity could reduce fees paid to outside lawyers.[138]

Litigation in US courts. Litigation is an inherent risk of doing business in the United States, and US lawyers play an indispensable role in assisting clients to navigate the complex adjudicatory system. Given the unpredictability and volatility of litigation work, even companies with competent in-house legal staff must outsource it, let alone average Chinese companies operating in the United States.[139] However, heavy reliance on US legal services comes at a high cost. To explore the relationship between the amount of US litigation of a Chinese company and its US legal expenses, I use the hand-collected data on all federal lawsuits involving Chinese companies that responded to the China General Chamber of Commerce USA (CGCC) 2019 survey.[140] As shown in Table 3.3 in the Appendix, an average Chinese company in the sample experienced 1.54 federal cases since their entering into the US market.

Business reorganization. Apart from litigation, companies typically rely on outside lawyers for major business reorganizations such as mergers or acquisitions. As such special service needs are unpredictable and temporary, it is generally more cost-efficient to delegate them to outside lawyers. Therefore, Chinese companies in the United States that have recently undergone a business reorganization are likely to report higher legal costs.[141]

[137] Wilkins, *supra* note 4, at 2080; Craig B. Glidden, *The Evolution and Influence of Corporate Legal Departments*, 12 Fla. St. U. Bus. Rev. 131, 134 (2013). However, in the past few decades the in-house movement coincided with the escalation of spending on outside law firms in the United States. Wilkins, *supra* note 4, at 2084.

[138] To test these conflicting hypotheses, I use the dummy variable that equals one if a responding firm has employed a full-time legal manager licensed to practice law in the United States, and zero otherwise.

[139] Ribstein, *supra* note 9, at 758.

[140] The following chapters will analyze in greater detail litigation by Chinese companies in US courts.

[141] From the survey data I construct a dummy variable that equals one if a Chinese company engaged in mergers or acquisitions in the previous two years, zero otherwise.

Size of US investment. Large companies often deal with legal and regulatory issues that smaller firms rarely encounter (e.g., antitrust law). Additionally, within the same legal area, companies with larger US operations have more legal service needs (e.g., labor and employment disputes). Therefore, I hypothesize a positive link between business size and external legal expenses. However, due to economies of scale, large companies should enjoy a lower ratio of legal costs to operating costs.[142]

Listing status. As noted earlier, additional oversight by securities regulators magnifies US legal risks for listed Chinese companies, which might incentivize them to purchase more legal services in the United States.[143]

Sectoral regulation. As previously mentioned, firms tend to be less cost-conscious when purchasing legal services for "betting the company" matters.[144] Consistent with the argument, the preceding subsection just demonstrated that Chinese companies in heavily regulated sectors are less fee sensitive. Hence, it is plausible that such Chinese companies also report higher US legal expenses.[145]

Entry mode. The mode of entry chosen by a Chinese company may affect its US legal expense. Arguably, those that acquire an established US business do not have to deal with as many novel legal and regulatory

142 To test these two hypotheses, I use US revenue as a measure of the size of a Chinese company's US business. The data are derived from a scale question on the total US revenue of a CGCC survey respondent. The survey subjects chose one of five levels of revenue, with the lowest level being "below one million dollars" and the highest level "above 100 million dollars."

143 From the 2019 survey data, a dummy variable was created and assigned the value of one if a Chinese business in the United States is managed by a listed company, zero otherwise. One may reasonably argue that US securities regulation is uniquely consequential. Hence, I create an alternative listing status dummy that equals one if a Chinese investor is listed in the United States, zero otherwise. Tests using this alternative dummy return similar results.

144 Coates, et al., *supra* note 5, at 1021.

145 The 2019 survey data contain detailed sectoral information so I could rely on the regulation intensity index compiled by McLaughlin and colleagues. Each of the survey respondents is assigned to an industry designated by a two-digit NAICS (North American Industry Classification System) code, which corresponds to a regulatory intensity index number. All the respondents report their industries. I checked all their official websites or, when such websites are not available, third-party reports to ascertain their industries. For those operating in multiple industries, I use the one most heavily regulated. As typical with this type of proxy measure, the index is not perfect. For instance, real estate is a relatively heavily regulated industry, but because it is normally regulated at the state and local level, the industry appears to be subject to light federal regulation. For more details, *see* Patrick A. McLaughlin & Oliver Sherouse, RegData US 3.1 Annual (dataset), QuantGov, Mercatus Center at George Mason University, Arlington, VA, 2018. https://quantgov.org/regdata-us/.

issues as those engaging in greenfield investments. Therefore, I hypothesize that Chinese companies that build their US operations from scratch are likely to incur higher legal service costs.[146]

Investment duration. Investment duration may be related to US legal expense in nuanced ways. On the one hand, earlier Chinese investors may have adapted to paying expensive US legal bills. By contrast, those that have recently ventured abroad may be more budget-conscious due to the undervaluation of legal services in China. On the other hand, newcomers may encounter unfamiliar legal issues, leading to additional legal cost, while established businesses have learned to take preventive measures to mitigate US legal risks and lower expenses.[147]

3.3.2.2 *Analysis of Test Results*

The ownership structure of Chinese investors does not appear to be a significant factor in any of the model specifications (see Table 3.4 in the Appendix). Although the finding is inconclusive due to the limited sample size, it suggests that state-owned Chinese companies are similar to their privately owned counterparts in terms of US legal expenses, with all the other variables held constant.[148] Recall the earlier finding of a positive association between the ownership type and legal fee sensitivity.[149] One would expect to see a similar connection between the ownership type and Chinese companies' US legal service expenses. The absence of such an association may be attributable to the two opposing hypothetical effects offsetting each other. I contend, however, that Chinese companies' lack of bargaining power over US law firms offers a better explanation.[150] Under the isomorphic pressure of the US legal service market, state-owned Chinese investors must adapt, and their fee sensitivity does not significantly affect the total service costs. In other words, the host-state institutional pulls are much

[146] To measure the variation, I create a dummy variable that equals one if a Chinese multinational entered the US market via a merger or an acquisition or by forming a joint venture, zero otherwise.

[147] To evaluate this hypothesis, I include in the tests the number of years a Chinese multinational has operated in the United States.

[148] Though the sample size limits the power of the models, significance is highly unlikely even with larger samples given the large error terms relative to the coefficients for the state ownership variables.

[149] Li & Zhang, *supra* note 62, at 107–8.

[150] Given the overrepresentation of large Chinese companies in the sample, the average US legal expense of all Chinese companies with direct investment in the United States should be lower than the figure presented here.

stronger in this subject area, and the force of the US legal market overpowers variant institutional pressure from China and lawyer selection preferences of the Chinese companies.

The test results revealed demand-driven variations in Chinese companies' US legal expenditure. First, litigation in the United States is costly. In all the model specifications, the amount of federal litigation is highly significant and positively associated with the legal expenses. As previously discussed, given the complexity and unpredictability of litigation, even large US companies typically outsource such work.[151] Moreover, the service needs generated by US litigation tend to fluctuate, making it cost-effective to hire outside lawyers to meet the sporadic demand surge.[152] The same logic applies to Chinese companies in the United States.

Second, major business reorganizations drive up US legal expenses. Chinese companies that have recently engaged in major transactions, such as mergers or acquisitions, report higher legal costs. The finding is unsurprising, as in a country with sophisticated legal and regulatory systems, mergers and acquisitions invariably require extensive law firm support.[153] Only the largest US corporations can produce such services internally,[154] so the vast majority of Chinese companies in the United States must rely entirely on outside lawyers and incur high legal costs.

Third, Chinese companies with more expansive US investments report higher external legal costs. This finding confirms the conventional view that larger operations inevitably encounter more legal and regulatory issues, the resolution of which incurs higher costs. Of course, such companies can also afford expensive legal services.[155]

Similar tests using "ratios of legal costs to operating costs" as the dependent variable have returned results that reaffirm the market-driven conclusion (see Table 3.5 in the Appendix). The ownership structure of Chinese investors remains insignificant, which dovetails with the previous finding. One may therefore tentatively infer that Chinese state-owned investors do not differ from privately owned Chinese companies in their US legal expenses when the other variables are held

151 Omari Scott Simmons & James D. Dinnage, *Innkeepers: A Unifying Theory of the In-House Counsel Role*, 41 Seton Hall L. Rev. 77, 126 (2011).

152 Rosen, *supra* note 61, at 508.

153 De Fontenay, *supra* note 23, at 396–97.

154 Steven L. Schwarcz, *To Make or to Buy: In-House Lawyering and Value Creation*, 33 J. Corp. L. 497, 530 (2007).

155 None of the other variables is significant, and robustness tests excluding outliers in the sample return similar results.

constant. However, the variable for cultural difference is significant and positively associated with the legal expense ratio. The cultural gaps generate frictions and raise the legal service needs relative to other operating costs, resulting in a higher legal cost ratio.

Intuitively, a merger or acquisition would significantly raise the ratio of legal expenses to operating costs. This echoes the finding that major corporate restructuring gives rise to complex legal and regulatory issues that are more efficiently handled by outside lawyers. Relatedly, the entry mode variable is also significant in four tests and negatively associated with the legal cost ratio. As anticipated, Chinese companies that entered the United States by building businesses from scratch, instead of acquiring or partnering with local firms, must tackle myriad costly legal issues. As a result, they record a higher ratio of legal costs to operating costs.

Moreover, the size of Chinese companies' US operations significantly correlates with their legal expense ratio. However, the coefficient has turned negative, suggesting that larger US businesses report lower ratios of legal to operating expenses. Economies of scale are apparently at work here. Legal problems that may bankrupt a small business often have no major revenue impact on a large company. Furthermore, the litigation variable is weakly significant in only one of the models.[156] While large Chinese companies attract more lawsuits, the additional legal service expense only marginally alters the firms' larger operating costs, hence the low level of significance.

To summarize, Chinese companies in the United States rely extensively on local legal professionals to navigate the complex legal and regulatory regime. In this process, the influence of formal and informal home-state institutions manifests in their US lawyer selection preferences. However, with insignificant legal service budgets, Chinese companies are usually treated by established US law firms as "low-quality clients."[157] Without much bargaining power, Chinese companies' lawyer selection preferences, which vary according to state ownership and other home-state institutional influence, have limited impact on their US legal costs, and the costs largely reflect the companies' objective demand for legal services. Moreover, cultural differences appear to increase the ratio of legal to operating costs for Chinese companies in the United States.

[156] The results are weakly significant at the 15 percent level in the other tests, so it is possible that future tests using larger samples may return significant results.

[157] Interview with a partner of a US law firm (June 7, 2020).

3.4 CONCLUSION

Lawyers play an essential role in the proper functioning of the US legal system, and their assistance is crucial for Chinese companies to negotiate legal risks in the United States. However, we know nothing about the relationships between these companies and their US lawyers. Within the dual institutional framework, this chapter found a significant influence of the home-state institutions on Chinese managers' attitudes toward US lawyers and their selection preferences. Moreover, Chinese companies typically spend insignificant amounts on US legal services and therefore are largely market followers.[158] They must adapt to the US legal market in order to acquire high quality legal services, and their US legal expenditures mostly reflect varying legal service demands generated in the host state.

The findings also revealed nuanced institutional effects of the companies' home and host states. In the tug of war between the institutional pull and push, the home-state inertia is evident in the managers' views and preferences when dealing with US lawyers. However, when it comes to the consumption of US legal services, the host-state institutional pressure dominates, obscuring not only the varying institutional attributes of the companies' home state but also their different internal legal capacities in the United States.

These findings are crucial to understanding how Chinese companies navigate the US legal system, and some of them will be re-examined in relation to the other topics explored in this book. For instance, lawyer's role in US litigation by Chinese companies will be analyzed in following chapters. Beyond this book, the findings of this chapter also contribute more broadly to the literature on US legal profession, the legal service market, SOEs, and MNCs with the new empirical insights about how MNCs, especially state-owned MNCs and those from emerging markets, select US lawyers and consume US legal services.

[158] This is not to deny the influence of Chinese companies' preferences on the practices of US legal service providers on the margin. Multiple interviewees reported flexible fee arrangements as key to attract Chinese clients. For instance, one US lawyer, a litigation partner at a small US law firm, offers a hybrid cap that includes contingency fee with a relatively low hourly rate (interview on July 28, 2022).

APPENDIX

TABLE 3.1 Summary statistics

Variable	Mean	Standard deviation	Min.	Max.	Observations
Consider legal fees important	0.503	0.501	0	1	177
Consider lawyer or law firm's prestige important	0.345	0.477	0	1	177
Consider lawyer's Chinese background important	0.198	0.399	0	1	177
Consider lawyer's government background important	0.119	0.324	0	1	177
Consider recommendation by acquaintances important	0.203	0.404	0	1	177
Consider headquarters' recommendation important	0.113	0.317	0	1	177
State ownership (50%)	0.393	0.490	0	1	191
Investment duration	9.239	9.114	0	36	201
US revenue	2.452	1.610	1	5	188
In-house counsel	0.284	0.452	0	1	190
Intensity of sectoral regulation	0.381	0.487	0	1	210
Listing status	0.484	0.501	0	1	184
Cultural differences	0.234	0.424	0	1	167

Note: Data source is 2017 CGCC survey.

TABLE 3.2 Test results for varying US lawyer selection preferences

Variable	Legal fee	Lawyer or law firm reputation	Recommendation by acquaintances	Chinese background	US government background	Recommendation by Chinese headquarters
State ownership	2.415**	1.218	1.041	2.207	6.112***	5.114**
	(1.026)	(.527)	(.535)	(1.206)	(3.967)	(3.855)
Cultural differences	0.958	2.310*	1.223	2.713**	2.332	4.415**
	(0.422)	(1.016)	(.608)	(1.382)	(1.412)	(3.070)
Sectoral regulation	0.438**	2.327**	0.580	0.828	1.449	5.966**
	(0.177)	(.921)	(0.274)	(0.405)	(0.796)	(4.196)
Size of US investment	0.891	1.348**	1.007	0.796	0.798	1.479*
	(0.127)	(0.191)	(0.160)	(0.150)	(0.168)	(0.323)
Investment duration	1.032	0.995	0.987	0.974	0.960	0.965
	(0.026)	(0.024)	(0.029)	(0.031)	(0.034)	(0.037)
In-house counsel	0.659	0.472	0.389	0.378	0.425	0.426
	(0.314)	(0.235)	(0.245)	(0.258)	(0.329)	(0.346)
Listing status	2.845**	0.472*	0.643	3.137**	1.527	0.521
	(1.189)	(0.201)	(0.307)	(1.647)	(0.891)	(0.363)
Constant	0.552	0.244***	0.512	0.1872***	0.095	0.009***
	(0.211)	(0.100)	(0.221)	(0.096)	(0.059)	(0.008)
N	142	142	142	142	142	142
Pseudo R^2	0.112	0.075	0.052	0.119	0.137	0.216

Note: Data source is 2017 CGCC survey, logit tests, reporting odds ratio.

TABLE 3.3 Summary statistics

Variable	*Mean*	*Standard deviation*	*Min.*	*Max.*	*Number of observations*
Investment duration	10.271	8.325	1	38	218
State ownership (50%)	0.304	0.461	0	1	230
State ownership (10%)	0.078	0.269	0	1	230
Listing status	0.398	0.491	0	1	226
Annual US revenue	2.535	1.587	1	5	202
M&A in the past two years	0.270	0.445	0	1	178
Professional in-house legal manager	0.346	0.477	0	1	188
Legal fees	356,282.8	1,219,213	0	1.10E+07	113
ln(legal fees)	10.663	2.036	5.704	16.213	110
Legal fee ratio scale (1–4)	1.6	0.842	1	4	155
Sectoral regulation	50,656.02	52,294.36	511.455	214,953.4	230
Number of lawsuits	1.539	4.296	0	30	206
Entry mode	0.214	0.411	0	1	220
Cultural challenge	0.275	0.447	0	1	193

Note: Data source is 2019 CGCC survey.

TABLE 3.4 Regression results (dependent variable: log fees paid to US law firms)

Variable	1	2	3	4	5
State ownership (50%)	–0.016	–0.028	–0.049	–0.040	–0.040
	(0.402)	(0.404)	(0.419)	(0.513)	(0.516)
State ownership (10%)	0.946*	0.922	0.911	0.817	0.816
	(0.563)	(0.575)	(0.559)	(0.575)	(0.576)
Number of cases	0.135***	0.135***	0.136***	0.146***	0.146***
	(0.040)	(0.041)	(0.041)	(0.044)	(0.055)
Mergers & acquisitions	10.039***	10.043***	10.036***	10.019**	10.018**
	(0.374)	(0.380)	(0.386)	(0.396)	(0.394)
US revenue	0.416***	0.414***	0.412***	0.4133***	0.413***
	(0.131)	(0.134)	(0.135)	(0.150)	(0.151)
In-house legal manager	0.429	0.424	0.411	0.379	0.379
	(0.371)	(0.374)	(0.376)	(0.434)	(0.435)
Cultural difference	–0.049	–0.048	–0.073	–0.1545	–0.149
	(0.379)	(0.384)	(0.397)	(0.437)	(0.469)
Entry mode		–0.106	–0.102	–0.154	–0.153
		(0.426)	(0.432)	(0.449)	(0.457)
Listing status			0.143	0.131	0.133
			(0.367)	(0.388)	(0.394)
Investment duration				–0.013	–0.013
				(0.024)	(0.024)
Sectoral regulation					–2.27e-07
					(3.94e-06)
Constant	8.836***	8.867***	8.828***	9.012***	9.019***
	(0.408)	(0.436)	(0.427)	(0.524)	(0.524)
N	96	95	95	90	90
R-square	0.39	0.387	0.388	0.371	0.371

Note: Data source is 2019 CGCC survey; OLS test results reporting robust standard error.

TABLE 3.5 Regression results (dependent variable: ratio of legal fees to operating costs, scale one to four)

Variable	1	2	3	4	5	6
State ownership (50%)	0.017	0.017	0.042	0.008	0.045	0.131
	(0.159)	(0.166)	(0.183)	(0.411)	(0.417)	(0.448)
State ownership (10%)	0.549	0.549	0.377	10.139	10.239	0.824
	(0.393)	(0.409)	(0.418)	(0.741)	(0.767)	(0.814)
Number of cases	0.024	0.024	0.027*	0.047	0.045	0.059
	(0.016)	(0.016)	(0.016)	(0.046)	(0.046)	(0.049)
Mergers & acquisitions	0.282*	0.282*	0.314*	0.814**	0.847**	0.985**
	(0.167)	(0.170)	(0.174)	(0.398)	(0.404)	(0.432)
US revenue	–0.097**	–0.097**	–0.106**	–0.259**	–0.252*	–0.278**
	(0.049)	(0.049)	(0.051)	(0.128)	(0.129)	(0.139)
In-house legal manager	0.012	0.012	0.043	0.080	0.109	0.172
	(0.146)	(0.149)	(0.166)	(0.387)	(0.391)	(0.414)
Entry mode	–0.284**	–0.284**	–0.338**	–0.644	–0.639	–0.796*
	(0.143)	(0.143)	(0.138)	(0.443)	(0.443)	(0.462)
Cultural difference	0.362**	0.362**	0.392**	0.727*	0.744*	0.768*
	(0.176)	(0.176)	(0.192)	(0.386)	(0.388)	(0.428)
Listing status		–0.0003	–0.009		–0.216	–0.269
		(0.160)	(0.165)		(0.382)	(0.395)
Investment duration			0.0004			–0.007
			(0.012)			(0.028)
Sectoral regulation			–5.38e-07			–1.19e-06
			(1.76e-06)			(4.12e-06)
Constant	1.631***	1.631***	1.647***			
	(0.163)	(0.164)	(0.195)			
N	131	131	125	131	131	125
R^2/Pseudo R^2	0.133 (OLS)	0.133 (OLS)	0.147 (OLS)	0.059 (ordered logit)	0.06 (ordered logit)	0.068 (ordered logit)

Note: Data source is 2019 CGCC survey; ordered logit tests, and OLS test results reporting robust standard error.

CHAPTER FOUR

US LITIGATION BY CHINESE COMPANIES

I tell my Chinese client sometimes you need to be a bully and litigate … but they always want to settle.

—Lawyer for a Chinese company in the United States

To litigate or not to litigate, that is the question any Chinese companies operating in the United States long enough must contemplate. For American companies, litigation is nothing but an unavoidable business risk and often a vital competition strategy, routinely dealt with by legal and managerial professionals applying monetarized cost-benefit analysis. Such analysis typically incorporates attorney fees and other litigation expenses, potential reputational damage, time and human resource consumption, and the present value of expected litigation gains or losses.

In contrast, litigation in China carries complex social meanings and is often avoided to preserve long-term cooperative relationships or to signal desirable attributes to uninformed third parties. When lawsuits do occur, they are often handled by stakeholders without professional legal assistance. Disputants consider a wide range of material and non-material interests that are shaped by both formal institutions undergoing significant transformation and complex, entrenched social norms governing dispute resolution.

How do Chinese companies immersed in these two disparate institutional environments approach legal disputes in the United States? Although dispute resolution in a transnational context has attracted a great deal of academic attention, the existing literature has largely overlooked developing country multinational companies (MNCs), much less those that invest in developed host countries with robust, sophisticated adjudicatory systems. Moreover, the existing literature, premised largely on comparative cultural research, fails to articulate an analytical framework that incorporates or evaluates the possible dual institutional effects.

This Chapter 4 aims to narrow these gaps. It begins by making the baseline inquiry about the likelihood of Chinese companies experiencing justiciable disputes in the United States. As revealed below, many Chinese investors entered the US market relatively recently and have been growing their businesses incrementally. Thus, a slight majority of them have either managed to avoid any justiciable dispute or are unaware of their existence due to their limited knowledge of the US legal environment. Many Chinese investors with disputes in the United States cannot "name" the cause of legal action or "blame" a specific party for the loss, let alone press judicial claims.[1]

Next, if a justiciable dispute does occur to a Chinese company, who decides on the resolution method: its outside US lawyers, in-house legal manager, local managers, or the Chinese headquarters? How does the dual institutional influence, if any, manifest in the making of important decisions concerning US litigation? To answer this question, this chapter revisits the roles of in-house legal managers and outside lawyers serving Chinese companies in the United States. Additionally, it examines the litigation experience of Chinese companies and identifies institutional and organizational factors associated with their varying odds of US litigation.

The remainder of this chapter is organized as follows. Section 4.1 takes stock of the cumulative research on cross-border dispute resolution and conflict management and situates the insights within the dual institutional framework articulated in Chapter 1. Section 4.2 provides an overview of the survey data on Chinese companies' dispute resolution and litigation in the United States, and supplements it with in-depth interviews. Section 4.3 further examines the inter-company variations in two critical aspects: the allocation of the power to make US litigation decisions and the likelihood of US litigation experience. In doing so, it focuses on state ownership of Chinese companies and other variables representing the dual institutional tensions and major firm-specific attributes. Finally, Section 4.4 concludes this chapter.

[1] William L.F. Felstiner, et al., *The Emergence and Transformation of Disputes: Naming, Blaming, Claiming*, 15 Law & Soc'y Rev. 631, 631 (1980).

4.1 LITERATURE ON CROSS-BORDER DISPUTE RESOLUTION AND LITIGATION

A considerable body of research has examined disputes in transnational settings from various perspectives. One stream of such research highlights the social cognitive differences between disputants from East Asian and Western cultures. Those from the former, accustomed to "high-context communications, collective interests, and hierarchical power distributions," tend to prefer indirect dispute resolution.[2] Conversely, those from Western cultures, used to "low-context communications, self-interest, and egalitarian power distributions," generally favor direct confrontation for resolving disputes.[3]

Of course, no large country fits these cultural and normative prototypes neatly. For instance, while the United States exemplifies a culture of adversarial dispute resolution,[4] scholars have located and explored various close-knit communities within the country that persistently steer disputes away from adjudication.[5] The same is true for China, where empirical research has documented regional variations in litigation preferences or behavior.[6] However, viewed from afar, the two countries differ vastly in their informal institutions regulating dispute resolution and litigation, which raises the question of whether these differences and the tensions they generate have an effect on the litigation preferences, behavior, and experience of Chinese companies operating in the United States.

[2] *See, e.g.*, JEANNE M. BRETT, NEGOTIATING GLOBALLY: HOW TO NEGOTIATE DEALS, RESOLVE DISPUTES, AND MAKE DECISIONS ACROSS CULTURAL BOUNDARIES (2007); John Barkai, *What's a Cross-Cultural Mediator to Do? A Low-Context Solution for a High-Context Problem*, 10 CARDOZO J. CONFLICT RESOL. 43 (2008).

[3] *Id.*

[4] LEE AXELRAD & ROBERT A. KAGAN, REGULATORY ENCOUNTERS: MULTINATIONAL CORPORATIONS AND AMERICAN ADVERSARIAL LEGALISM 3–4 (2000).

[5] *See, e.g.*, ROBERT C. ELLICKSON, ORDER WITHOUT LAW: HOW NEIGHBORS SETTLE DISPUTES (1991); Lisa Bernstein, *Opting Out of the Legal System: Extralegal Contractual Relations in the Diamond Industry*, 21 J. LEGAL STUD. 115 (1992); Caryn Litt Wolfe, *Faith-Based Arbitration: Friend or Foe? An Evaluation of Religious Arbitration Systems and Their Interaction with Secular Courts*, 75 FORDHAM L. REV. 427 (2006); Michael A. Helfand, *Religious Arbitration and the New Multiculturalism: Negotiating Conflicting Legal Orders*, 86 N.Y.U. L. REV. 1231 (2011).

[6] *See, e.g.*, Ji Li, *Suing the Leviathan? An Empirical Analysis of the Changing Rate of Administrative Litigation in China*, 10 J. EMPIRICAL LEGAL STUD. 815 (2013). Thomas Talhelm, et al., *Large-Scale Psychological Differences Within China Explained by Rice Versus Wheat Agriculture*, 344 SCI. 603 (2014).

Though comparative cultural research on cross-border dispute resolution has not addressed this question, empirical studies exist on a related one: normative and cognitive adaptation in a foreign setting. Some found that individuals exposed to a foreign cognitive system are capable of learning and adapting, even though they remain versed in the home-state system.[7] In the same vein, international business scholars contend that bicultural managers are better able to analyze and resolve complex transnational conflicts. The literature, however, has not fully explored variations in the adaptation by transnational actors in their dual institutional contexts. Moreover, the literature has largely neglected formal institutional pressure, which, according to sociological institutionalists, inevitably induces coercive isomorphism.[8]

Several other lines of research have explored cross-border litigation. Chapter 1 has already reviewed them, but a brief recapitulation may be helpful. First, some legal scholars have investigated judicial bias against foreign parties and reached contradictory conclusions.[9] Secondly, a vast literature has accumulated on the jurisdictional boundary of US courts in light of foreign parties' frequent access. Much of the scholarship, however, is doctrinal or policy-driven and explores the applicability of US law, such as the *Alien Torts Statute*, for foreign victims to seek remedy in US courts against alleged wrongdoing of MNCs.[10] Thirdly, more relevant to the topics of this book, international business scholars have begun to investigate the relative frequency of foreign-company litigation in the United States. Mezias found that foreign-invested companies in the United States are sued more often in US courts than domestic firms and attributed the finding to the "liability of foreignness"

[7] *See, e.g.*, Richard Nisbett, The Geography of Thought: How Asians and Westerners Think Differently... and Why (2004); Marjorie Faulstich Orellana, et al., *Accessing Assets: Immigrant Youth's Work as Family Translators or "Para-Phrasers*," 50 Soc. Problems 505 (2003).

[8] Paul J. DiMaggio & Walter W. Powell, *The Iron Cage Revisited: Institutional Isomorphism and Collective Rationality in Organizational Fields*, 48 Am. Socio. Rev. 147 (1983).

[9] Kevin M. Clermont & Theodore Eisenberg, *Xenophilia or Xenophobia in US Courts? Before and After 9/11*, 4 J. Empirical Legal Stud. 441 (2007); Kevin M. Clermont & Theodore Eisenberg, *Xenophilia in American Courts*, 109 Harv. L. Rev. 1120 (1996). Compare them with Kimberly A. Moore, *Xenophobia in American Courts*, 97 Nw. U. L. Rev. 1497 (2002).

[10] *See, e.g.*, Donald Earl Childress III, *The Alien Tort Statute, Federalism, and the Next Wave of Transnational Litigation*, 100 Geo. L.J. 709 (2011); Christopher A. Whytock, *The Evolving Forum Shopping System*, 96 Cornell L. Rev. 481 (2010).

suffered by most foreign companies.[11] Lastly, a nascent scholarship, branching out from the enduring debate about US judicial deference to foreign sovereigns,[12] has analyzed US cases involving foreign parties that give rise to a growing tension between variant legal regimes and political values.[13]

To summarize, the existing literature has explored cross-border dispute resolution and litigation in the United States from a variety of perspectives and generated valuable insights. However, it falls short of answering the questions raised in this book. Specifically, no scholar has systematically examined the litigation preferences and behavior of MNCs in US courts, let alone those headquartered in China, a developing country with vastly different legal and cultural institutions. Moreover, most of the existing scholarship has taken as the unit of analysis a culture, a country, or a group of firms sharing the same country of origin or cultural background. Few scholars have rigorously explored inter-company variations in their US litigation preferences or behavior. To narrow these gaps, Section 4.2 below analyzes the interviews and descriptive survey data to examine dispute resolution and litigation by Chinese companies in the United States.

4.2 CHINESE COMPANIES AND THEIR DISPUTE RESOLUTION IN THE UNITED STATES

In the United States, disputants normally have to go through a complex and protracted legal process before reaching the trial stage in court, and alternative resolution methods are often available for quicker settlement. Despite the country's reputation for being notoriously litigious, the vast majority of filed cases are settled.[14] And the decision to litigate usually depends on myriad factors, and multiple parties may be involved. To concentrate on the most important aspects of

[11] John M. Mezias, *Identifying Liabilities of Foreignness and Strategies to Minimize Their Effects: The Case of Labor Lawsuit Judgments in the United States*, 23 Strategic Mgmt. J. 229 (2002).

[12] *See, e.g.*, Malvina Halberstam, *Sabbatino Resurrected: The Act of State Doctrine in the Revised Restatement of US Foreign Relations Law*, 79 Am. J. Int'l L. 68 (1985); Michael J. Bazyler, *Abolishing the Act of State Doctrine*, 134 U. Pa. L. Rev. 325 (1986).

[13] *See, e.g.*, Diego Zambrano, *Foreign Dictators in U.S. Court*, 89 U. Chi. L. Rev. 157 (2022); Mark Jia, *Illiberal Law in American Courts*, 168 U. Pa. L. Rev. 1685 (2020).

[14] Theodore Eisenberg & Charlotte Lanvers, *What Is the Settlement Rate and Why Should We Care?*, 6 J. Empirical Legal Stud. 111 (2009).

the complex process, this section examines Chinese companies' experience with disputes and litigation in the United States, their allocation of decision-making power regarding US litigation, and their litigation preferences in the United States.

4.2.1 Dispute and Litigation Experience

Anecdotal reports have lately portrayed Chinese companies as adaptive and savvy users of the US adjudicatory system.[15] For instance, TikTok's meticulous execution of litigation strategies allowed it to enjoin Trump's executive order aimed at excluding the popular app from the US market.[16] However, interviews with Chinese executives have revealed significant variations in their approach to litigation in the United States. A sizable Chinese company with more than two decades of US operation had initiated only one lawsuit, seeking to recover a substantial loss from a contractual default. According to the manager, "We always try to resolve disputes without litigation, which is too expensive in the United States … we have been defendants more often."[17] The manager of another Chinese company agreed, "We have only been sued occasionally. We have never sued anyone [in the United States]. Our customers are X and Y [both large US companies in the auto industry]; they always pay. But we are sued by others on product liability issues."[18] By contrast, some interviewees reported frequent litigation. According to a senior executive of a Chinese-invested firm: "We often have disputes in the United States, and often litigate as well … everything is handled by lawyers … we always follow lawyers' advice."[19]

The narrative largely affirms the descriptive survey data, which indicates that Chinese companies have had varied experiences in resolving disputes in the United States. As Table 4.1 shows, slightly more

[15] *See, e.g.*, Rachel Lerman, *TikTok Asks Court for Injunction to Stall Impending Ban*, Washington Post (September 23, 2020), at www.washingtonpost.com/technology/2020/09/23/tiktok-requests-injunction-ban/; Wendy Lee, *TikTok Sues Trump Administration, Calls Ban Unconstitutional*, L.A. Times (August 24, 2020), at www.latimes.com/entertainment-arts/business/story/2020-08-24/la-et-ct-tiktok-lawsuit-trump.

[16] See Chapter 6 for more discussion of TikTok's success in US courts.

[17] Interview with CEO of the US subsidiary of a large Chinese MNC (April 7, 2019).

[18] Interview with a senior executive of the US subsidiary of a large Chinese MNC (May 24, 2018).

[19] Interview with an executive of a US subsidiary of a large Chinese state-owned MNC (June 23, 2017).

than half of Chinese companies have not encountered any legal disputes in the United States. This finding can be attributed to several factors. First, some Chinese companies have a limited presence in the US market, which reduces the likelihood of disputes. As highlighted in Chapter 1, many Chinese investors have only recently entered the US market, with some operating in niche areas serving pre-existing clients. Second, and relatedly, Chinese companies testing the US market, unlike high-profile ones such as Huawei and TikTok, may not draw enough attention from plaintiff lawyers. Third, as noted in Chapter 1, the survey data were collected from executives of Chinese companies, so bias and a lack of knowledge about US law could also explain why some respondents reported no prior legal dispute experience. Chinese managers ignorant about US law may fail to name any violation of their legal rights, or place the blame on the proper infringing party, much less make judicial claims,[20] and therefore they could have under-reported justiciable disputes and litigation experiences in the United States. Therefore, readers should consider the percentages in Table 4.1 as setting the bounds of the actual figures, that is, *at least* 46.5 percent of Chinese companies have experienced US legal disputes, and *at least* 16.5 percent have litigated in the United States.

Among Chinese companies that reported justiciable disputes, a slightly higher number opted for arbitration than litigation. Given the focus of this chapter, an in-depth analysis of arbitration by Chinese companies in the United States is reserved for a separate research project.[21] Nonetheless, it is worth noting that a majority of Chinese companies, ranging from 67.9 to 79.8 percent, included arbitration provisions in their business contracts in the United States,[22] which inevitably redirects business and contractual disputes away from litigation.[23] However, even with arbitration provisions in place, Chinese companies are not entirely immune to US litigation, especially since many disputes fall outside the scope of arbitration. As a result, at least 16.5 percent of the Chinese companies have had some US litigation experience.

20 Felstiner, et al., *supra* note 1.

21 Ji Li & Carrie Menkel-Meadow, *Dispute Process Choices Among Chinese Companies in the United States: Some Preliminary Data and Analysis*, 27 HARV. NEGOT. L. REV. 295(2022).

22 *Id.*

23 Parties may still litigate on limited grounds such as the validity of the arbitration provision or the arbitration procedure.

TABLE 4.1 Dispute and litigation experience in the United States

Has your firm experienced any legal disputes in the United States? (multiple choices allowed)	Response (%)
No	53.5
Yes, and all have been settled	16.5
Yes, and some have been resolved through arbitration	18.8
Yes, and some have been resolved through litigation	16.5
Yes, and the disputes have not been resolved	8.2

Note: Data source: China General Chamber of Commerce USA (CGCC) 2017 Survey; 170 responded to this question.

4.2.2 Allocation of Power over US Litigation Decisions

In US lawsuits involving Chinese companies, human agents ultimately make all the decisions, often in a collective manner. Given the complexity and technicality of the US adjudicatory system, legal professionals, either in-house or external, are expected to play a significant role in the process. Besides these professionals, managers of both the US subunits and the Chinese headquarters may also have a say in the litigation decision. The presence of multiple parties raises important questions about the allocation of decision-making power, which should reflect and modify the dual institutional influence over Chinese companies.

In the United States, formal institutions such as statutes and common law at the federal and state levels govern most corporate litigation. Under the enormous coercive pressure, Chinese companies should delegate much of the litigation decision to US lawyers. Interviews with knowledgeable informants partially confirm this conjecture. For instance, a senior executive spoke about his firm's ongoing dispute with a US government agency and possible reactions. He would consider litigation only because the outside lawyer had suggested it as a viable option.[24] Another Chinese manager echoed this observation. Her firm was involved in a complex business dispute with a foreign developer, which sued in a US court. Throughout the litigation process, the Chinese company delegated most of the major decisions to a team of US lawyers and eventually managed to have the case dismissed.[25]

[24] Interview with CEO of the US subsidiary of a Chinese state-owned Chinese MNC (May 31, 2019).

[25] Interview with a senior executive of the US subsidiary of a Chinese state-owned MNC (June 23, 2017).

However, the influence of home-state institutions is also evident in the decision-making process. According to several interviewees, some Chinese companies have utterly failed to appreciate the importance of professional legal services in resolving US disputes. For instance, a US litigator noted that he would sometimes recommend litigation to his client, a sizable Chinese company with more than two decades of operation in the United States, but the client consistently sought to settle.[26] During another interview, a Chinese manager recounted a case where the seasoned US litigator hired by the firm advised against litigation due to the weakness of the legal claim, yet the Chinese company filed a lawsuit anyway.[27] "The board distrusts lawyers," explained the interviewee, "they built a successful business by taking risks, not by following the advice of risk-averse lawyers and consultants."[28]

The interviews also shed light on the variable role of in-house legal managers and the shifting tensions of conflicting institutional pressure. One US lawyer with years of experience advising Chinese clients remarked that he rarely worked with general counsel, as "they either don't exist or don't matter."[29] Similarly, one in-house counsel noted that her employer had not taken in-house legal advice seriously, though the situation improved after the company suffered several setbacks in the United States.[30] However, some interviewees suggested the opposite. For instance, a large Chinese company with substantial US investment in the manufacturing sector never questioned the judgment of its US in-house legal manager on matters of US law.[31]

The variable dual institutional pulls also manifest in the allocation of decision-making power between the headquarters and local managers. Some Chinese companies heavily rely on local managers for resolving US disputes. The manager of a large Chinese company commented that the headquarters rarely opined on US litigation.[32] In contrast, some other Chinese investors deprive the US affiliates of the power to make decisions about US lawsuits. An experienced US litigator, for instance, voiced his frustration at serving Chinese-invested businesses

26 Interview with a US lawyer (September 14, 2016).

27 Interview with a manager of the US subsidiary of a large Chinese MNC (May 31, 2020).

28 *Id.*

29 Interview with a partner at the US office of a large Chinese law firm (April 8, 2021).

30 Interview with an in-house counsel of the US subsidiary of a large Chinese MNC (May 14, 2017).

31 Interview with a senior executive of the US subsidiary of a large Chinese MNC (May 24, 2018).

32 *Id.*

TABLE 4.2 Allocation of decision-making power re US litigation

In deciding to litigate a dispute in the United States, whose opinion plays a major role? (multiple choices allowed)	Response (%)
In-house counsel	22.9
US lawyers	79.9
Local managers	46.5
Chinese headquarters	32.6

Note: Data source: 2017 CGCC Survey; 144 responded to this question.

as they would report everything back to the headquarters, seeking the superiors' instructions.[33]

In summary, comments from interviewees portrayed a variable allocation of decision-making power concerning US litigation among the four key parties: local managers, the headquarters, in-house counsel, and US lawyers. Some Chinese companies defer to local professionals, which not only reflects adaptation but also enables isomorphism. Other Chinese companies, however, appear to act under the influence of their home-state institutions, distrusting US lawyers and local managers on matters as important, complex, and technical as US litigation.

The descriptive survey data (see Table 4.2) provides further insight into the relative importance of the parties involved in making US litigation decisions. As expected, most Chinese companies consider US lawyers as key decision-makers, although some interviewees expressed disagreement on this point. The coercive US institutions governing litigation compel Chinese companies to adapt. This finding is consistent with the preceding chapter, where it was noted that the vast majority of Chinese companies would immediately consult US lawyers once a legal dispute arises. Thus, the survey data demonstrate that once a US dispute escalates, most Chinese companies value outside lawyers' advice regarding its resolution.

In-house counsel play a significant role in US litigation decisions for 23 percent of Chinese companies, which may seem low compared with US firms that typically delegate such decisions to their general counsel.[34] However, this figure should be interpreted in the context

[33] Interview with a lawyer at the US office of a Chinese international law firm (June 11, 2012).

[34] Jonathan C. Lipson, *Who's in the House? The Changing Role and Nature of In-House and General Counsel*, 2012 Wis. L. Rev. 237.

that, as discussed in Chapter 2, only a minority of Chinese companies in the United States employ full-time legal managers. Additionally, recall that some Chinese companies have lay managers overseeing their US legal matters, and their opinions may not add much value to decisions concerning US litigation.

Furthermore, the survey data reveal that 46.5 percent of Chinese companies give local managers a major voice in the litigation decision, compared with 32.6 percent that reserve it for the headquarters. These two figures should be interpreted together. The headquarters can theoretically dictate major decisions concerning US affiliates via its legal and management control, but doing so regularly can be inefficient due to information asymmetry, high communication cost, and the agency problem. Moreover, as just discussed, the US subunits are subject to intense isomorphic pressure from formal US adjudicatory institutions. A Chinese company sued in a US court will find its options stipulated or circumscribed by complex US laws and regulations, ignoring or deviating from which will prove costly. Hence, according to the descriptive survey data, more Chinese companies have chosen to localize US litigation decisions.

However, despite the apparent inefficiency of centralized decision-making and the coercive isomorphic pressure from the host-state formal institutions, 32.6 percent of the surveyed Chinese firms still defer to the headquarters on US litigation matters, which may be attributable to certain home-state institutional influence and intra-organizational control. First, as will be detailed in a moment, the State-Owned Assets Supervision and Administration Commission (SASAC) and its local equivalents have issued formal rules on the management of overseas state assets that require reporting of major foreign lawsuits not only to the headquarters but also to the supervisory governmental agency. These rules with extraterritorial effects may pressure state-owned Chinese investors to intervene in their US subunits' litigation decisions. Second, US lawsuits may materially implicate the global business of a Chinese MNC, incentivizing its headquarters to overreach. In such a scenario, the information asymmetry is reversed, and local managers usually lack knowledge about the interests at stake. For example, Huawei's decision to litigate against the federal government was ultimately made not by its US team, but by the senior executives of its Chinese headquarters, partly because the lawsuit was crucial to the MNC's global business.[35]

[35] Paul Mozur & Austin Ramzy, *Huawei Sues U.S. Government over What It Calls an Unfair Ban*, N.Y. Times (March 6, 2019), www.nytimes.com/2019/03/06/business/huawei-united-states-trade-lawsuit.html.

In summary, the interviews and survey data have demonstrated the dual institutional influence on Chinese companies' US litigation decisions. While formal host-state institutions pressure most Chinese companies to delegate the decisions to local agents, a significant minority reserve the power to their headquarters. One may ascribe hierarchical control in this subject area to the influence of home-state institutions, but such control also amplifies the influence. Executives in China inevitably bring Chinese norms and rules to bear when deciding whether and how to litigate disputes in the United States.

4.2.3 Litigation Preferences in the United States

The dual institutional influence may also modify the litigation preferences of Chinese companies in the United States. Those deeply immersed in the US environment may have fully adapted, basing their litigation decisions on a monetarized cost-benefit analysis. However, for those under stronger influence from home-state institutions, litigation is an action imbued with social meanings. A lawyer described her Chinese clients' response to US lawsuits as nothing short of a "cultural shock."[36] "In the US, litigation is a routine part of business, not in China."[37] A senior executive of a Chinese company attributed the reluctance to sue to potential reputational damage, "We operate in a small circle; lawsuits with business partners are bad for reputation."[38] In a rare lawsuit where the company served as defendant, he repeatedly proposed to settle, but the US plaintiff insisted on a trial, probably misinterpreting the eagerness to settle as a sign of legal weakness. However, with evidence clearly in its favor, the Chinese company easily prevailed at trial.[39]

Not all Chinese companies would refrain from litigation in the United States. As mentioned earlier, one Chinese manager noted that her company would strictly follow legal advice and sue whenever doing so would make business sense. Readers should also keep in mind that the home-state institutional influence does not always lead to litigation aversion. Given its intricate social meanings, litigation may, in certain circumstances, be the preferred option. A lawyer described a Chinese

[36] Interview with a partner at an international law firm (February 19, 2019).
[37] *Id.*
[38] Interview with CEO of the US subsidiary of a Chinese state-owned MNC (September 16, 2020).
[39] *Id.*

client who was personally offended by a lawsuit threat to his company and insisted on "litigating the other party to death."[40]

According to another US lawyer, "The difference is that American companies think litigation is just a cost of doing business; they assess by the dollar cost of litigation and settle when it's cheaper. Chinese clients are less concerned about those things. They don't see litigation as normal way of doing business. They are more willing to stand on principle. American companies don't care about principles, they just want to get over it."[41]

To further examine their litigation preferences, the executives were asked the following survey question: In comparison with the preference in China, in the United States your company shows (i) a stronger preference for settlement; (ii) a stronger preference for litigation; or (iii) the same preference in dispute resolution. As shown in Figure 4.1, 20 percent observed that their reactions in the United States would be the same as in China. Meanwhile, 64 percent expressed a stronger preference for settling disputes in the United States, and 16 percent showed a stronger inclination to litigate.

Why are the majority of the Chinese managers more inclined to settle disputes in the United States than in China, despite their shared perception of US judicial power and independence? Existing theories offer different answers. Rational choice theorists generally ascribe reluctance to sue to higher costs of litigation in the United States, which incentivizes disputants to settle and split the saved cost.[42] Others may attribute the aversion to litigation to the "liability of foreignness," as foreign investors lack adequate institutional knowledge about the host state. However, as indicated by some of the interviews, the settlement preference in the United States may also reflect the inclinations of Chinese managers shaped by their home-state institutional context.

Data from the 2014 and 2017 surveys unpack this settlement preference. As shown in Figure 4.2, the overwhelming majority of Chinese managers (88.2 percent for 2014 and 83.1 percent for 2017) attributed their stronger preference to settle in the United States to higher

[40] Interview with a partner at the US office of a Chinese international law firm (April 8, 2021).

[41] Interview with a partner at a US law firm (September 16, 2020).

[42] *See, e.g.*, Richard A. Posner, *An Economic Approach to Legal Procedure and Judicial Administration*, 2 J. LEGAL STUD. 399 (1973); Steven Shavell, *Suit, Settlement and Trial: A Theoretical Analysis Under Alternative Methods for the Allocation of Legal Costs*, 11 J. LEGAL STUD. 55 (1982).

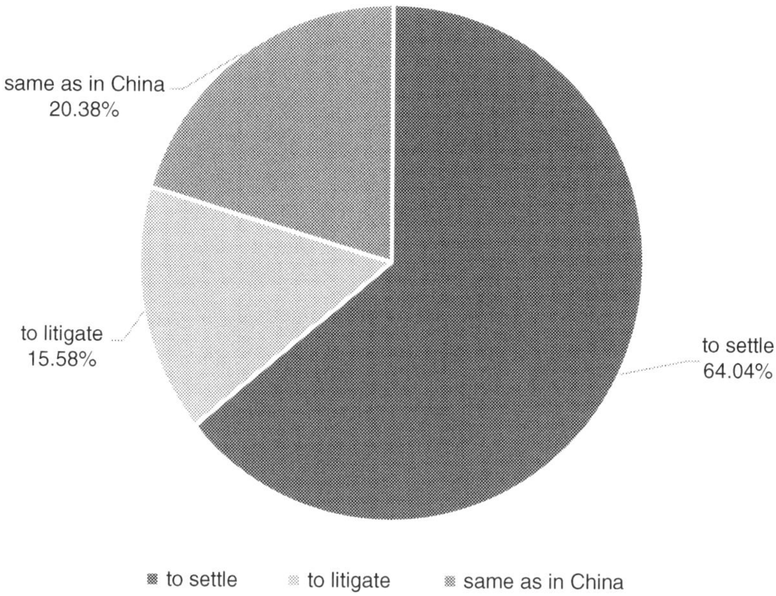

Figure 4.1 Litigation preference in the United States [Survey question: Compared to the preference in China, when a legal dispute occurs in the United States, your firm is more likely to __?][43]
Source: 2017 CGCC survey; 167 responded to this question.

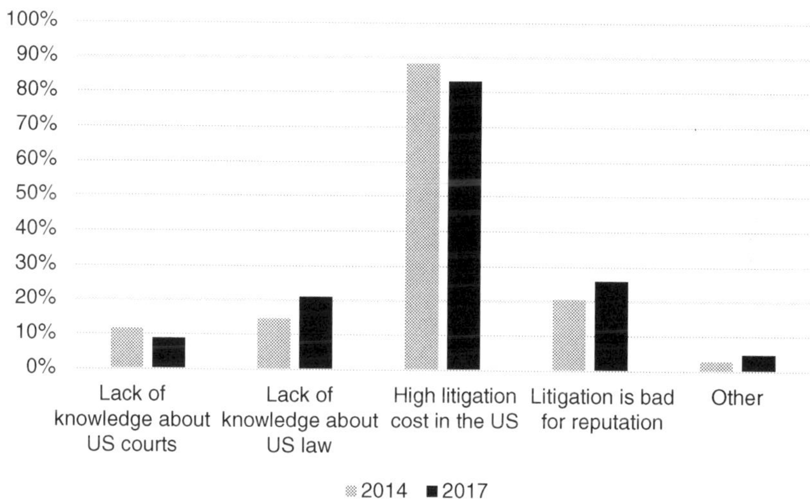

Figure 4.2 Explanation for settlement preference [Survey question: If your company is more likely to settle disputes in the United States, it is mainly because __? (multiple choices allowed)]
Note: 68 answered the question in 2014 survey; 124 answered the question in 2017 survey.
Source: 2014 CGCC survey and 2017 CGCC survey.

[43] The question in Chinese is the following: (与在中国相比)当涉及法律的纠纷在美国发生时,贵公司会更倾向于: A. 和解; B. 诉讼; C. 和在中国国内没什么不同.

litigation costs. This finding supports the litigation selection theory, which predicts that high litigation costs induce settlement of disputes.[44] Navigating the US adjudicatory system is more costly than in China due to lengthy process and hefty lawyer fees and the costs associated with highly uncertain litigation outcomes.[45]

Meanwhile, a significant minority of the respondents (20.6 percent in 2014 and 25.8 percent in 2017) expressed a preference to avoid litigation in the United States to prevent reputational damage. This association of litigation with "bad reputation" evinces the influence of home-state normative institutions. As discussed earlier, dominant Chinese culture and norms generally denigrate litigation and assign to it socially constructed interpretations such as hostility and intent to terminate cooperative relationships.[46] By contrast, in the United States, litigation and the threat thereof are routinely employed by companies as an effective negotiation strategy and an integral part of dispute resolution. To illustrate, consider the following description of a litigation experience by an in-house counsel of a large Chinese company in the United States:

> Chinese firms don't want to litigate. They are concerned with the cost and reputational damage. They don't even want to be plaintiffs. There is a cultural fear for litigation. The other [US] party knew about this, so they kept doubling down on their unreasonable demand. We were cornered and had no other choice, so we drafted an attorney letter, laying out our legal claims. Even then, the management hesitated, for fear of jeopardizing cooperative relationship (*pa shang le he qi*) … they didn't know that in the United States business can continue despite litigation. They thought face would be torn by a lawsuit (*da guan si jiu si po lian le*).[47]

Granted, being sued is probably an unpleasant experience even in the United States, but the corporate community rarely interpret the filing of a lawsuit (against a corporate party) as a personal offense or a signal of hostility. Put differently, except for some close-knit communities, social norms regulating contemporary US business society do

[44] John P. Gould, *The Economics of Legal Conflicts*, 2 J. LEGAL STUD. 279 (1973).

[45] J. MARK RAMSEYER, SECOND-BEST JUSTICE: THE VIRTUES OF JAPANESE PRIVATE LAW (2015).

[46] Ji Li, *Interactions Between Domestic Social Norms and International Law on Trade Dispute Resolution*, in *THE RULE OF LAW AT THE NATIONAL AND INTERNATIONAL LEVELS: CONTESTATIONS AND DEFERENCE* (M. Kanetake & A. Nollkaemper, eds., 2016).

[47] Interview with an in-house counsel of the US subsidiary of a large Chinese MNC (December 2, 2017).

not associate litigation with hostility *to the same degree* as the Chinese norms governing business dispute resolution. The reputational concern expressed by the Chinese managers also resonates with the literature on cross-cultural negotiations and conflict management.[48] It is worth noting that the survey question is posed as a hypothetical, so actual concern with reputational damage caused by any particular corporate wrongdoing, which may motivate US firms to settle, do not explain this survey result.

Furthermore, ignorance about the US adjudicatory system also partly explains the settlement preference. Chinese companies are less familiar with substantive US law than with the judicial institution itself. Around 21 percent of the 2017 survey respondents (14.7 percent for the 2014 survey) attributed their relative settlement preference to a lack of knowledge about US law, compared with 8.9 percent (11.8 percent) to ignorance about US courts. This finding adds nuances to the "liability of foreignness" literature. While inadequate institutional knowledge constitutes a major liability of foreignness, it appears to reduce rather than increase lawsuits. One way to reconcile the contradictory empirical findings is to distinguish the companies by their role in US courts (plaintiff versus defendant), which the following chapter will do.[49]

To summarize, the interviews and survey data have revealed nuanced dual institutional influence on Chinese companies' litigation preferences and behaviors. On the one hand, formal US legal rules and procedures exert considerable isomorphic pressure, compelling Chinese companies to adapt by delegating litigation decisions to American lawyers and engaging in cost-benefit analyses in litigation decisions. On the other hand, home-state institutions appear to have a notable impact, as a significant minority of Chinese companies have retained control over US litigation matters at their headquarters and others have opted for settlement to mitigate culturally constructed reputational damage.

[48] Wendi L. Adair & Jeanne M. Brett, *The Negotiation Dance: Time, Culture, and Behavioral Sequences in Negotiation*, 16 ORG. SCI. 33 (2005); Jeanne M. Brett & Tetsushi Okumura, *Inter- and Intracultural Negotiation: US and Japanese Negotiators*, 41 ACAD. MGMT J. 495 (1998); Catherine H. Tinsley & Jeanne M. Brett, *Managing Workplace Conflict in the United States and Hong Kong*, 85 ORG. BEHAV. & HUMAN DECISION PROCESSES 360 (2001).

[49] Mezias, *supra* note 11.

4.3 VARIATIONS IN LITIGATION DECISION POWER ALLOCATION AND US LITIGATION EXPERIENCE

The interviews and survey data have revealed a range of approaches taken by Chinese companies when it comes to litigation in the United States. While some companies have expressed faith in the US adjudicatory system and confidence in litigating disputes, others have displayed skepticism and hesitation. Moreover, their reactions to a US dispute vary as well. While some would immediately report back to the headquarters in China and await instructions, others attempt to resolve the issue locally without notifying the home office. Still others would play ostrich, ignoring the problem entirely or "kicking the can down the street" – passing it off to the next expatriated manager.[50]

To further analyze these inter-company variations, this section conducts two sets of tests. The first set focuses on decision-making power concerning US litigation, and the second examines the probability of experiencing US litigation. Again, in line with the focus of this book, the analysis will pay special attention to the key institutional variables, including the ownership structure of Chinese investors and US–China cultural difference.

4.3.1 Power to Make Litigation Decisions

This subsection examines the variable allocation of decision-making power concerning US litigation. Specifically, it investigates why some retain the power for the headquarters and others delegate to outside lawyers. While the power allocated to in-house legal counsel is an important topic, the truncated sample size forecloses rigorous statistical analysis.[51] Additionally, as the decision-making power of the headquarters and local managers are two sides of the same coin, it makes sense to investigate the more puzzling retention of power by the headquarters.

4.3.1.1 Chinese Headquarters

Around 32.6 percent of Chinese companies give their headquarters a strong role in deciding whether to litigate in the United States, setting them apart from the rest that delegate this power to local managers or external lawyers. This hierarchical control over US litigation arguably

[50] Interview with a lawyer at the US office of a Chinese international law firm (June 11, 2012).

[51] As noted in Chapter 2, only a minority of Chinese MNCs have employed full-time US legal managers.

reflects, enables, and amplifies home-state institutional influences on the preferences and behaviors of the US subunits.[52] But what may explain this allocation of power? The answer may reside in the following variables (see Table 4.3 in Appendix for the summary statistics).

State ownership. Under the rational choice framework, profit-driven MNCs would expand their control over foreign affiliates to the point where the marginal cost of doing so equals the marginal benefit. This same logic should apply to US litigation decisions of privately-owned Chinese MNCs, where the anticipated commercial loss stemming from inefficient dispute resolution should discourage excessive intervention by the headquarters. State ownership of Chinese investors, however, complicates the analysis. As previously discussed, state-owned Chinese investors are subject to unique home-state institutional restraints imposed by the SASAC and its regional equivalents. These agencies have issued a whole set of directives for preserving state-owned assets that apply to the foreign operations of state-owned Chinese MNCs. In particular, legal scandals involving Chinese state-owned enterprises (SOEs) triggered specific disclosure rules in 2005, under which SOEs subject to SASAC supervision must report any lawsuit or arbitration (or dispute that may lead to litigation or arbitration) that may result in damages exceeding fifty million RMB (approximately US$7 million).[53] Following the SASAC model, many regional governments have also imposed reporting obligations on SOEs within their jurisdictions. These reporting rules may motivate the headquarters of Chinese MNCs to assert tighter control over the resolution of foreign disputes. Moreover, the acute agency problem inherent in SOEs may also explain the extraordinary deference of local managers to headquarters' opinions. An informant described the hierarchical control: "SOEs are administrative bodies where leaders dictate. Every decision is made at the top, so the process is very slow … lower level staff shirk responsibilities and direct any questions to outside

[52] For the tests, I create a dependent dummy variable that equals one if a survey respondent reported an important role of the headquarters in the US litigation decisions, zero otherwise.

[53] Measures for the Management of Major Legal Disputes Cases between Central Enterprises, SASAC Rule #43 (effective August 1, 2023), at www.sasac.gov.cn/n2588035/c28266275/content.html; previously Interim Measures for the Management of Major Legal Disputes Cases between Central Enterprises, SASAC Rule #11 (effective March 1, 2005), at www.gov.cn/zhengce/2022-01/13/content_5718595.htm.

lawyers."[54] Another interviewee, a US in-house counsel for a Chinese state-owned company, generally agreed, "Because of the nature of my company, its decisions are mostly made top-down. The HQs sets the tone, and you can only make decisions within that range. You feel you did a lot, but it's not factored into the decision-making."[55] In short, state-owned Chinese MNCs may be more likely to centralize the power to decide on US litigation.[56]

Cultural difference. Competing pressure from informal institutions may also play a role. As previously noted, social and cultural institutions are essential in regulating dispute resolution, especially in countries such as China where the modern adjudicatory system is a patchwork of institutional transplants. Given that Chinese social and cultural institutions differ significantly from those of the United States, those deeply immersed in the home-state normative environment may approach US litigation decisions differently. To be specific, it is plausible that Chinese companies confronting cultural challenges in the United States prefer a hierarchical governance style and defer to the headquarters when making decisions about US litigation.[57]

In-house legal capacity. Presumably, Chinese companies with professional in-house counsel in the United States would be better equipped to make localized litigation decisions. However, as demonstrated in Chapter 2, some Chinese investors expatriate their in-house legal managers to administer personnel control and communicate with local managers. Moreover, in-house lawyers are often corporate law specialists lacking expertise in US litigation.[58] These factors suggest that having full-time US legal managers may not necessarily affect how the

[54] Interview with a lawyer at the US office of a Chinese international law firm (June 11, 2012).

[55] Interview with an in-house counsel of the US subsidiary of a Chinese state-owned MNC (May 11, 2023).

[56] To test this hypothesis, I use the same state ownership dummy created in prior chapters from the 2017 survey data, which takes the value of one if a Chinese government body owns more than 50 percent of the equity of the investor.

[57] As in previous chapters, for testing the hypothesis about the varying cultural gaps, I use the dummy variable that equals one if a Chinese MNC reported cultural differences as a major challenge to running its US business.

[58] I opt not to use the data for in-house counsel's opinion in decision-making power allocation, as objective data is preferable for the tests and the correlation tests between the two scales from the survey question, i.e., the importance levels for in-house counsel opinions and those for the headquarter management have already shown very low correlation.

power to make US litigation decisions is allocated. The statistical analysis will shed light on the indeterminate effect and add to the empirical findings of Chapter 2.[59]

US investment duration. New entrants to the US market may rely more heavily on headquarters for any major decisions, including litigation decisions, due to the lack of a trusted local workforce. In contrast, those with an extended operating history in the United States may have fully localized their operations and earned the trust of the headquarters. Additionally, investment duration may serve as an objective measure of acculturation or adaptation to the host-state institutional context.[60] It may also be correlated with state ownership, further justifying its inclusion as a control.

Listing status. As previously discussed, companies whose securities are listed on major securities exchanges must comply with enhanced reporting requirements, including timely disclosure of lawsuits that may materially implicate the stock price.[61] This obligation may motivate listed Chinese companies to tighten internal control over decisions concerning US litigation, which tend to be consequential and unpredictable. Additionally, listing status can serve as a proxy for the overall size of a Chinese MNC and control for potential correlation with the ownership structure of Chinese investors.[62]

Sectoral regulation. The effect of sectoral regulation on the allocation of litigation decision-making is unclear. On the one hand, heavily regulated sectors may exert more coercive pressure on Chinese companies to implement localized decision-making, which pulls the decision power away from the headquarters. On the other, extensive sectoral regulation may amplify the implications of the business conduct, and the increased corporate stake may motivate the headquarters to scrutinize local decisions.

Size of US investment. The size of a Chinese company's US business may impact headquarters participation in US litigation decision-making. A larger US operation may raise the stakes, pressuring the headquarters to impose

[59] For this variable, the dummy equals one if a Chinese company has employed a full-time in-house legal manager who is licensed to practice law in the United States, the dummy equals zero if otherwise.

[60] As in previous chapters, this variable is measured by the number of years a Chinese firm has invested in the United States.

[61] *See, e.g.*, Paragraph 1, section 11, Rules re Listing of Shares on the Shenzhen Stock Exchange; Paragraph 1, section 11, Rules re Listing of Shares on the Shanghai Stock Exchange.

[62] Ji Li, *"Going Out" and Going In-House: Chinese Multinationals' Internal Legal Capacity in the United States*, 46 Law & Soc. Inquiry 487, 504 (2021).

tighter hierarchical control. Conversely, from an efficiency point of view, a large, complex US operation requires responsive, localized management. Larger US investments may also result in greater immersion in the host-state institutional environment and isomorphic pressure.[63]

4.3.1.2 *Analysis of Test Results*

The statistical tests have returned interesting results. As Table 4.4 shows (see Appendix), Chinese companies of state ownership are more likely than those of private ownership to concentrate litigation decision-making power in the headquarters. This finding of hierarchical control resonates with those from the two previous chapters and is largely consistent with the qualitative evidence. While the exact wording varies, the interviewees generally agreed that decisions to litigate in the United States must go through a lengthy reporting and approval process at state-owned Chinese companies.

Moreover, Chinese companies with professional in-house counsel in the United States tend to prioritize their professional opinions over the headquarters when making decisions regarding US litigation. Put differently, US in-house lawyers facilitate localized decision-making. The complexity and idiosyncrasies of the US legal system present significant challenges to Chinese executives at the headquarters who typically lack necessary knowledge and expertise to evaluate and compare dispute resolution methods in the United States. Delegating this responsibility to a legal professional familiar with firm-specific information is a logical solution. The availability of professional in-house counsel also provides a layer of protection for local managers. Should anything go wrong with a US lawsuit, the managers could blame it on the in-house counsel, who would probably point the finger at the outside lawyer.[64]

[63] Apart from testing these two conflicting hypotheses, the variable also controls for possible correlation between state ownership and investment size, since Chinese SOEs historically dominated large-scale outbound investment. Ji Li, The Clash of Capitalisms? Chinese Companies in the United States (2018). As described in earlier chapters, the variable is measured on a scale of US revenue.

[64] Recall that some Chinese MNCs would have lay managers supervising the legal matters of their US subunits. Additional tests indicate that only in-house "lawyers" can shift the decision away from the headquarters. Replacing the variable with one that includes in-house legal managers unlicensed to practice US law, the result is no longer significant. As discussed in Chapter 2, the Chinese MNCs employ lay managers to fulfill tasks of control and coordination. Intuitively, such managers cannot overcome the information asymmetry in making US litigation decisions. So, adding them to the variable dilutes its effect on the localization of the decision-making power.

This finding adds to the analyses of Chapters 2 and enriches our understanding about the internal legal capacity of Chinese MNCs.[65]

4.3.1.3 *Outside US Lawyers*

Readers may recall that Chapter 3 explored Chinese companies' selection of US lawyers and consumption of their services. Earlier in this chapter, the interviews and descriptive survey data underscored the critical role of US lawyers in making US litigation decisions for most Chinese companies. But we also observed significant inter-company variations. This raises the question of why some Chinese companies undervalue professional legal advice when litigating in such a complex institutional environment. This subsection attempts some answers.

State ownership. State-owned Chinese companies are subject to distinct home-state institutional influence, which, as just demonstrated, leads to tighter hierarchical control over their US litigation decisions. The same logic implies that state-owned Chinese companies would defer less to US lawyers. Moreover, US lawyers are usually clueless about the intricate governance of Chinese SOEs and their home-state institutional context, resulting in the provision of generic legal advice that often cannot meet the idiosyncratic needs of state-owned Chinese clients. An in-house counsel of a Chinese state-owned company stated, "US lawyers are ignorant about the regulatory environment we face at home, so they sometimes cannot give us sound legal advice."[66] Therefore, due to both the home-state institutional effect and the perceived inadequacy of US legal services, state-owned Chinese companies may be less inclined to delegate US litigation decisions to local professionals.

Cultural difference. As reiterated earlier, informal institutions in China assign a relatively low social status to lawyers and undervalue legal services. Therefore, Chinese managers closely affiliated with their home-state culture may continue to undervalue professional legal advice, even on matters concerning US litigation. By contrast, the US culture assigns lawyers an elevated social status,[67] and Chinese investors that are culturally immersed in this context may show more deference to local lawyers regarding litigation matters.

[65] None of the other variables is significant. But due to the limited sample size, more definitive inference awaits future research.

[66] Interview with a manager of the US subsidiary of a Chinese state-owned MNC (January 9, 2020).

[67] Deborah L. Rhode, Lawyers as Leaders 1 (2013).

In-house legal capacity. The attitude of Chinese executives toward outside lawyers might also be influenced by their in-house legal capacity. Although in-house legal managers are generally corporate lawyers rather than litigators, they have invested in firm-specific knowledge and therefore are more capable than outside lawyers of assessing the pros and cons of a US lawsuit. Consequently, one could expect Chinese companies equipped with professional US legal managers to rely less on external lawyers in making litigation decisions.

Other relevant variables. The duration of an investment may also impact the delegation of litigation decisions to US lawyers. Arguably, Chinese companies that have operated in the US market for an extended period may have adapted to the home-state legal environment and learned to value professional legal advice. Moreover, sectoral regulation can also play a role in the reliance on outside lawyers for making litigation decisions. Heavily regulated sectors create a heightened compliance burden, which pressures or educates Chinese managers to appreciate the importance of professional legal advice. Hence there is a hypothetical connection between sectoral regulation and the delegation of litigation decisions to US lawyers. The size of a Chinese company's US investment may also have an effect. As discussed in Chapter 3, companies' limited legal service budgets disincentivize US lawyers from investing in firm-specific information and tailoring their services. This lack of attention could breed distrust in lawyers. By contrast, Chinese companies with substantial US investments attract more devoted lawyers. They are also more embedded in the host-state institutional environment and therefore subject to greater isomorphic pressure, which may alter their attitude toward professional legal advice. Lastly, heightened regulations for publicly traded companies complicate the analysis of US litigation, which may lead to heavier reliance on local professionals.[68]

4.3.1.4 *Analysis of Test Results*

The test results show that state-owned Chinese companies are less likely to assign outside lawyers a major role in US litigation decisions (see Table 4.5 in the Appendix).[69] This finding aligns with the enhanced hierarchical control at such companies and is consistent with the qualitative evidence. Several US lawyers have lamented the diminished

[68] Again, listing status may correlate with state ownership of Chinese MNCs, necessitating its inclusion as a control.

[69] The variable is highly significant and robust across all the model specifications.

role and complained about the slow pace and uncertainties in working with the US subunit of a Chinese SOE, stating that "everything must be reported back to China, and we have to learn to be very patient."[70] As previously noted, Chinese SOEs often have concerns beyond profit maximization, and US lawyers accustomed to cost-based analysis of lawsuits may provide advice that is deemed highly inadequate or irrelevant by such clients. A senior executive at the New York subsidiary of a state-owned Chinese company commented that US lawyers often had no clue as to the intricate rules governing its actions.[71]

Moreover, the presence of professional in-house legal managers is significantly and negatively correlated with reliance on US lawyers. Although these managers usually lack US litigation experience, their involvement appears to shift legal decisions away from outside lawyers. This finding, combined with the previous tests showing less headquarters control over US litigation at companies with internal legal capacity, suggests that, contradicting anecdotal reports, *professional* in-house legal managers of Chinese companies operating in the United States are not merely cosmetic. Instead, they play a nuanced and sometimes effective role in facilitating the firms' adaptation to the host-state legal institutions.

Furthermore, Chinese companies in heavily regulated sectors are more likely to delegate US litigation decisions to outside lawyers. Businesses in these sectors often face complex legal issues that require regular consultation with legal experts. This ongoing relationship cultivates a high level of trust and appreciation for professional opinions. Additionally, lawsuits involving such companies may have far-reaching implications, justifying extensive reliance on US lawyers. In short, the coercive isomorphic pressure from heavy regulation induces adaptation by Chinese companies to the host-state institutional environment.

4.3.2 US Litigation Experience

Chinese companies report vastly different litigation experiences in the United States. While some engage in frequent court battles, others have not participated in any lawsuit at all. This subsection aims to explore possible reasons for this inter-company variation. Factors such as state ownership of Chinese investors, cultural differences encountered, and the size and duration of Chinese investments, among other relevant considerations, will be examined.

[70] Interview with a US lawyer (June 11, 2012).

[71] Interview with manager of the US subsidiary of a Chinese state-owned MNC (January 9, 2020).

State ownership. The ownership type of Chinese companies has an indeterminate effect on their litigation experiences within the United States. On the one hand, as previously demonstrated, state-owned Chinese companies tend to centralize the management of their US operations, including litigation decisions. The hierarchical control of the headquarters, due to high transaction costs and information asymmetry, may result in more disputes and hinder efficient resolutions, leading to an increase in US lawsuits. Additionally, severe agency problems plaguing Chinese SOEs may also amplify the likelihood of US litigation. One experienced lawyer elaborated on the rationale, stating:

> Suppose you [could] settle a dispute for a million dollars, and if fully litigated, it would cost you ten million dollars. You would still want to litigate. Why? Because if you settle, the headquarters, without adequate contextual information and trust, would blame you for the loss of state assets. But if you litigate, everything is in the open, and Beijing is less likely to blame or punish you for cutting an under-the-table deal.[72]

Another lawyer made similar observations, highlighting a lawsuit where the plaintiff clearly sued to extract settlement money, and the reasonable reaction in that lawyer's opinion was to "pay the jerk to walk away."[73] But the client, a state-owned Chinese company, insisted on litigation, partly because they feared that the headquarters would interpret a settlement offer as "acknowledging wrongdoing."[74]

On the other hand, due to the distinct home-state governmental supervision (e.g., SASAC rules on reporting of foreign lawsuits), state-owned Chinese companies may consider US litigation especially costly and detrimental to their executives' careers, thus striving to avoid it. Also, relatively centralized control over the US operations, including US litigation, may channel more home-state normative influence, resulting in an aversion to dispute escalation. To test these conflicting arguments, a working hypothesis was adopted that, all else being equal, state-owned Chinese companies would be less likely to experience US litigation.

[72] Interview with a partner at the US office of a Chinese international law firm (April 8, 2021).

[73] Interview with general counsel of the US affiliate of a Chinese state-owned MNC (July 16, 2019).

[74] *Id.*

Cultural difference. Chinese companies facing cultural challenges in the United States may experience more conflicts, a portion of which inevitably land in court. It is therefore reasonable to hypothesize a positive correlation between reported cultural differences by Chinese companies and a higher probability of litigating in the United States. However, the causal relationship may not be straightforward. Chinese companies that face cultural barriers tend to be more closely tied to home-state institutions, which may lead to litigation aversion in the United States and less litigation experience. However, the preferences of Chinese parties may not hold significant weight. The encompassing and compulsory jurisdiction of US courts means that it is easy to drag a Chinese company into a lawsuit. As discussed in Chapter 3, the coercive pressure of US legal institutions may outweigh the influence of informal Chinese institutions, and evidence of adaptation obscure that of home-state institutional inertia.

Sectoral regulation. Chinese companies operating in heavily regulated sectors in the United States may be sued more often due to a higher probability of violations and a broader statutory basis for pressing legal claims that fall beyond arbitration provisions usually included in the companies' business contracts.[75] Moreover, the coercive pressure from extensive formal regulations compels adaptation by Chinese companies to the host-state environment. This pressure may also subdue competing pulls from the home-state institutions that may have litigation aversion effects. Hence, I hypothesize that sectoral regulation is positively associated with the probability of experiencing litigation in the United States.

In-house legal capacity. Corporate internal legal capacity may be related to a firm's litigation experience.[76] The presence of professional in-house legal managers signals an awareness of host-country legal risks and sufficient needs for US legal services that justify vertical integration of their production,[77] implying a positive association between Chinese companies' internal legal capacity and their US litigation experience. Also, as alluded to in Chapter 2, management awareness of US legal risks, and the need for strengthening internal legal capacity may result from costly litigation in the host country. Conversely, in-house legal

[75] Li & Menkel-Meadow, *supra* note 21.

[76] This variable is not included in the 2018 survey data.

[77] Steven L. Schwarcz, *To Make or to Buy: In-House Lawyering and Value Creation*, 33 J. Corp. L. 497 (2007).

managers may take preventive measures that reduce litigation risk, leading to a negative correlation between the two variables. The tests will shed light on the indeterminate effect.

Listing status. The listing status of a Chinese company may also affect its US litigation experience in variable ways. First, publicly traded companies are typically obligated to report lawsuits that may materially impact their stock price,[78] which may motivate them to settle or to prevent disputes from occurring in the first place. Second, information about listed companies is easily available, reducing the cost of suing them. Third, the listing status serves as a good proxy for the overall size of a Chinese MNC, and large, high-profile companies tend to attract US lawsuits. All these factors indicate a complex association between listing status and the probability of experiencing US litigation.

Size of US investment. The size of a Chinese company's US investment may be positively associated with its litigation experience. Larger companies typically have more US legal issues and justiciable disputes. Moreover, due to the peculiar features of the US adjudicatory system, such as contingency fee arrangements and the general lack of fee shifting, lawsuits tend to chase deep pockets. Chinese companies with substantial US operations are easy targets, especially in the increasingly hostile host-state political and regulatory environment.[79]

US investment duration. Investment duration should be positively associated with the odds of US litigation. Litigation is an unavoidable risk for most businesses operating in the US market. It follows naturally that Chinese companies that entered the market early are more likely to have been involved in some lawsuits. Conversely, new entrants may initially avoid US lawsuits due to a lack of justiciable disputes or limited knowledge about their rights or how to access the court system. As mentioned in Chapter 1, even TikTok managed to circumvent lawsuits at the early stage of its US expansion.

Litigation preference. The effect of litigation preferences is unclear.[80] As previously demonstrated, many Chinese managers who express a preference for settling cite cost concerns, meaning they will not shy away from litigation when the expected benefits from litigation

[78] RAMSEYER, *supra* note 45.

[79] Ji Li, *In Pursuit of Fairness: How Chinese Multinational Companies React to U.S. Government Bias*, 62 HARV. INT'L L.J. 375 (2021).

[80] This variable is not included in the 2018 survey data.

outweigh the costs. Additionally, as Chapter 5 will show, most Chinese companies go to court as defendants in the United States, so their litigation preference may not determine whether and how others litigate against them. In fact, rational disputants aware of Chinese managers' settlement preference would have a stronger incentive to sue Chinese companies in order to extract concessions.

4.3.2.1 Analysis of Test Results

I run tests of these hypotheses using two separate sets of data derived from the CGCC surveys of 2017 and 2018. As noted in Chapter 1, the survey questionnaires included different sets of questions each year to meet CGCC's shifting needs and interest. Therefore, the two datasets do not allow for tests on identical variables (see Tables 4.3 and 4.7 in the Appendix). Nonetheless, they complement each other and, more importantly, each reveals new information and serves as robustness checks of the findings from the other. The 2017 survey inquired about the Chinese companies' cumulative litigation experience in the United States, and the resulting data generated a binary variable that equals one if a Chinese company had litigated at least one lawsuit in the United States prior to the survey, zero if it had never litigated before. In comparison, the 2018 survey asked whether a Chinese company had been involved in any US lawsuit in the previous year (2017). From the responses, a dummy variable was constructed that equals one if a Chinese company litigated in 2017, zero otherwise. Obviously, this data reflects a company's one-year US litigation experience.[81]

The test results using the 2017 survey data (see Table 4.6 in Appendix) indicate that Chinese companies reporting cultural differences as a major challenge are more likely to have past litigation

[81] For both the ownership structure variable and the litigation preference variable, it is important to condition the discussion with some more knowledge about the probability of dispute occurrence. For instance, if state ownership is found to be negatively associated with litigation, is it because state-owned Chinese investors are less likely to litigate a dispute, or they are less likely to be involved in disputes in the first place? I ran tests for potential connections between a series of variables and the probability of dispute occurrence in the United States and found no significant evidence that state-owned Chinese investors are different in this regard. Intuitively, investment duration and the size of US investments both are significant and positively associated with the likelihood of having experienced disputes in the United States. Then I added a measure of cultural difference, and the variable is significant. Chinese MNCs that consider cultural differences to be a major challenge for doing recruiting and retaining US workforce are more likely to be involved in a dispute in the United States.

experience in the United States. While Chinese companies subject to stronger pulls of the home-state norms and culture may exhibit notable aversion to litigating disputes, the wide cultural gaps also generate miscommunication, misunderstanding, and judgment errors. The latter effect appears to dominate, and Chinese companies under the intense competing pressure of the dual normative institutions of the home and host states are more likely to experience disputes and lawsuits in the United States.

Moreover, the size of a Chinese company's US business is significantly and positively associated to the probability of its involvement in US lawsuits. The finding is intuitive, as large companies naturally encounter frequent and complex legal issues, a portion of which inevitably result in litigation. Additionally, deep pockets of these companies likely attract lawsuits due to the unique features of the US adjudicatory regime.

As expected, investment duration is also significant. Veteran Chinese investors in the United States are more likely to report some litigation experience. Given the constantly positive US legal risk, the longer a Chinese company is exposed to it, the more likely the risk will materialize into US lawsuits. Also intuitively, investment duration is not significant when only one-year litigation data is tested, as will be shown in a moment.

None of the other variables are significant. However, due to the limited sample size, one cannot draw definitive reference from the null findings. Also, as will be explained below, coding the Chinese companies' US litigation experience into a binary variable results in the loss of important information. To address this drawback, the following Chapter 5 will analyze hand-collected objective litigation data (i.e., number of federal lawsuits involving Chinese companies), and the tests therein will reveal more interesting results.

By comparison, the 2018 survey inquired about the companies' litigation experience only for the year 2017 and used a different set of questions, leading to different model specifications yet generally consistent test results (see Table 4.8 in the Appendix).[82] The variable measuring cultural differences remains highly significant and positively associated with the likelihood of Chinese companies' experiencing US

[82] The 2018 data allow the coding of state ownership with two dummies, 50 percent state ownership and 10 percent state ownership. Also, the size of the US investment can be assessed with two variables, US revenue and the number of US employees.

litigation in 2017.[83] This result confirms the findings from the tests on Chinese companies' cumulative litigation experience, suggesting that cultural challenges increase the risk of US litigation, which in turn supports the argument that US–China cultural gaps give rise to more disputes and escalate them.[84]

Furthermore, the variable measuring the size of a Chinese company's US investment remains highly significant and positive. Larger US businesses tend to face a higher volume of complex legal issues that may result in litigation, and their abundant financial resources both enable them to afford costly litigation and attract lawsuits in the unique legal environment of the United States. As expected, the duration of US investment is no longer significant, for the dependent variable only measures the Chinese companies' litigation experience in 2017, not their cumulative litigation experience since entering the US market. The result also indicates that the US litigation risk for Chinese companies does not exhibit any significant linear temporal change when the effects of the other variables are held constant.[85]

4.4 CONCLUSION

High-profile lawsuits involving prominent Chinese companies, such as Huawei and TikTok, have captured a great deal of public attention, and anecdotal accounts abound. These lawsuits have had significant impacts, from determining the survival of China's most competitive companies to changing US laws in subject areas closely tied to national security and foreign relations, and even modifying the escalating US–China geopolitical rivalry. However, few scholars

[83] The 2018 survey contained a specific question about the perceived effect of the cultural differences on the responding firm's US business. The respondents chose one of three answers: negative effect, positive effect, no effect. I created a dummy variable that equals one if the respondent chose "negative effect," i.e., the cultural difference between China and the United States had negative influence on the responding firm's US business. The dummy equals zero if the other two answers were selected.

[84] The insignificance of the litigation preference variable underscores the complexity of the nuanced effects of Chinese companies' home-state normative institutions, which may be obscured by strong coercive isomorphic pressure of host-state institutions.

[85] As will be shown in the following chapter, the case studies suggest a curvilinear association between the investment duration and the number of lawsuits a year involving a Chinese MNC's US subunit. To test this hypothetical association, I ran tests of the 2018 data including both investment duration and its square. Neither is significant, suggesting that the curvilinear pattern shared by the three Chinese MNCs studied extensively in Chapter 5 is not representative.

have systematically explored the litigation preferences, behavior, and experience of Chinese companies in the United States. This chapter has taken the first step toward filling that gap. The survey data has clearly shown that less than half of Chinese companies reported justiciable disputes, and even fewer have litigated in US courts. However, once involved in a lawsuit, Chinese companies rely heavily on US lawyers to navigate the complex adjudicatory system. Interestingly, Chinese managers revealed a stronger preference to settle disputes in the United States than in China, primarily due to high litigation costs, cultural aversion to litigation, and a lack of knowledge about the US legal system.

Further statistical analysis has revealed hierarchical control by state-owned Chinese investors over US litigation decisions and less delegation to US lawyers. Professional in-house counsel, where they exist, facilitate localized litigation decision-making. However, the actual effect of tight home-state control on the companies' litigation experience is less clear, as the test results showed no significant connection between the ownership structure of Chinese investors and their US litigation experience, roughly measured by a binary variable.

By contrast, informal home-state institutions appear to matter less in the decision-making allocation but more in shaping the varying litigation experiences. Specifically, Chinese companies that have adapted to the host-state environment are less likely to have US litigation experience. This finding is not attributable to the normative aversion to litigation, which would have predicted the opposite test result. Moreover, the variable "litigation preference," included in one of the tests using the 2017 survey data, turned out to be insignificant. Together, the findings suggest larger cultural gaps give rise to more conflicts and suboptimal dispute management, which leads to their escalation.

However, with the dependent variable being a collapsed binary variable, important information about the US litigation of Chinese companies is lost.[86] Moreover, as previously noted, the survey data is subjective, which could suffer bias and errors. Although running tests on both the 2017 and 2018 survey data, which used different measures of the interested variables, and supplementing the tests with in-depth interviews

[86] In an earlier annual survey, the CGCC attempted to collect more detailed data on litigation from its members. Unfortunately, the response rate for that question was low, and the quality of the collected data was poor. Thus, later survey questionnaires were revised to inquire only about the overall US litigation experience with a yes or no question.

should mitigate such problems, underreporting and bias may be systematic issues tainting both the surveys and the interviews. To address these concerns, especially the information loss due to the nature of the binary data, I hand-collected all federal cases involving the Chinese companies that responded to the 2019 survey and analyzed the data. The findings will be presented in Chapter 5, along with three detailed case studies.

APPENDIX

TABLE 4.3 Summary statistics

Variable	Mean	Standard deviation	Min.	Max.	Number of observations
State ownership	0.393	0.490	0	1	191
Cultural difference	0.304	0.461	0	1	191
Investment duration	9.239	9.114	0	36	201
Size of US investment	2.452	1.610	1	5	188
US in-house legal capacity	0.284	0.452	0	1	190
Listing status	0.484	0.501	0	1	184
Sectoral regulation	0.381	0.487	0	1	210
US litigation preference	0.155	0.363	0	1	168
HQ playing a major role in US litigation decisions	0.326	0.471	0	1	144
US lawyers playing a major role in US litigation decisions	0.799	0.402	0	1	144
US litigation experience	0.157	0.365	0	1	166

Note: Data source 2017 CGCC Survey.

TABLE 4.4 Test results (dependent variable: headquarters playing a major role in US litigation decisions)

Variable	Model 1	Model 2	Model 3	Model 4
State ownership	6.031***	4.862***	4.748***	5.363***
	(2.587)	(2.162)	(2.364)	(2.899)
Cultural challenge	1.291	1.219	1.292	1.281
	(0.581)	(0.563)	(0.602)	(0.600)
US in-house legal capacity	0.317**	0.219*	0.184***	0.192*
	(0.163)	(0.129)	(0.117)	(0.123)
Sectoral regulation	1.178	1.106	1.149	1.164
	(0.520)	(0.497)	(0.533)	(0.542)

TABLE 4.4 (cont.)

Variable	Model 1	Model 2	Model 3	Model 4
Size of US investment		1.181	1.196	1.207
		(0.170)	(0.184)	(0.187)
Investment duration			0.992	0.990
			(0.026)	(0.026)
Listing status				0.669
				(0.325)
Constant	0.224***	0.178***	0.180***	0.211***
	(0.092)	(0.088)	(0.091)	(0.109)
Pseudo R2	0.146	0.149	0.147	0.146
N	131	127	124	121

Note: Data source 2017 CGCC Survey; logit model; odds ratio reported.

TABLE 4.5 Test results (dependent variable: US lawyers playing a major role in US litigation decisions)

Variable	Model 1	Model 2	Model 3	Model 4
State ownership	0.211***	0.126***	0.119***	0.131***
	(0.110)	(0.080)	(0.079)	(0.092)
Cultural challenge	0.759	0.615	0.591	0.619
	(0.395)	(0.345)	(0.334)	(0.351)
US in-house legal capacity	0.335**	0.162***	0.1943**	0.178**
	(0.178)	(0.104)	(0.129)	(0.122)
Sectoral regulation	7.412***	7.654***	6.592**	7.042***
	(5.275)	(5.717)	(4.982)	(5.364)
Size of US investment		1.566**	1.582**	1.626**
		(0.325)	(0.338)	(0.361)
Investment duration			1.021	1.016
			(0.035)	(0.036)
Listing status				0.975
				(0.582)
Constant	9.676***	5.751***	4.790***	4.299**
	(4.955)	(3.373)	(2.928)	(2.683)
Pseudo R^2	0.171	0.210	0.202	0.206
N	131	127	124	121

Note: Data source 2017 CGCC Survey; logit model; odds ratio reported.

TABLE 4.6 Test results (dependent variable: having previously litigated in the United States)

Variable	Model 1	Model 2	Model 3	Model 4
State ownership	0.405	0.324	0.325	0.327
	(0.257)	(0.228)	(0.229)	(0.238)
Cultural challenge	3.381**	3.337**	3.362**	3.490**
	(1.896)	(1.989)	(2.031)	(2.127)
US in-house legal capacity	1.150	1.133	1.133	1.128
	(0.754)	(0.787)	(0.786)	(0.802)
Investment duration	1.069**	1.080**	1.080**	1.078**
	(0.033)	(0.037)	(0.037)	(0.037)
Size of US investment	1.680**	1.617**	1.614**	1.611**
	(0.342)	(0.343)	(0.345)	(0.346)
US litigation preference		2.149	2.175	2.384
		(1.524)	(1.581)	(1.765)
Sectoral regulation			1.049	1.057
			(0.663)	(0.673)
Listing status				0.964
				(0.614)
Constant	0.013***	0.012***	0.012***	0.0126***
	(.010)	(.010)	(.010)	(.011)
Pseudo R^2	0.220	0.236	0.236	0.237
N	145	139	139	137

Note: Data source 2017 CGCC Survey; logit model; odds ratio reported.

TABLE 4.7 Summary statistics

Variable	Mean	Standard deviation	Min.	Max.	Number of observations
State ownership (50%)	0.308	0.462	0	1	247
State ownership (10%)	0.060	0.238	0	1	247
Cultural difference	0.393	0.489	0	1	214
Investment duration	10	9.091	1	37	243
Size of US investment	2.509	1.598	1	5	212
Number of employees	719.134	4,458.701	0	45,000	246
US market importance	2.193	0.926	1	4	212
Litigation experience in 2017	0.227	0.420	0	1	220

Note: Data source 2018 CGCC Survey.

TABLE 4.8 Test results (dependent variable: having litigated in the United States in 2017)

Variable	Model 1	Model 2	Model 3	Model 4
State ownership (50%)	0.524	0.553	0.557	0.587
	(0.255)	(0.277)	(0.279)	(0.303)
State ownership (10%)			1.435	1.417
			(1.024)	(1.026)
Cultural difference	5.327***	5.433***	5.343***	5.443***
	(2.276)	(2.351)	(2.286)	(2.358)
Investment duration	1.020	1.025	1.020	1.025
	(0.024)	(0.025)	(0.024)	(0.025)
Size of US investment	1.954***	1.880***	1.939***	1.867***
	(0.274)	(0.266)	(0.272)	(0.265)
Number of employees		1.000		1.000
		(0.0001)		(0.00006)
US market importance		0.777		0.778
		(0.189)		(0.190)
Constant	0.017***	0.031***	0.016***	0.030***
	(0.010)	(0.024)	(0.010)	(0.023)
Pseudo R^2	0.237	0.240	0.238	0.241
N	190	186	190	186

Note: Data source 2018 CGCC Survey; logit model; odds ratio reported.

CHAPTER FIVE

CHINESE COMPANIES IN US FEDERAL COURTS

File a lawsuit; that's how you can resolve any dispute in the US. It's not personal.
—Experienced US litigator on advising Chinese clients

"A lawsuit [involving a Chinese party] has a million moving parts," observed an experienced US litigator.[1] Litigation is undoubtedly a complex matter, calling for more sophisticated inquiries than what can be measured by a binary variable, namely, whether or not a Chinese company had experienced US lawsuits. The dichotomy glossed over crucial aspects of Chinese companies' interactions with the US adjudicatory system. For instance, while prominent Chinese companies such as Huawei have litigated hundreds of lawsuits in the United States, most others were involved in no more than a few cases. However, the coding in Chapter 4 grouped them together in terms of US litigation experience. In fact, those that litigate infrequently may have more in common with Chinese companies that have managed to avoid US lawsuits altogether (hence no US litigation experience) than prominent repeat players such as Huawei and TikTok. To unveil important information lost from collecting and coding the data as a binary variable and to ameliorate possible biases in survey data concerning sensitive topics, this chapter explores a hand-collected objective dataset: federal lawsuits involving Chinese companies. More details of the methodology follow.

I searched on Bloomberg Law litigation database for lawsuits involving each of the Chinese companies that responded to the China

[1] Interview with a US lawyer with a China-focused litigation practice (April 17, 2020).

General Chamber of Commerce USA (CGCC) 2019 survey.[2] The search focused on cases filed in federal courts only, as state, municipal, and local courts in the United States often have inconsistent practices when it comes to publicizing court files.[3] Although federal courts maintain better records, nonpublication of court documents still occurs for various reasons,[4] such as withholding a judgment to avoid setting a precedent.[5] However, it is reasonable to assume that the nonpublication of federal court documents does not correlate with the hypotheses being tested here (e.g., the effect of state ownership and cultural difference). For each of the Chinese companies, I reviewed all the federal court documents associated with the lawsuits and gleaned data from them. In addition to the federal judicial archives and the CGCC survey data, I also used the extensive corporate information about the Chinese companies compiled by Bloomberg Law and the in-depth interviews.[6]

Before analyzing the data, this chapter presents three detailed case studies to demonstrate how Chinese companies with direct investments in the United States navigate the complex host-state legal system. These case studies (i.e., Lenovo, Huawei, and Fuyao Glass) will revisit the hypotheses of prior chapters and substantiate the findings therein. They will also contextualize the questions to be investigated and highlight the inter-company variations in the US litigation experiences of Chinese companies.

The rest of this chapter proceeds as follows. Section 5.1 presents a detailed investigation of three Chinese companies with substantial US investments. These three companies occupy different sectors and feature varied ownership structures. More importantly, their experiences

[2] Due to the escalation of the US-China trade war and the outbreak of the COVID-19 pandemic, the sample size shrank in 2020 and remained small thereafter, so I rely primarily on the 2019 survey data.

[3] Alexandra Natapoff, *Criminal Municipal Courts*, 134 Harv. L. Rev. 967 (2020).

[4] *See, e.g.*, Daniel N. Hoffman, *Nonpublication of Federal Appellate Court Opinions*, 6 Just. Sys. J. 405 (1981); Donald R. Songer, *Nonpublication in the United States District Courts: Official Criteria Versus Inferences from Appellate Review*, 50 J. Pol. 206 (1988).

[5] Hoffman, *supra* note 4, at 406.

[6] Some Chinese companies have several subsidiaries in the United States. For instance, Sany has Sany America and Putzmeister America Inc. Similarly, Huawei has four subsidiaries in the US. In the surveys, it may happen that several subsidiaries responded separately, for example, Sinopec subsidiaries in the United States. For this section, I look at the primary subsidiaries of Chinese companies. So, for Huawei, I look at Huawei Technologies USA, which has the highest number of lawsuits, and more importantly, it is the party that sued the US government.

in US federal courts differ. Analyzed together, these three cases provide a mosaic portrait of the dynamic interactions between Chinese companies and the US adjudicatory system within the dual institutional context. Next, Section 5.2 will present key summary statistics about federal lawsuits involving all the Chinese companies that responded to the CGCC survey in 2019. It will then statistically examine the significant inter-company variations in the number of the federal suits, with a focus on the major institutional factors of interest such as state ownership of Chinese investors and the cultural differences they experience in the United States. Finally, Section 5.3 will conclude the chapter by summarizing the findings and discussing their contributions.

5.1 LITIGATION OF THREE CHINESE COMPANIES IN US FEDERAL COURTS

Foreign litigants often appear in US courts, and their US litigation experiences raise important theoretical and policy questions. However, systematic research in this area remains patchy. As discussed in previous chapters, the debates have primarily revolved around xenophobia, liability of foreignness, and access to US jurisdiction by foreign parties. The existing literature reviewed in Chapter 4 overlooks Chinese companies' litigation experiences in US courts. In fact, "just what business does in the courts has long eluded systematic analysis ... business use of law has simply not been a major object of study."[7] The scarcity of reliable information likely explains the dearth of rigorous research. Businesses, especially foreign-invested ones, are typically hesitant to disclose detailed information about their US litigation,[8] leaving unanswered many crucial questions: How often does an average Chinese company litigate in United States? When appearing in US courts, are Chinese companies more likely to be defendants than plaintiffs? Why do their litigation experiences vary significantly in the United States? Do major institutional factors such as state ownership of Chinese investors make a difference? The rest of this chapter will attempt some answers.

Before analyzing the quantitative data, however, this chapter will closely examine the litigation experiences of three Chinese businesses

[7] Terence Dunworth & Joel Rogers, *Corporations in Court: Big Business Litigation in US Federal Courts, 1971–1991*, 21 Law & Soc. Inquiry 497, 517–518 (1996).

[8] *Id.* See also the discussion at the end of Chapter 4 about the low quality of data about US litigation experience of Chinese CGCC members collected from the survey and the subsequent change of the survey question.

that have invested in the United States: Lenovo, Huawei, and Fuyao Glass. As will be discussed, these three companies operate in distinct sectors, feature varying ownership structures, and had dramatically different experiences investing in the United States. Although I have interviewed knowledgeable informants affiliated with all these three companies, to preserve confidentiality, I rely on public sources to gather pertinent corporate information[9]; interviews with unaffiliated parties will be used to supplement the discussion. This section will begin with a background description of the three companies' US investments. Subsequently, details will be presented about the federal lawsuits involving the three companies, the personal backgrounds of their in-house counsel, and the outside lawyers representing them in US federal courts. A comparison will be made within the dual institutional framework.

5.1.1 US Investments of Lenovo, Huawei, and Fuyao Glass

Lenovo Group, the foremost personal computer vendor globally, predominantly operated within China before its acquisition of IBM's personal computer business in 2005.[10] This purchase, partially driven by the Chinese government's "Go Global" policy,[11] defied widespread skepticism and marked a crucial turning point in Lenovo's triumphant globalization initiatives.[12] The Chinese government, which still owns a significant minority stake of Lenovo's holding company, offered financial backing for the acquisition.[13] Following the transaction, Lenovo Group retained most of IBM's former employees and established a global headquarters in North Carolina.[14] This Chinese investor then expanded its US workforce and prioritized local recruitment, with only a minimal portion of US management being expatriated from China.[15]

[9] Note that the three companies are the US subunits, not the global conglomerates.

[10] Neil Gough & David Gelles, *Lenovo Agrees to Buy IBM Server Business for $2.3 Billion*, N.Y. Times (January 23, 2014), http://dealbook.nytimes.com/2014/01/23/lenovo-buys-ibm-server-business-for-2-3-billion/.

[11] Chuan Zhi Liu, *Lenovo: An Example of Globalization of Chinese Enterprises*, J. Int'l Bus. Stud. 573, 573 (2007).

[12] *Id.*, at 574.

[13] Ping Deng, *Why Do Chinese Firms Tend to Acquire Strategic Assets in International Expansion?* 44 J. World Bus. 74, 80 (2009).

[14] *Lenovo in the United States*, at www.lenovo.com/transactions/pdf/Lenovo-USA-Fact-Sheet.pdf.

[15] Lawrence Yu, director of Lenovo Global Marketing, presentation at Rutgers Business School, March 2016.

Capitalizing on the momentum of its US expansion, Lenovo acquired Motorola Mobility in 2014 for $2.91 billion, ascending to the position of the world's third-largest smartphone manufacturer and incorporating an additional 2,800 US employees into its workforce.[16] Moreover, Lenovo procured IBM's lower-end server business for $2.3 billion, once again retaining a significant portion of the seller's staff.[17] Lenovo's US investments markedly altered the geographic composition of its globalized enterprise, as the company reported greater revenue from the Americas in recent years than the Chinese domestic market.[18] In essence, Lenovo surmounted considerable institutional challenges and metamorphosed into a competitive China-based multinational company (MNC), or as one of its executives aptly described, a "global company with Chinese heritage."[19]

As a pioneer in Chinese direct investment in the United States, Lenovo has garnered immense public and scholarly scrutiny. Although national security concerns regarding its products have occasionally surfaced, they have consistently been resolved without impacting Lenovo's core US operations,[20] which have continued to grow despite the deterioration of US–China relations.[21]

In contrast, Huawei's foray into the US market has encountered incessant treacherous currents. Aspiring to achieve global market

16 *Lenovo Completes Acquisition of Motorola Mobility from Google*, Lenovo Newsroom (October 30, 2014), news.lenovo.com/pressroom/press-releases/lenovo-completes-full-acquisition-motorola-mobility-from-google/.

17 Gough & Gelles, *supra* note 10.

18 Annual Report of Lenovo Group Limited for Fiscal Year of 2020–21, at 220, https://doc.irasia.com/listco/hk/lenovo/annual/2021/ar2021.pdf.

19 Yu, *supra* note 15.

20 In 2014, CFIUS approved the acquisition by Lenovo of IBM's server business. Alex Barinka & David McLaughlin, *IMB Obtains US Approval for Sale of Server Business to Lenovo*, Bloomberg Technology (August 15, 2014), www.bloomberg.com/news/articles/2014-08-15/ibm-gets-u-s-approval-for-sale-of-server-business-to-lenovo. In 2005, CFIUS reviewed but raised no objections to the acquisition of the IBM PC business. Mike Musgrove, *US Panel Clears IBM Deal with Chinese Firm*, Washington Post, March 10, 2005, at 5; Eva Dou, *US Navy Looks to Replace IBM Servers for Security after Lenovo Purchase*, Wall Street J. (May 19, 2015), www.wsj.com/articles/u-s-navy-looks-to-replace-ibm-servers-for-security-after-lenovo-purchase-1432047582.

21 Ryan McMorrow & Kathrin Hille, *Lenovo's Sales Strong Despite Growing Threat of US Sanctions*, Financial Times (August 13, 2020), www.ft.com/content/a5f5f290-04c9-4776-ae8d-ee881b13bb3a.

dominance, Huawei established its US headquarters as early as 2001[22] and has since persistently endeavored to acquire well-established US businesses. However, the US government has consistently impeded its efforts.[23] For instance, in 2011, after Huawei bought some assets from the bankrupt US firm, 3Leaf, the Committee on Foreign Investment in the United States (CFIUS) investigated the acquisition and subsequently mandated divestiture, invoking national security threats.[24] The US government has also intervened to curtail Huawei's sale of telecommunication equipment.[25]

Huawei has strived to assuage the national security concerns. Like Lenovo, Huawei's US subsidiaries employed local talent to manage its US operations. Virtually all senior executives in the United States were American, recruited from its US competitors or partners.[26] The company also "enacted an all-out lobbying effort in Washington."[27] Their efforts, however, proved mostly futile. In 2012, the House Intelligence Committee issued a report recommending that the US government block Huawei from acquiring US assets and exclude its equipment from the market.[28] This marked a turning point for Huawei's US strategy. Ren Zhengfei, Huawei's founder, declared the company's withdrawal from the US market, expressing concerns that its US business could compromise US–China relations.[29] Nonetheless,

22 Cecilia Kang, *Huawei's US Competitors Among Those Pushing for Scrutiny of Chinese Tech Firm*, Washington Post (October 10, 2012), www.washingtonpost.com/business/technology/huaweis-us-competitors-among-those-pushing-for-scrutiny-of-chinese-tech-firm/2012/10/10/b84d8d16-1256-11e2-a16b-2c110031514a_story.html.

23 Steven R. Weisman, *Sale of 3Com to Huawei is Derailed by US Security Concern*, N.Y. Times (February 21, 2008), www.nytimes.com/2008/02/21/business/worldbusiness/21iht-3com.1.10258216.html.

24 Sinead Carew & Jessica Wohl, *Huawei Backs Away from 3Leaf Acquisition*, Reuters (February 19, 2011), www.reuters.com/article/us-huawei-3leaf-idUSTRE71I38920110219.

25 Joann S. Lublin & Shayndi Raice, *Security Fears Kill Chinese Bid in US*, Wall Street J. (November 5, 2010), www.wsj.com/articles/SB10001424052748704353504575596611547810220.

26 Ashlee Vance & Bruce Einhorn, *At Huawei, Matt Bross Tries to Ease US Security Fears*, Bloomberg Businessweek (September 15, 2011), www.bloomberg.com/news/articles/2011-09-15/at-huawei-matt-bross-tries-to-ease-u-dot-s-dot-security-fears.

27 *Id.*

28 David E. Sanger & Nicole Perlroth, *N.S.A. Breached Chinese Servers Seen as Security Threat*, N.Y. Times (March 22, 2014), www.nytimes.com/2014/03/23/world/asia/nsa-breached-chinese-servers-seen-as-spy-peril.html?_r=0.

29 Kathrin Hille, *Huawei "Not Interested in the US Any More,"* Financial Times (April 23, 2013), www.ft.com/content/7b212314-ac28-11e2-a063-00144feabdc0.

the Chinese MNC maintained a presence in the United States, concentrating on research and development and servicing existing clients primarily in rural areas. For years, the dispute between Huawei and its US critics revolved around allegations that the Chinese company acted as an agent of the Chinese government, rendering its equipment untrustworthy. Shortly after Ren's announcement, however, Edward Snowden disclosed that the National Security Agency (NSA) had infiltrated all major telecommunication systems and had been spying on Huawei since 2007. The revelations temporarily "leveled the playing field between Huawei and the US government and US-based competitors. It has caused a reset of the trust issues on both sides."[30] Nonetheless, the narratives shifted once more as US–China rivalry intensified. Rather than substantiating evidence of wrongdoing, the US government asserted that Huawei's products and services could potentially constitute a national security risk. The Trump administration added Huawei to the "entity list," barring its sale in the US market and any usage of US technology without government approval.[31]

Similar to Lenovo, Huawei is also a China-based MNC with a global workforce of 194,000.[32] However, due to political obstacles, Huawei's US investments never truly flourished, and the US market constitutes a negligible portion of its international business.[33] Nonetheless, Huawei has maintained several US subsidiaries conducting businesses with no national security implications.[34]

In contrast to Lenovo and Huawei, Fuyao, the world's second-largest glass manufacturer and China's largest, with a global workforce

[30] Joseph Kovar, *Huawei and US Spying: "Snowden Revelations Level Playing Field on Both Sides,"* CRN (May 2, 2014), www.crn.com/news/channel-programs/300072702/huawei-and-u-s-spying-snowden-revelations-level-playing-field-on-both-sides.htm.

[31] David Shepardson & Karen Freifeld, *China's Huawei, 70 Affiliates Placed on U.S. Trade Blacklist*, REUTERS (May 15, 2019), www.reuters.com/article/us-usa-china-huaweitech-idUSKCN1SL2W4.

[32] HUAWEI INVESTMENT & HOLDING CO., LTD. 2019 SUSTAINABILITY REPORT, p. 6, www-file.huawei.com/-/media/corp2020/pdf/sustainability/2019-sustainability-report-en-v2.pdf?la=zh.

[33] Michael Hiltzik, *Suspicions Keep Chinese Telecom Firm Huawei out of U.S. Market*, L.A. TIMES (December 5, 2014), www.latimes.com/business/hiltzik/la-fi-hiltzik-20141207-column.html.

[34] Linda Deng, *Huawei to Open New Office in Seattle, Go on Hiring Spree*, CHINA DAILY (March 4, 2016), http://usa.chinadaily.com.cn/2016-03/04/content_23740864.htm.

exceeding 27,000,[35] entered the United States relatively recently.[36] In 2014, the privately-owned Chinese company invested $230 million to refurbish a former General Motors plant in Ohio, converting it into an auto glass manufacturing facility.[37] Unlike Huawei and Lenovo, the Chinese glassmaker was never perceived as a national security threat to the United States. Nonetheless, Fuyao has faced its share of controversies. In 2019, an Academy Award-winning documentary, *American Factory*, chronicled Fuyao's entrance into the US market, highlighting the "clashing cultures and work ethics" between the US employees and the expatriated workforce, and more broadly, the attempts of Chinese companies to establish their dominance globally.[38]

Fuyao initiated its investment in the Ohio factory with great enthusiasm and optimism. Its chairman and founder, Mr. Cao, expressed his admiration for the host country and commitment to the US market. "To succeed in the United States," Mr. Cao once proclaimed to a large assembly of Chinese investors at the Waldorf Astoria in New York, "you need to love this country."[39] He spared no effort in fostering goodwill among relevant US constituencies.[40] Fuyao's US subsidiaries have predominantly employed American workers, with only 10 percent of the workforce expatriated from China.[41] Nonetheless, as depicted in the documentary, the Chinese owner encountered conflicts with various

[35] Russell Flannery, *"American Factory" Owner Fuyao Glass to Raise $550 Million, Eyes Solar Market*, FORBES (May 2, 2021), www.forbes.com/sites/russellflannery/2021/05/02/american-factory-owner-fuyao-glass-to-raise-550-mln-eyes-solar-market/?sh=2e5eba3b422b.

[36] Fuyao Global has listed its shares on both the Shanghai Stock Exchange and the Hong Kong Stock Exchange.

[37] Hassan A. Kanu & Alex Ebert, *Obama-Backed Netflix Documentary Causes Headaches for Fuyao Glass*, BLOOMBERG LAW (August 30, 2019), https://news.bloomberglaw.com/daily-labor-report/obama-backed-netflix-documentary-causes-headaches-for-fuyao-glass.

[38] David Alm, *"American Factory" Shows What Happens When One Multibillion Dollar Chinese Company Opens Shop in an Ohio Town*, FORBES (August 12, 2019), www.forbes.com/sites/davidalm/2019/08/12/american-factory-shows-what-happens-when-one-multibillion-dollar-chinese-company-opens-shop-in-an-ohio-town/?sh=3dfa6874863c.

[39] JI LI, THE CLASH OF CAPITALISMS? CHINESE COMPANIES IN THE UNITED STATES 149 (2018).

[40] Ylan Q. Mui, *A Chinese Billionaire Is Staking His Legacy – And Thousands of American Jobs – On This Factory in Ohio*, WASHINGTON POST (October 26, 2016), www.washingtonpost.com/news/wonk/wp/2016/10/26/a-chinese-billionaire-is-staking-his-legacy-and-thousands-of-american-jobs-on-this-factory-in-ohio/.

[41] *Id.*

local stakeholders. Fuyao initially appointed an American executive to manage the Ohio plant, but Cao later dismissed him for allegedly "squandering his money."[42] Aggrieved, the former executive sued Fuyao for wrongful termination.[43] Fuyao also confronted union issues, and Cao lamented that he could not manage US workers because "when we try to manage them, they threaten to get help from the union."[44] He promised to "shut down the factory if [a] union comes," which legal experts regard as a "hallmark violation" of US labor law.[45] Although employment and labor disputes persistently plagued Fuyao's US business, the company eventually turned profitable.[46] And despite the dramatic conflicts with local constituencies, Fuyao plans to further expand its US investments.[47]

5.1.2 Federal Lawsuits Involving the Three Companies

Lenovo, Huawei, and Fuyao Glass differ significantly in terms of their sectors and possess varying ownership structures and positions in the geopolitical tensions between China and the United States. As anticipated, their US litigation experiences diverge (see Figure 5.1). Lenovo encountered the most federal lawsuits from 2007 to 2020, while Fuyao had the least, despite the cultural clash portrayed in the award-winning documentary. For both Lenovo and Huawei, the number of federal lawsuits followed an upward trajectory, peaking in 2015, which roughly coincided with the phases of accelerated US investments. Both companies saw fewer cases after 2015. However, in 2020, Huawei bucked the trend by initiating a series of legal challenges against the US government. Examined longitudinally, the litigation experiences of the two Chinese companies display an inverted V shape. This pattern also aligns with Fuyao's federal litigation from 2015 to 2020. The company faced an increased number of lawsuits as it expanded its US operations and fewer cases following the peak in 2017.

42 Noam Scheiber & Keith Bradsher, *Culture Clash at a Chinese-Owned Plant in Ohio*, N.Y. Times (June 10, 2017), www.nytimes.com/2017/06/10/business/economy/ohio-factory-jobs-china.html.

43 *Id.*

44 Kanu & Ebert, *supra* at note 37.

45 *Id.*

46 Thomas Gnau, *Fuyao Glass America Profitable in 2020 Despite Pandemic*, Dayton Daily (April 26, 2021), www.daytondailynews.com/local/fuyao-glass-america-profitable-in-2020-despite-pandemic/MKCGGON2X5G2TLIUT3KU2JMD5U/.

47 George Lewis, *Fuyao Glass America in $45 Million Ohio Plant Expansion*, Glass Int'l (September 14, 2020), www.glass-international.com/news/fuyao-glass-america-in-45-million-ohio-plant-expansion.

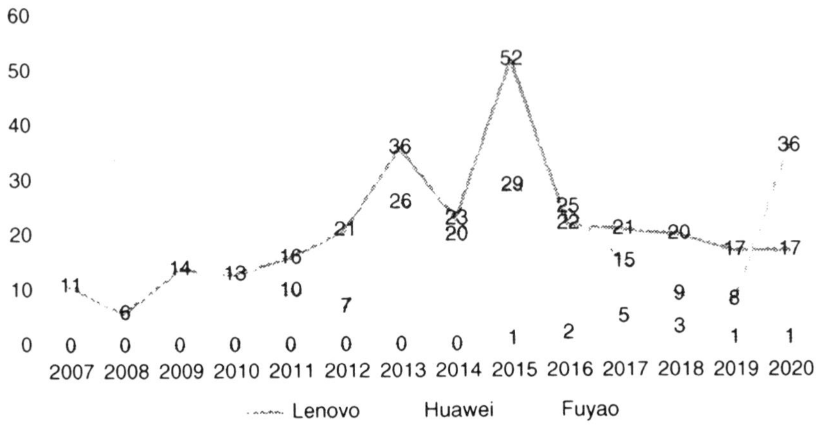

Figure 5.1 Number of federal lawsuits
Note: Data collected from Bloomberg Law. The exact names of the three companies are Lenovo United States Inc., Huawei Technologies USA Inc., and Fuyao Glass America Inc. The data comprises all the cases these entities and their subsidiaries in the United States have litigated in federal courts from 2007 to 2020.

As Chapter 4 has shown, substantial organizational changes often result in conflicts and US lawsuits. The cases of Fuyao and Lenovo are consistent with the finding, new investments by Chinese investors or major reorganizations in the US market generate frictions with US institutions and entrenched constituencies. During the transition period, lawsuits are more likely to arise as individuals affiliated with the acquiring party, influenced by strong home-state institutional factors, extensively interact with the target and other related parties embedded in the host-state institutional environment. After the adjustment period, during which the investors adopt adaptive measures such as hiring skilled professionals and implementing risk management programs, disputes occur less frequently, and those that do emerge tend to be addressed more effectively. Fuyao's experience serves as another illustrative case. After major operational challenges, the company hired a Chinese American manager capable of bridging cultural gaps and engaged professional consultants to tackle contentious unionization issues.[48] Furthermore, it learned from past lawsuits and rectified violations, thereby reducing the potential for future litigation in the United States.

[48] *Exclusive Interview: Jeff Daochuan Liu, President of Fuyao Glass America*, 81 GLASS WORLDWIDE 56 (2019), www.glassworldwide.co.uk/Articles/exclusive-interview-jeff-daochuan-liu-president-fuyao-glass-america.

5.1.3 Types of Federal Lawsuits

In addition to varying numbers of federal lawsuits, the three Chinese companies also confront diverse types of cases, as shown in Table 5.1. For Lenovo's US subsidiary, the majority of its federal lawsuits pertain to patent disputes. As one of the most competitive Chinese companies, Lenovo has invested heavily in research and development, recently ranking 82nd on the global list of patent holders.[49] Among Chinese companies, Lenovo is second only to Huawei in terms of patent holdings. Moreover, since patent law is predominantly federal, patent cases make up over 70 percent of all federal cases involving Lenovo's US subsidiary. In contrast, only around 5 percent of the federal lawsuits were related to product liability. This percentage is significantly lower than what would be expected for large US firms.[50] One possible explanation is that Lenovo's US affiliates focus more on research and development, which is not prone to generating tort claims. Contract cases account for a small percentage of Lenovo's federal lawsuits, contradicting empirical findings from previous research on US business litigation. For instance, an earlier empirical study found more than 20 percent of federal cases litigated by large US corporations revolve around contractual disputes.[51] This discrepancy may be partially attributed to Chinese companies' inclination to include arbitration clauses in their business contracts,[52] which steers most of their contractual disputes away from US courts. It is worth noting that Lenovo had few federal lawsuits concerning labor and employment issues. This might be due to the nature of its US operations, which mainly consist of management, research, and sales, with mass production kept in low-labor cost countries.[53]

Similar to Lenovo, the vast majority of Huawei's federal lawsuits involve patent claims. As mentioned above, Huawei holds the most patents among Chinese firms. In the United States, litigation plays a

[49] *IFI 250: Largest Global Patent Holders*, IFI Claims Patent Services, at www.ificlaims.com/rankings-global-assets-2020.htm.

[50] Dunworth & Rogers, *supra* note 7, at 526.

[51] *Id.*

[52] Ji Li & Carrie Menkel-Meadow, *Dispute Process Choices Among Chinese Companies in the United States: Some Preliminary Data and Analysis*, 27 HARV. NEGOT. L. REV. 295, 312 (2022). Also, contracts are generally governed by state law and adjudicated in state courts, and only a portion of those are handled by federal courts exercising diversity jurisdiction.

[53] More details about Lenovo's global operations can be found on the company's official website, at www.lenovo.com/us/en/about/locations.

TABLE 5.1 Major types of federal lawsuits

Lenovo		Huawei		Fuyao	
Case type	Percentage	Case type	Percentage	Case type	Percentage
Patent	71.0	Patent	93.0	Employment	23.1
Unknown	9.1	General contract	2.7	Labor	23.1
Other statutes	7.4	Unknown	2.1	Unknown	15.4
Product liability	4.8	Other statutes	1.1	Other civil rights	7.7
General contract	1.7	Enforcement of judgment	0.5	Marine	7.7
Antitrust	1.7	Labor	0.5	Antitrust	7.7
Fraud	1.7			Arbitration	7.7
Others	2.7			Others	7.7

Note: Data source is Bloomberg Law database. The percentages were calculated on June 21, 2021. By that date, the target US affiliates of Lenovo, Huawei, and Fuyao had been involved in 297, 187, and 13 federal cases respectively.

central role in the competition among high-tech companies.[54] As a leader in the design and production of telecommunication equipment and 5G technology, Huawei frequently resorts to US federal courts to defend its interests. Again, due to the prevalence of arbitration provisions in the business contracts of Chinese companies, only a small percentage of Huawei's federal cases are contractual in nature.[55] As will be detailed in Chapter 6, Huawei also sued the federal government for its alleged wrongful actions.

In contrast to Huawei and Lenovo, Fuyao's US investment focuses on mass manufacturing, which inevitably leads to labor and employment disputes that occasionally reach federal courts. Meanwhile, the manufacturing of auto glass, a relatively mature industry, does not require or continuously generate cutting-edge technology. As a result, the majority of legal cases involving Fuyao relate to federal employment and labor law claims, such as employment discrimination, rather than patent infringements. Fuyao has been implicated in few contract cases, as the US auto industry relies on relational contracts that prevent disputants from going to court.[56] Additionally, the company is likely to have contractual provisions for arbitration.[57] Despite Fuyao's prominence and the "cultural clashes" it has experienced, the company has successfully averted a substantial volume of lawsuits, at least at the federal level. The investor's willingness to adapt to the host-state environment has certainly helped to mitigate potential frictions, thus reducing the probability of disputes arising in the first place. This inclination to adapt is also evident in the company's internal management of legal risks. As will be elaborated upon shortly, the first employee Fuyao hired for the investment in Ohio was its in-house legal counsel.

5.1.4 In-House Counsel of the Three Companies

Recall the empirical findings in Chapter 2, which indicate that Chinese companies with substantial investments in the United States are more likely to employ full-time professionals to manage their US legal matters. Moreover, business internationalization is positively

[54] Colleen V. Chien, *Of Trolls, Davids, Goliaths, and Kings: Narratives and Evidence in the Litigation of High-Tech Patents*, 87 N.C. L. Rev. 1571, 1603 (2008).

[55] Li & Menkel-Meadow, *supra* note 52.

[56] Susan Helper & Rebecca Henderson, *Management Practices, Relational Contracts, and the Decline of General Motors*, 28 J. Econ. Persp. 49 (2014).

[57] Li & Menkel-Meadow, *supra* note 52.

correlated with the likelihood of developing US internal legal capacity. Therefore, it is not surprising that all the three Chinese companies, given their expansive US presence and globalized operations, have cultivated internal legal capacity within the United States.

The general counsel for Lenovo's North American business joined Lenovo as senior counsel in 2005 after serving as the assistant general counsel of the Federal Communications Commission for six years.[58] This self-branded "global company with Chinese heritage" also appointed a US lawyer as its vice president and general counsel, responsible for the Chinese MNC's global legal and compliance functions. This global general counsel, who joined Lenovo in 2012 after twelve years at eBay, oversees approximately eighty in-house legal professionals across fifteen countries.[59] Having a US lawyer as a top executive for Lenovo's global operations undoubtedly facilitates the company's adaptation to the US institutional environment.

The head in-house counsel for Huawei Technologies USA also has extensive government work experience. After working as senior trial attorney at the Office of the General Counsel of the Federal Labor Relations Authority for three years, he held the position of labor relations specialist at the Federal Aviation Administration for six years. He then spent five months in private practice before joining Huawei Device USA, another US affiliate of Huawei, as its general counsel. He stayed in this role for over eight years before being promoted to chief counsel of Huawei Technologies USA.[60] In contrast, the general counsel for Huawei's global operations does not have US legal credentials. Although Huawei has expansive overseas business, its global general counsel at the Chinese headquarters was trained as an engineer and subsequently became a self-taught Chinese lawyer specializing in Chinese intellectual property (IP) law. Despite his lack of US legal training, this Chinese IP lawyer has actively participated in developing and implementing Huawei's US legal strategies.[61] While such intensive headquarters intervention by non-US lawyers may not be the sole cause of Huawei's impediments, it likely played a role.

[58] Self-reported education background on LinkedIn profile.
[59] Executive biography published on Lenovo's official website.
[60] Biographical information on LinkedIn profile.
[61] Dan Strumpf, *Huawei Founder Ren Zhengfei Takes Off the Gloves in Fight against U.S.*, WALL STREET J. (June 6, 2020), www.wsj.com/articles/huawei-founder-ren-zhengfei-takes-off-the-gloves-in-fight-against-u-s-11591416028.

As briefly mentioned above, the first employee of Fuyao Glass America was its Director of Legal Affairs and Government Relations. Chairman Cao selected the deputy chief of the Office of Strategic Business Investments of Ohio Development Services Agency, who also had some prior experience working for the federal government and the Ohio Attorney General's Office. However, this non-practicing lawyer remained at Fuyao for only two years. Succeeding her was a Chinese American lawyer who had led the China practice of a medium-sized US law firm.[62] She left China as an adult, pursued graduate legal education in the United States, and then worked at the US law firm for over fifteen years before joining Fuyao Glass America.[63] Though Chairman Cao seems to recognize the importance of in-house legal capacity for conducting business in the United States, in China he has excluded in-house lawyers from the senior executive team of Fuyao Group.[64] In other words, lawyers do not participate in making the most important corporate decisions at the Chinese parent company. Thus, overcoming the vast institutional gaps between confronting Fuyao's headquarters and its US subsidiary necessitates US legal counsel with bicultural background who can function as an effective bridge.

5.1.5 US Law Firms and Lawyers Representing the Three Companies

As discussed in Chapter 3, Chinese companies rely heavily on the assistance of external law firms and lawyers to traverse the intricate US legal landscape. The outsourcing of the legal services, however, varies considerably, as shown in Table 5.2. Lenovo, for example, has engaged five US law firms to handle about 50 percent of its litigation work in federal courts. In contrast, Huawei has distributed its federal litigation work rather evenly across various law firms. Fish Richardson, Huawei's primary legal service provider, was responsible for a mere 7.4 percent of its total litigation work, whereas Akin Gump, Lenovo's foremost go-to law firm, handled 15.6 percent of the client's litigation work. The allocation strategy employed by Huawei suggests an intention to stimulate competition among law firms, which helps

62 Biographical information on LinkedIn profile, at www.linkedin.com/in/athena-hou-73986b20/.

63 *Id.*

64 For details of the biographies of the executive team, see www.fuyaogroup.com/team.html.

TABLE 5.2 Major law firms for the three Chinese companies

Lenovo		Huawei		Fuyao	
Law firm	Percentage	Law firm	Percentage	Law firm	Percentage
Akin Gump	15.6	Fish Richardson	7.4	Littler Mendelson	30
Vinson Elkins	8.8	Sidley Austin	6.8	Thompson Hine	20
Potter Anderson	7.4	Gillam Smith	6.3	Bricker Eckler	10
Findlay Craft	7.1	Locke Lord	6.3	Fisher Phillips	10
Sheppard Mullin	6.2	Lee Tran Liang	5.7	Freeborn Peters	10
K&L Gates	5.4	McGuireWoods	5.7	Sheppard Mullin	10
Morris Nichols	4.0	Leydig Voit	4.5	Taft Stettinius	10
Kilpatrick Townsend	2.8	Munck Wilson	3.4		
Womble Bond	2.3	Potter Minton	3.4		
Others	40.5	Others	50.6		

Note: Data source is Bloomberg Law database. Percentages were calculated on August 31, 2020.

to reduce short-term service costs.[65] As discussed in Chapter 3, the procurement of legal services in China often hinges on stringent cost management.[66] The US subsidiary's adoption of this approach likely reflects greater hierarchical oversight exerted by the headquarters. In comparison, Fuyao has not litigated many federal lawsuits. The law firm it has relied on the most is Littler, renowned for its expertise in labor and employment law.

Since corporate clients tend to place their trust in competent lawyers rather than entire law firms,[67] it is necessary also to investigate the identities of the legal advocates representing these three Chinese companies in US courts.[68] The ten lawyers enlisted most frequently by each of the three corporations, determined by their frequency of court appearance, are discussed in the remainder of this subsection. As shown in Table 5.3, Lenovo relies heavily on a select few lawyers for court appearances, which aligns with its preference for partnering with a panel of US law firms. Key attributes of the top ten lawyers enlisted by Lenovo, largely corroborate the findings presented in Chapter 3 regarding Chinese companies' lawyer selection preferences. First, Lenovo values the practice experience of US lawyers, as evidenced by its engagement of partners or senior counsels who specialize in IP litigation (see Table 5.3). Given that the majority of the cases pertain to patent claims, possessing a background in the US government is deemed less relevant. Additionally, since both Lenovo Group and its US subsidiary employ experienced US lawyers as general counsel, there is no apparent need for external litigators with Chinese backgrounds. Chapter 3 also found that Chinese companies do not appear to emphasize credentials when selecting US lawyers. Echoing that finding, none of the top three lawyers engaged most frequently by Lenovo graduated from a prestigious national law school,[69] and only two out of the ten boasted federal clerkship experience.

[65] David B. Wilkins, *Team of Rivals-Toward a New Model of the Corporate Attorney-Client Relationship*, 78 FORDHAM L. REV. 2082 (2009).

[66] See Chapter 3 for more discussion about the centrality of cost control in the purchase of legal services in China.

[67] John C. Coates, et al., *Hiring Teams, Firms, and Lawyers: Evidence of the Evolving Relationships in the Corporate Legal Market*, 36 LAW & SOC. INQUIRY 999 (2011).

[68] The lawyer information for these case studies was collected from their LinkedIn profile pages or their law firms' websites.

[69] In this category are law schools that are repeatedly ranked in the top fourteen of ABA accredited US law schools by U.S. News & World Report.

TABLE 5.3 Profiles of litigators for Lenovo

Attorney name	Appearances[a] (%)	Law firm	Status	Law school	Graduation year	Government background	Chinese background	Practice area	Main office location	Federal clerkship
Fred I. Williams	10.8	Williams Simons & Landis pllc	Founding partner	Brigham Young University	1995	No	No	IP litigation	Texas	No
Eric J. Klein	9.1	Vinson & Elkins llp	Partner	Texas Tech University	2003	No	No	IP litigation	Texas	No
David E. Moore	3.5	Potter Anderson Corroon llp	Partner	Temple University	1999	No	No	IP litigation	Delaware	No
Richard L. Horwitz	2.5	Potter Anderson Corroon llp	Of Counsel	Duke University	1982	No	No	IP litigation	Delaware	No
Todd E. Landis	2.2	Williams Simons & Landis pllc	Founding partner	Franklin Pierce Law Center	1997	No	No	IP litigation	Texas	No
Daniel J. Stephenson	2.0	K&L Gates	Senior Of Counsel	University of Michigan	1982	No	No	IP litigation	North Carolina	No
Jack B. Blumenfeld	1.8	Morris Nichols Arsht & Tunnell	Partner	Yale University	1977	No	No	IP litigation	Delaware	Yes
Kellie M. Johnson	1.8	Akin Gump	Associate	SMU Dedman School of Law	2009	No	No	IP litigation	Texas	No
Stephanie E. O'Byrne	1.3	Potter Anderson Corroon llp	Counsel	Rutgers-Camden	2003	No	No	IP litigation	Delaware	Yes
Ashley Edison Brown	1.2	Akin Gump	Associate	University of Texas	2011	No	No	IP litigation	Texas	No

Note: [a] Percentage of a total of 595 appearances as of August 31, 2020.
Source: Bloomberg Law database and the lawyers' online profile pages.

Huawei's distribution of litigation work to US lawyers conforms to a pattern akin to its law firm engagements, with no litigators distinctly dominating in terms of their share of federal court representations on the company's behalf. Again, this strategy signifies a cost-oriented approach that stimulates intense competition among legal service providers,[70] which can be ascribed to the centralized management of US legal matters by the company's headquarters in China. A former executive at Huawei's US subsidiary has remarked that the ingrained corporate culture in addressing US issues is the "HQ knew better."[71] The heightened competition bolsters Huawei's bargaining power, culminating in US lawyers exhibiting "deference to the point of hesitancy. Recommendations were made almost nervously, and at times backed away from all-too-quickly, depending on how they were received."[72] The lawyers' profiles also affirm the selection preferences identified in Chapter 3. All the litigators possessed over a decade of practice experience. The vast majority had neither government work experience nor a Chinese background. Notably, none of the three most relied-upon lawyers graduated from a top national law school, and none of the ten on the list ever clerked for a federal judge (Table 5.4).

In comparison with Lenovo and Huawei, Fuyao litigates much less frequently in US federal courts, making it difficult to extrapolate comprehensive inferences from the limited lawyer profiles available. Given that Fuyao has predominantly faced lawsuits for violating US labor and employment law, most of its outside counsel specialize in these two practice areas. Analogous to Lenovo and Huawei, Fuyao seems to prioritize practice experience over US lawyers' government work experience or Chinese background; however, as noted earlier, the company did take these factors into account when hiring its inaugural US in-house counsel. Most of Fuyao's lawyers had extensive practice experience. Three of the lawyers graduated from prestigious national law schools, and two of them clerked for federal judges. The majority of these lawyers practice in Ohio, the state where Fuyao's factory is located (Table 5.5).

In summary, Section 5.1 presented an in-depth examination of the interactions between three prominent Chinese companies and the US adjudicatory system at the federal level. This analysis has underscored

[70] Wilkins, *supra* note 65, at 2082.
[71] William B. Plummer, Huidu – Inside Huawei 123 (2018).
[72] *Id.*, at 15.

TABLE 5.4 Profiles of litigators for Huawei

Attorney name	*Appearances*[a] (%)	*Law firm*	*Status*	*Law school*	*Graduation year*	*Government background*	*Chinese background*	*Practice area*	*Main office location*	*Federal clerkship*
Shaun W. Hassett	3.1	McGuireWoods	Counsel	University of Dayton	2009	No	No	IP litigation	Texas	No
Jason W. Cook	3.1	McGuireWoods	Partner	University of Texas	2000	No	No	IP litigation	Texas	No
Tyler T. VanHoutan	2.8	McGuireWoods	Partner	University of Missouri-Kansas City	2001	No	No	IP litigation	Texas	No
Thomas H. Reger	2.8	Fish Richardson	Principal	SMU Dedman School of Law	2001	Yes	No	IP litigation	Texas	No
David M. Airan	2.4	Leydig Voit	Shareholder	Northwestern	1993	No	No	IP litigation	Chicago, IL	No
John P. Wisse	2.4	Sidley & Austin	Associate	University of Houston	2007	No	No	IP litigation	Texas	No
H. Michael Hartmann	2.1	Leydig Voit	Shareholder	Depaul	1976	No	No	IP litigation	Chicago, IL	No
Leonard Z. Hua	2.1	Leydig Voit	Shareholder	NYU	2010	No	Yes	IP litigation	Chicago, IL	No
Jeffrey M. Olson	2.1	SOA	Partner	University of Michigan	1981	No	No	IP litigation	California	No
Tung T. Nguyen	2.1	Sidley	Counsel	SMU Dedman School of Law	1998	No	No	IP litigation	Texas	No

Note: [a] Percentage of a total of 290 appearances as of August 31, 2020.
Source: Bloomberg legal database and other sources such as lawyers' online profile pages.

TABLE 5.5 Profiles of litigators for Fuyao

Attorney name	Appearances[a] (%)	*Law firm*	*Status*	*Law school*	*Graduation year*	*Government background*	*Chinese background*	Practice area	Main office location	Federal clerkship
Michael T. Short	15.8	Littler	Shareholder	Ohio State	1998	No	No	Labor and employment	Ohio	No
Timothy S. Anderson	5.3	Littler	Shareholder	University of Michigan	1999	No	No	Labor and employment	Ohio	No
Thomas F. Bush	5.3	Freeborn	Partner	University of Chicago	1979	No	No	Complex litigation	Chicago, IL	Yes
Sarah C. Leyshock	5.3	Taft Stettinius	Partner	Northern Kentucky University	2006	No	No	Labor and employment	Ohio	No
Kofi A. Semenya	5.3	Bricker Eckler	Associate	Vanderbilt	2014	No	No	Labor and employment	Ohio	No
Evan T. Priestle	5.3	Taft Stettinius	Associate	Northern Kentucky University	2012	No	No	Labor and employment	Ohio	No
Rena Andoh	5.3	Sheppard Mullin	Partner	NYU	2003	No	No	Complex litigation	New York	No
Curtis G. Moore	5.3	Fisher Phillips	Associate	University of Dayton	2013	No	No	Labor and employment	Ohio	No
George B. Musekamp	5.3	Thompson Hine	Partner	University of Cincinnati	2010	No	No	Labor and employment	Ohio	Yes
Megan S. Glowacki	5.3	Thompson Hine	Partner	University of Cincinnati	2010	Yes	No	Labor and employment	Ohio	No

Note: [a] Percentage of a total of 19 appearances as of August 31, 2020.
Source: Bloomberg Law database and lawyers' online profile pages.

significant inter-company variations and suggested stylized litigation patterns. However, to what degree do Huawei and Lenovo exemplify the majority of Chinese companies operating in the United States? Or, does Fuyao Glass serve as a more accurate benchmark for analyzing US litigation involving Chinese companies? What institutional and firm-specific variables might be associated with the observed inter-company variations? The subsequent section seeks to offer preliminary insights by analyzing the hand-collected dataset of federal lawsuits.

5.2 FEDERAL LAWSUITS INVOLVING CHINESE COMPANIES

As previously mentioned, I collected data on all federal lawsuits involving the 209 Chinese companies that responded to the 2019 CGCC membership survey.[73] For the purposes of this study, federal lawsuits encompass cases filed at federal district courts, appeal courts, and the Supreme Court, as well as federal special courts. I collected three key data points: (1) the total number of federal suits involving the Chinese companies since their entry into the US market, (2) the number of cases in which the Chinese companies served as plaintiffs, and (3) the number of cases where the companies acted as defendants.[74]

As illustrated in Figure 5.2, the majority of Chinese companies have not been involved in any litigation in federal courts, which corroborates the finding of the preceding chapter based on the binary data from the 2017 CGCC survey.[75] To a certain degree, this distribution aligns with the litigation experiences of US companies in federal courts, which also display significant inter-company variations, with the majority litigating infrequently.[76]

In the majority of the federal suits, the Chinese companies litigated as defendants, which may be attributable to several factors. First, corporations frequently face claims such as consumer rights violations

[73] The limit to federal cases is due to lack of data from state courts, though state courts adjudicate many more lawsuits than federal courts.

[74] Multiple parties are often involved in a lawsuit.

[75] Note that some disparities between the archival data from Bloomberg Law and the survey data analyzed in the prior chapter are probably attributable to misreporting or litigation by Chinese MNCs in state or local courts, a topic awaiting future research.

[76] Dunworth & Rogers, *supra* note 7.

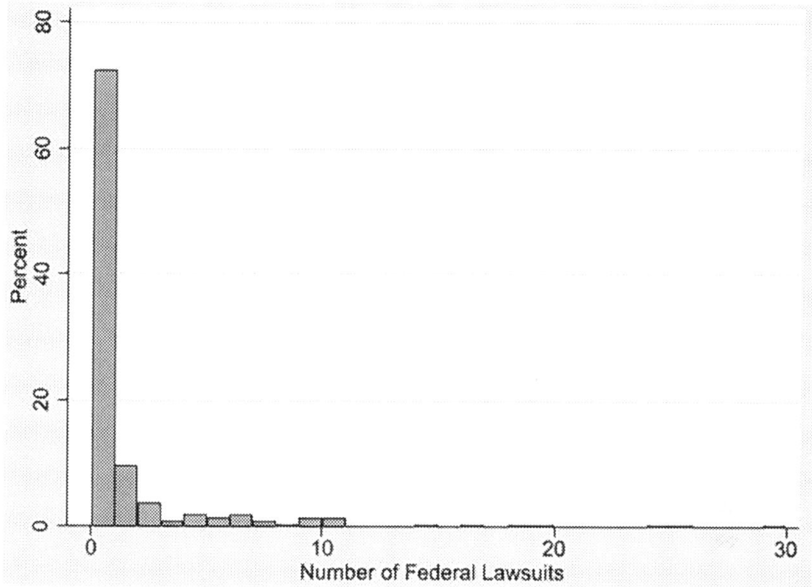

Figure 5.2 Distribution of Chinese companies by number of federal lawsuits
Source: Bloomberg legal database.

and employment discrimination that typically position corporations as defendants. Second, as highlighted in the preceding chapter, Chinese companies demonstrate a strong aversion to litigation in the United States due to high litigation costs, reputational concerns, and limited knowledge of the US legal system. This reluctance to sue naturally turns Chinese companies away from filing legal claims to resolve disputes. Nevertheless, the preference for alternative dispute resolution does not preclude other US parties from initiating lawsuits against Chinese companies. In fact, it may fuel opponents' legal aggression, as they could misinterpret the Chinese party's litigation aversion as indicating legal vulnerability or intentionally exploit this aversion.

5.2.1 Variations in Federal Litigation Experiences

Chinese companies demonstrate considerable disparities in their litigation experiences within US federal courts. While the majority have not faced any federal lawsuits, others have been involved in numerous legal proceedings, ranging from dozens to even hundreds of cases. What factors might account for these divergent experiences? The preceding chapter evaluated a range of potential variables, and this section will reexamine these factors using the federal lawsuit data about the Chinese companies that responded to the 2019 CGCC survey. As noted earlier, each of the annual surveys included a combination of recurring and novel questions, so the 2019 data allow the examination of several variables unavailable in the 2017 and 2018 data. Once again, the analysis begins with an exploration of the ownership type of Chinese investors.

State ownership. In the preceding chapter, the influence of ownership structure on the US litigation experience was examined as a binary variable (i.e., whether or not a company has previously engaged in US litigation), without differentiating between cases where Chinese companies acted as plaintiffs and those as defendants. The federal litigation data presented herein contains this crucial information, thereby permitting a more refined analysis.

To reiterate, the effect of ownership type on US litigation experience remains uncertain. State-owned Chinese enterprises tend to centralize the management of their US operations, and this heightened hierarchical control by headquarters, due to high transaction costs and information asymmetry, may give rise to more disputes and impede their effective resolution, culminating in a greater number of US lawsuits. Also, as litigation is relatively transparent and easy to monitor, risk-averse local managers may opt for costly litigation to avoid suspicions from headquarters concerning settlement terms or implied admission of wrongdoing.[77] However, an alternative hypothesis could also be construed. Because of increased scrutiny from the home-state government, local managers at state-owned Chinese companies may perceive US litigation as detrimental to their careers, thereby striving to avert such legal proceedings. Moreover, the centralized control within state-owned Chinese companies may facilitate the transmission of home-state institutional influence to the US subsidiaries' litigation decisions, resulting in a marked reluctance to escalate disputes.

To assess these competing arguments, I put forth two working hypotheses positing that, all else being equal, state-owned Chinese companies engage in (1) fewer federal lawsuits as plaintiffs, and (2) fewer federal cases as defendants in comparison with privately-owned Chinese counterparts. The 2019 survey data enables the creation of two dummy variables that capture the ownership characteristics of Chinese companies,

[77] Interview with a partner at a Chinese international law firm (September 22, 2022).

with one representing majority or complete state ownership and the other denoting significant minority state ownership.[78]

Cultural difference. The preceding chapter unveiled a significant positive correlation between cultural challenges and the likelihood of a Chinese company litigating in the United States. More specifically, Chinese companies that are more rooted in their home-state normative environment, and as a result face substantial cultural barriers in the United States, exhibit a greater propensity to litigate in the host-state courts. Building on this empirical finding, I propose that a positive association exists between a Chinese company's cultural challenges in the United States and its frequency of litigation in US federal courts, in the roles of both plaintiffs and defendants.

Business expansion and reorganization. The case studies of Lenovo, Huawei, and Fuyao have demonstrated that when foreign-invested businesses undergo rapid expansion in the US market, disputes and lawsuits often ensue. This observation is corroborated by the reverse V-shaped pattern of the number of federal cases over time, as depicted in Figure 5.1. Thus, it is plausible that business expansion and reorganization foster increased friction between the home- and host-state institutions, leading to a greater number of lawsuits for Chinese companies undertaking such activities in the United States. Based on this reasoning, I hypothesize that positive associations exist between US expansion and the number of cases Chinese companies have litigated in federal courts, in the capacities of both plaintiffs and defendants.[79]

Sectoral regulation. Federal courts have limited subject matter jurisdiction and generally adjudicate cases arising out of federal law or with conditional diversity.[80] Presumably, all else being equal, the more heavily regulated a sector is by federal rules, the higher the likelihood

[78] As noted in previous chapters, the first dummy equals one if a Chinese government body owns more than 50 percent of a Chinese MNCs that has made direct investment in the United States. The second dummy equals one if the state ownership is between 50 percent and 10 percent. When the two dummies both equal zero, we have the baseline situation where a Chinese MNC reports insignificant or no state ownership.

[79] To test this hypothetical effect, I created a dummy variable that equals one if a Chinese MNC engaged in a merger or acquisition in the United States in the two years prior to the 2019 survey.

[80] Additional conditions are generally covered under the federal justiciability doctrine. F. Andrew Hessick, *Cases, Controversies, and Diversity*, 109 Nw. U. L. Rev. 59 (2014).

that a party could identify a cause of action against a Chinese company operating in that sector. The 2019 survey offers a breakdown of the responding firms' sectors, which allows for the use of an index measuring the degree of federal regulation in each sector.[81] Moreover, as previously discussed, pervasive host-state regulation exerts greater coercive isomorphic pressure on foreign-invested businesses, compelling conformation to local customs and practices. This hypothesis may yield divergent empirical implications. On the one hand, adaptation may mitigate conflicts with local constituencies, consequently reducing litigation. Conversely, Chinese companies that adapt in this manner may resolve disputes like their local counterparts, exhibiting less reluctance to litigate. The tests below will illuminate the validity of these conflicting suppositions.

In-house legal capacity. As elaborated in Chapter 2, Chinese companies operating in the United States vary in their internal legal capacity building. The question arises as to whether this capacity impacts their experience with US litigation. To pick up where I left off in Chapter 4, I explore two possible effects. Firstly, a Chinese company facing a steady stream of US lawsuits may be incentivized to develop in-house legal capacity to manage outside lawyers and implement concrete measures to prevent or mitigate legal risks. In this scenario, the function of in-house counsel is primarily defensive, which should lead to a positive correlation between its presence and the number of federal lawsuits involving Chinese companies as defendants. Conversely, in-house legal professionals may also enhance their employers' capacity to actively engage in litigation, resulting in the Chinese companies filing more cases as plaintiffs. In this scenario, we would expect to see a positive association between in-house legal

[81] As noted in Chapter 3, the regulation intensity index was compiled by McLaughlin and colleagues. Each of the survey respondents is assigned to an industry designated by a two-digit North American Industry Classification System (NAICS) code, which corresponds to a regulatory intensity index number. All the respondents report their industries. I checked all their official websites or, when such websites were not available, third-party reports, to ascertain their industries. For those operating in multiple industries, I use the one most heavily regulated. As typical with this type of proxy measures, the index is not perfect. For instance, real estate is a relatively heavily regulated industry, but because it is normally regulated at the state and local level, the industry appears to be subject to light federal regulation. For more details, see Patrick A. McLaughlin and Oliver Sherouse, RegData US 3.1 Annual (dataset). QuantGov, Mercatus Center at George Mason University, Arlington, VA, 2018. https://quantgov.org/regdata-us/.

capacity and the number of federal cases in which Chinese companies have participated as plaintiffs.

US market importance. As established in Chapter 2, Chinese companies that consider the US market important tend to assign expatriate US legal managers. The implications of this staffing arrangement on their US litigation experience, however, remain theoretically ambiguous. On the one hand, an emphasis on the US market may result in tight, suboptimal hierarchical control over US dispute resolution and litigation, which could spawn more federal lawsuits. On the other hand, tight top-down control exerted by Chinese headquarters might convey the home-state normative aversion to litigation to the US subsidiaries, thereby reducing the number of lawsuits. Additionally, Chinese companies that place significant importance on the US market may implement preventive and remedial measures to mitigate litigation risk, which would also contribute to a decrease in the number of lawsuits.

Listing status. As discussed in earlier chapters, publicly traded Chinese companies may be more concerned with the market implications of US lawsuits, potentially incentivizing them to pursue settlements. At the same time, due to their visibility, these listed companies are easy litigation targets. Moreover, as previously highlighted, a company's listing status can function as a proxy for the size of a Chinese MNC, rather than merely the size of its US operations. The resources available on a global scale may enable the US subsidiary to engage in litigation. Additionally, US securities law broadens federal jurisdiction to encompass a wide array of securities-related cases, so Chinese companies subject to this regulatory framework may be involved in more federal lawsuits, especially as defendants.[82]

Duration of US investment. Litigation constitutes an integral part of the US business landscape, and typically, the duration of a Chinese company's operations in the United States correlates with an increased likelihood of involvement in federal court cases. The test results of the previous chapter have affirmed this relationship, and the present chapter revisits this association by testing the federal lawsuit data.

Size of US investment. Large US businesses generally experience more disputes, which can consequently result in more federal lawsuits. They are also better equipped to engage in costly litigation. Moreover,

[82] In some of the tests I use listing on a US stock exchange as an alternative measure to assess any possible effect originating from the allegedly more heightened scrutiny and enforcement pressure from the US regulatory agency.

companies with extensive, high-profile US operations may attract lawsuits. The empirical findings of the preceding chapter have corroborated the positive correlation between the magnitude of Chinese companies' investments in the United States and their litigation experience. Thus, I incorporate this variable into the analysis.[83]

5.2.2 Chinese Companies as Plaintiffs

I bifurcated the federal lawsuit data by the Chinese company's role, as either plaintiff or defendant, and conducted two sets of negative binomial tests. This subsection analyzes the test results for Chinese companies as plaintiffs. First, Chinese companies that have recently expanded through mergers or acquisitions tend to file more cases in federal courts. Prior research has documented that substantial institutional differences obstruct the realization of potential synergies,[84] which could extend to post-merger dispute resolution for Chinese companies. Influenced by their home-state institutions, Chinese managers may underestimate or neglect the challenges and risks associated with acquiring and managing US firms, resulting in frictions that end up in federal courts. Even if, as exemplified by the Lenovo case, a merger or acquisition is well executed and synergies are realized, a Chinese-invested business undergoing expansion is still more susceptible to disputes and lawsuits than those maintaining static US operations.

Second, the perceived importance of the US market appears to be consequential. Holding all the other variables constant, Chinese investors who prioritize the US market are associated with filing fewer lawsuits in federal courts. This finding supports the hypothesis that Chinese investors that emphasize the US market implement preventive or mitigating measures either to reduce conflicts or to keep them out of federal courts. Alternatively, increased hierarchical control due to the perceived market importance may channel the home-state

[83] As in previous chapters, I measure the size of US operations by the revenue scale reported in the 2019 survey. An alternative measure I use is the number of local employees. The case study of Fuyao indicates that employment and labor cases abound at Chinese multinationals in the United States due to alleged regulatory and "cultural" clashes. Since all the Chinese-invested businesses in the United States are subject to federal employment and labor law, I included this alternative variable in some robustness tests of possible association with the varying numbers of federal lawsuits involving Chinese companies.

[84] Bülent Aybar & Aysun Ficici, *Cross-Border Acquisitions and Firm Value: An Analysis of Emerging-Market Multinationals*, 40 J. INT'L BUS. STUD. 1321 (2009).

normative litigation aversion to the US subunits, resulting in a reluctance to initiate legal action.

Third, as expected, investment duration is significant and positively correlated with the number of federal cases filed by Chinese companies. Intuitively, with all the other variables held constant, the longer a Chinese investor has conducted business in the US market, the more federal lawsuits it has filed. The outcome corroborates the test result from the preceding chapter.

Fourth, the size of US investment is also significant and positively associated with the number of lawsuits initiated by Chinese companies in federal courts. All else being equal, Chinese companies with larger US operations tend to experience more disputes, have more interests at stake in these disputes that justify litigation costs, and possess more resources to litigate in US courts. This positive association further confirms the empirical finding from the preceding chapter.

5.2.3 Chinese Companies as Defendants

When Chinese companies appear in US federal courts, they typically assume the role of defendants rather than plaintiffs. As such, the varying frequency with which they are sued holds greater practical and theoretical importance. The statistical tests (see Table 5.7 in the Appendix to this chapter) have revealed several interesting correlations.

First, state ownership of Chinese investors is positively associated with the number of federal cases they defend. As previously discussed, hierarchical control in state-owned companies and their acute agency problem hinder efficient dispute resolution. Local managers, who heavily discount corporate legal expenses, may prefer litigation to avoid the appearance of admitting wrongdoing or negligence (see more discussion in Chapter 4). Additionally, the extensive control exerted by headquarters at state-owned Chinese companies increases the transaction cost of dispute resolution, leading to escalation. As noted earlier, several interviewees have complained about the complex reporting and approval procedures at state-owned Chinese firms for matters concerning US litigation. One lawyer summarized it nicely, "SOEs make decisions very slowly and after multiple layers of approval; often the person dealing with you has no decision-making power… Every SOE employee wants to avoid taking responsibility for any mistakes."[85]

[85] Interview with a partner of a US law firm (August 18, 2021).

Second, cultural difference is positively associated with the likelihood of being sued in US federal courts.[86] In other words, all else being equal, Chinese companies struggling with the US culture are more likely to be legally challenged in US courts. As previously discussed, managers of Chinese companies more embedded in home-state normative institutions and poorly versed in the US culture are prone to miscommunication and misunderstanding, which give rise to conflicts and legal actions. For example, an in-house lawyer of a Chinese-invested firm recalled her dismay when her colleagues asked a female job candidate about her childbearing plans, an inquiry routinely made during the recruitment process in China.[87] These cultural differences also hamper pre-filing dispute resolution. As noted, in some cases, Chinese managers' behavior may even galvanize legal aggression. An eagerness to settle, for instance, might well be interpreted in the US cultural context as evidence of weakness in the Chinese party's legal position, boosting the US party's "optimism" about the outcome of litigation and consequently its willingness to escalate the dispute.[88]

Third, the tests revealed a positive association between the in-house legal capacity of Chinese companies and the number of lawsuits they defend in federal courts. Specifically, all else being equal, Chinese companies employing full-time professional legal managers at their US subsidiaries are sued more frequently in federal courts. Note that the preceding subsection found no significant link between the availability of in-house legal managers and the number of federal cases filed by Chinese companies (i.e., acting as plaintiff). The contrast suggests that the US in-house legal management position is established partially in response to coercive pressure from the host-state legal institution.[89] Recall that Chapter 2 highlighted the peculiar phenomenon of some Chinese companies sending expatriates to oversee the management of US legal matters. And due to the expatriates' lack of knowledge and qualification,

[86] The variable is significant at 5 percent and 10 percent levels (see Table 5.7 in Appendix).

[87] Interview with an in-house counsel at the US subsidiary of a large Chinese MNC (December 2, 2017).

[88] *See, e.g.*, Richard A. Posner, *An Economic Approach to Legal Procedure and Judicial Administration*, 2 J. LEGAL STUD. 399 (1973); Steven Shavell, *Suit, Settlement and Trial: A Theoretical Analysis Under Alternative Methods for the Allocation of Legal Costs*, 11 J. LEGAL STUD. 55 (1982).

[89] Note that this is only suggestive evidence, as the limited sample size does not allow the drawing of definitive conclusions from the insignificance of the result from the tests using data with Chinese multinationals as plaintiffs.

their primary functions were limited to control and coordination. Building on those insights, I further investigated the potential effects of this unusual personnel arrangement on the likelihood of federal litigation by replacing the professional in-house counsel dummy with two dummy variables that together codify the three scenarios: (1) having no full-time legal manager at the US subsidiary; (2) having an expatriate as the US legal manager; and (3) having a local recruit as the US legal manager. The test results confirm the findings from Chapter 2.[90]

Fourth, Chinese companies that prioritize US investment are more frequently sued in federal courts. Compare this with the finding from the preceding subsection that Chinese investors taking the US market seriously file fewer federal lawsuits. The contrast may be explained in two ways. First, Chinese companies with ambitious US investment plans may take more measures to prevent and mitigate legal risks in the host state, resulting in fewer claims to litigate. They may also have a long-term perspective on the US market and thus avoid end-game behavior such as litigation. Second, as illustrated in Chapter 2, Chinese companies that regard the US market as highly important tend to feature more centralized and hierarchical control over the US operations, which could channel the home-state normative litigation aversion to the US subsidiaries' filing decisions. Both rationales may still hold true. However, internal mechanisms to mitigate US legal risks may not stop others from suing, and enhanced hierarchical control may hinder dispute resolution. Moreover, Chinese companies that prioritize the US market are less likely to exit, so disputes that would have forced out a casual investor end up in US courts. Hence the positive association between US market importance and the frequency of being sued in federal courts.

Fifth, as expected, Chinese companies operating in sectors subject to extensive federal regulation are more likely to be sued in federal courts. Within the US political structure, federal courts enjoy only limited subject matter jurisdiction. Federal regulations provide either government or private parties, sometimes both, with jurisdictional bases to sue regulated Chinese companies. Hence the positive association between sectoral regulation and the frequency of being sued in federal courts.

Lastly, both investment size and duration are significant. Intuitively and in line with previous test results, Chinese companies with larger US operations tend to be sued more frequently when the other variables are

[90] The coefficient for expatriated legal managers is not significant, whereas the coefficient for local recruits is significant at 5 percent level.

held constant. Moreover, a lengthy business presence in the US market naturally increases the likelihood of being taken to a federal court.[91]

5.3 CONCLUSION

The US litigation experiences of Chinese companies vary significantly, raising interesting questions for scholars, practitioners, and policymakers. Building on what we have learned so far, Chapter 5 continued to investigate Chinese companies' US litigation by empirically analyzing their federal lawsuits. The analysis revealed that Chinese companies are much more likely to litigate as defendant than as plaintiff, and their federal litigation experiences differ in each case. As plaintiffs, US business expansion, US market importance, investment duration, and size are important variables. In contrast, the likelihood of being sued in federal courts is associated with the ownership structure of the Chinese investors, cultural differences, in-house counsel, US market importance, investment duration, and the size of their US operations.

The analysis also highlighted the dual institutional effects on Chinese companies' interactions with the US adjudicatory system. Distinct home-state formal rules governing state-owned Chinese companies and various ownership-related organizational traits lead to tight hierarchical control over their US subsidiaries and suboptimal dispute resolution and litigation, resulting in a higher frequency of being sued in federal courts. Normative institutions also play a role. Chinese companies that are less adaptive are sued more often, as the vast cultural gaps give rise to more conflicts and hinder effective dispute resolution. Meanwhile, host-state institutions such as federal regulations compel isomorphism and provide jurisdictional basis for filing federal lawsuits, so Chinese companies operating in heavily regulated sectors are sued more frequently in federal courts.

Moreover, the present chapter re-examined Chinese companies' in-house legal capacity in the United States. We have learned from Chapter 2 that the capacity varies across different Chinese companies and from Chapter 4 that professional legal managers facilitate

[91] It merits highlighting the differences in the two sets of test results in this section: one for Chinese companies litigating in federal courts as plaintiffs and the other as defendants. State ownership is significant when the companies are sued, but not when they sue. The same is true for the cultural difference variable. But it is premature to rule out the possible effects of state ownership and cultural tensions on the likelihood of filing lawsuits in federal courts.

the localization of US litigation decisions. Now, from the analysis of the federal judicial data and additional interviews, one may infer that Chinese investors build up US internal legal capacity partially in response to the risk of being sued in the United States.

While this chapter has addressed several important knowledge gaps, a significant and intriguing question remains open: How do Chinese companies fare in US courts? Do they typically win their cases in federal courts or suffer persistent losses? Chinese companies, like their US counterparts, often settle their lawsuits, and the terms of these settlements are usually undisclosed. Therefore, we cannot infer from the federal judgments whether they settled by satisfying the other parties' demands or with favorable terms. However, we can speculate about the outcome based on the empirical finding of the litigation aversion in Chapter 4 and the trial selection theory, which contends that cases often go to trial because both parties are overly "optimistic" about the outcome.[92] Assuming symmetric stakes, the theory predicts that in the limit, plaintiff win rate should approach 50 percent in tried cases.[93] While subsequent empirical research has found win rates to consistently deviate from 50 percent, the core causal relationships embodied in the model remain unchallenged.[94] So, all else being equal, a party's reluctance to litigate should increase its win rate. Due to their aversion to litigate in US courts, Chinese companies should only litigate cases that they highly expect to win. Thus, on average, they should prevail in US federal courts at a rate higher than 50 percent. Indeed, according to the data from the 2017 survey, the vast majority of Chinese companies won most or all of their lawsuits in the United States. But how federal lawsuits involving Chinese companies transpire remains an important yet complex topic for future research.

92 *Supra* note 88.

93 *Id.*

94 Keith N. Hylton, *Asymmetric Information and the Selection of Disputes for Litigation*, 22 J. Legal Stud. 187 (1993); Daniel Kessler, et al., *Explaining Deviations from the Fifty-Percent Rule: A Multimodal Approach to the Selection of Cases for Litigation*, 25 J. Legal Stud. 233 (1996); Peter Siegelman & John J. Donohue III, *The Selection of Employment Discrimination Disputes for Litigation: Using Business Cycle Effects to Test the Priest-Klein Hypothesis*, 24 J. Legal Stud. 47 (1995); Linda R. Stanley & Don L. Coursey, Empirical Evidence on the Selection Hypothesis and the Decision to Litigate or Settle (1990); Robert E. Thomas, *The Trial Selection Hypothesis Without the 50 Percent Rule: Some Experimental Evidence* 24 J. Legal Stud. 209 (1995).

APPENDIX

TABLE 5.6 Summary statistics

Variable	Mean	Standard deviation	Min.	Max.	Number of observations
Number of lawsuits (as plaintiff)	0.267	1.055	0	10	206
Number of lawsuits (as defendant)	1.306	3.863	0	25	206
State ownership (50%)	0.304	0.461	0	1	230
State ownership (10%)	0.078	0.269	0	1	230
Investment duration	10.271	8.325	1	38	218
Recent M&A	0.270	0.445	0	1	178
US revenue	2.535	1.587	1	5	202
US market importance	2.604	0.980	1	4	187
Sectoral regulation	50,656.02	52,294.36	511.455	214,953.40	230
Cultural challenge	0.275	0.447	0	1	193
Listing status	0.398	0.491	0	1	226
US in-house counsel	0.346	0.477	0	1	188

Note: Source: Bloomberg legal database; 2019 CGCC survey.

TABLE 5.7 Test results (dependent variable: number of federal lawsuits involving Chinese companies)

	Chinese company as plaintiff			Chinese company as defendant		
Variable	Model 1	Model 2	Model 3	Model 1	Model 2	Model 3
State ownership (50%)	0.665	0.657	0.642	10.172***	10.075***	10.124***
	(0.729)	(0.735)	(0.726)	(0.417)	(0.417)	(0.416)
State ownership (10%)	10.628	10.686	10.710	10.386**	10.188*	10.446**
	(10.067)	(10.109)	(10.094)	(0.643)	(0.657)	(0.668)
Investment duration	0.106***	0.110**	0.105**	0.102**	0.106***	0.101***
	(0.041)	(0.043)	(0.045)	(0.033)	(0.032)	(0.032)
Recent M&A	20.120**	20.134**	20.130**		–0.526	–0.271
	(0.870)	(0.880)	(0.871)		(0.441)	(0.471)
US revenue	0.742***	0.750***	0.767***	0.5193***	0.517***	0.529***
	(0.271)	(0.274)	(0.277)	(0.136)	(0.135)	(0.133)
US market importance	–10.333**	–10.360**	–10.351**	0.472**	0.497**	0.512**
	(0.536)	(0.551)	(0.546)	(0.218)	(0.218)	(0.214)
Sectoral regulation	20.11e-06	20.40e-06	20.25e-06	0.00001***	0.00001***	0.00001***
	(50.89e-06)	(50.98e-06)	(50.88e-06)	(30.40e-06)	(30.44e-06)	(30.45e-06)
Cultural challenge	0.418	0.416	0.329	0.794*	0.831**	0.899**
	(0.823)	(0.833)	(0.855)	(0.423)	(0.422)	(0.426)
Listing status		0.213	0.299			–0.586
		(0.674)	(0.721)			(0.423)
US in-house counsel			–0.286	10.536***	10.612***	10.699***
			(0.893)	(0.446)	(0.447)	(0.451)
Constant	–40.137***	–40.295***	–40.214***	–60.152***	–50.650***	–50.981***
	(10.472)	(10.588)	(10.576)	(10.008)	(0.984)	(0.982)
N	142	142	142	144	142	142
Pseudo R^2	0.271	0.272	0.273	0.178	0.180	0.186

Source: Bloomberg Law database; 2019 CGCC survey.

CHAPTER SIX

CHINESE COMPANIES' LEGAL STRATEGIES AGAINST US GOVERNMENT MISTREATMENT

When push comes to shove, we will sue the US government. After all, this is a country with the rule of law.

—CEO of a Chinese company in the United States

TikTok is a weapon by the Chinese Communist Party.

—Cathy McMorris Rodgers, Chair of the House Energy and Commerce Committee

Most US lawsuits involving Chinese companies are initiated by or against their customers, employees, or business counterparts. However, on occasion, Chinese investors may go to court against a US government entity to resolve a dispute. As US–China relations continue to deteriorate, Chinese companies are increasingly caught in the crossfire of the geopolitical rivalry. Being suspected as agents for the Chinese state, China-headquartered multinational companies (MNCs), especially those with ties to the Chinese government, have expressed growing frustration over what they perceive as unfair treatment by the US government.[1]

Chinese companies that entered the US market since the early 2000s made long-term investment plans and were unprepared for the anti-China policies that emerged after the election of Donald Trump as US president in 2016.[2] Granted, international business executives routinely complain about host-country bureaucratic overreach and

[1] Ji Li, *In Pursuit of Fairness: How Chinese Multinational Companies React to U.S. Government Bias*, 62 Harv. Int'l L.J. 375, 376 (2021).

[2] Ji Li, The Clash of Capitalisms? Chinese Companies in the United States 40 (2018).

malfeasance; US investors with businesses in China have been vocal about official prejudice for years, and their protests have fueled the escalating confrontation between the two governments.[3] Unexpected, however, is the hostile turn of the political and regulatory environment for Chinese companies doing business in the United States. According to the China General Chamber of Commerce USA (2019) survey, most Chinese investors in the United States consider the enforcement of host-state laws and policies unfair.[4] As the bilateral relations are trapped in a downward spiral, more Chinese companies will perceive or actually experience discriminatory treatment from the US government and respond with mitigating measures. Huawei is a prime example of this. Under unrelenting US government pressure, this prominent Chinese company hired lobbyists,[5] launched a media campaign,[6] sought diplomatic assistance,[7] and finally filed lawsuits against the federal government in US courts.[8] More recently, TikTok adopted similar strategies against what they viewed as "unfair" measures by the US government.[9] Although Huawei's legal tactics have largely failed, TikTok has successfully blocked Trump's presidential order banning its use in

[3] Zach Coleman, *US Companies in China Complain of Official Bias*, NIKKEI ASIAN REV. (February 26, 2019), https://asia.nikkei.com/Economy/Trade-war/US-companies-in-China-complain-of-official-bias.

[4] In the 2019 survey conducted by the China General Chamber of Commerce, 59 percent of the survey subjects responded "poor" or "very poor" to the question regarding the fairness of law and policy enforcement toward Chinese companies in the United States.

[5] Ben Brody, *Huawei Lobbying Spend Hits Record with Hire of Trump Fundraiser*, BLOOMBERG (October 21, 2019), www.bloomberg.com/news/articles/2019-10-22/huawei-lobbying-spend-hits-record-with-hire-of-trump-fundraiser.

[6] Janhvi Bhojwani, *Huawei Broadens Its Campaign to Win over American Public and Media*, NPR (March 1, 2019), www.npr.org/2019/03/01/699307312/huawei-broadens-its-campaign-to-win-over-american-public-and-media.

[7] Dan Strumpf, *Huawei Warns US of Retaliation by Beijing; Profit Growth Slows*, WALL STREET J. (March 31, 2020), www.wsj.com/articles/huawei-warns-u-s-of-retaliation-by-beijing-profit-growth-slows-11585658329.

[8] Paul Mozur & Austin Ramzy, *Huawei Sues US Government over What It Calls an Unfair Ban*, N.Y. TIMES (March 6, 2019), www.nytimes.com/2019/03/06/business/huawei-united-states-trade-lawsuit.html.

[9] On the report about TikTok's lobbying, *see*, *e.g.*, Cecilia Kang, *TikTok Enlists Army of Lobbyists as Suspicions over China Ties Grow*, N.Y. TIMES (July 15, 2020), www.nytimes.com/2020/07/15/technology/tiktok-washington-lobbyist.html; on its litigation threat, *see*, *e.g.*, Naomi Xu Elegant, *TikTok Threatens Legal Action in Response to Trump's Executive Order Banning the App*, FORTUNE (August 7, 2020), https://fortune.com/2020/08/07/tiktok-ban-trump-executive-order-lawsuit-legal-action-response/.

the United States.[10] However, whether TikTok can survive the continuous political onslaught in the post-Trump era remains uncertain.

Lawsuits against US government bodies are of great policy and theoretical importance. Yet, scholars have largely neglected the topic because, until recently, almost all Chinese investors had considered the United States as a haven for foreign investment.[11] This chapter aims to narrow the knowledge gap by examining the legal reactions of Chinese companies to perceived official bias in the United States in the context of growing geopolitical tensions.

It is important to note that "fairness" and "bias" are essentially subjective concepts, and what may be viewed as "unfair" or "biased" by Chinese investors may be considered neutral, lawful, and justifiable actions by the US government or an independent third party. This chapter does *not* judge whether the US government indeed treats Chinese investors unfairly. Rather, it focuses on how the investors may consider legal resistance to *perceived* mistreatment by the host state. After all, it is the managers' first-person perception that initiates their legal reactions. Hence, unless otherwise noted, the terms "fairness," "prejudice," "discriminatory," and "bias" are all used to describe the perceptions of Chinese executives throughout this chapter.

The remainder of this chapter is organized as follows. Section 6.1 introduces readers to the dual institutional contexts for litigating disputes with state actors, with a focus on the evolving Chinese institutional environment since the US context has been thoroughly explored. Next, Section 6.2 presents four case studies about the legal reactions of prominent Chinese companies (e.g., Huawei, China Telecom, and TikTok) to perceived "unfair" treatment by the US government. Despite differing in several major aspects, including sector, ownership structure, US investment duration, and the size of their US operations, all four Chinese companies chose to sue the US government when they felt its actions had caused or would cause them imminent and substantial harm. However, as will be detailed, their legal strategies and actions, as well as the political contexts, varied significantly and led to vastly different outcomes. Section 6.3 then analyzes the quantitative evidence on the contemplated coping strategies of Chinese companies against "unfair" US government treatment, with a focus on litigation in US courts and the inter-firm variations. Statistical tests will investigate

[10] See more details in Section 6.2.
[11] Li, *supra* note 2.

the possible effects of key institutional factors such as the ownership structure of Chinese investors and the cultural challenges they encounter in the United States. The analysis is followed by a brief discussion about Chinese companies' actual responses to US government bias. Finally, Section 6.4 concludes the chapter.

6.1 GOVERNMENT MISTREATMENT AND INVESTORS' REACTIONS

Conflicts between foreign investors and host-state governments are a longstanding issue, and the management and resolution of such conflicts has spawned research in a variety of topical areas including economic diplomacy,[12] investor-state arbitration,[13] and political risk management.[14] Nonetheless, there has been limited exploration of how MNCs, particularly those from developing countries, pursue legal recourse against host-state governments for official malfeasance or nonfeasance. Several factors may have contributed to this research gap. First, until the early 2000s, MNCs headquartered in the United States, Europe, and Japan dominated global investment, leaving little to explore for those interested in developing-country MNCs.[15] Second, discriminatory government treatments have traditionally been associated with countries lacking robust legal institutions.[16] In the United States and other industrialized nations, it was assumed that domestic and foreign investors operate on a level playing ground, hence few

[12] *See, e.g.*, Geoffrey Gertz, *Commercial Diplomacy and Political Risk*, 62 INT'L STUD. Q. 94 (2018); Jing-Lin Duanmu, *State-Owned MNCs and Host Country Expropriation Risk: The Role of Home State Soft Power and Economic Gunboat Diplomacy*, 45 J. INT'L BUS. STUD. 1044 (2014).

[13] See generally ALEC STONE SWEET & FLORIAN GRISEL, THE EVOLUTION OF INTERNATIONAL ARBITRATION: JUDICIALIZATION, GOVERNANCE, LEGITIMACY (2017); Thomas Schultz & Cédric Dupont, *Investment Arbitration: Promoting the Rule of Law or Over-Empowering Investors? A Quantitative Empirical Study*, 25 EUR. J. INT'L L. 1147 (2014).

[14] *See, e.g.*, Jiann-jong Guo, et al., *Do China's Outward Direct Investors Prefer Countries with High Political Risk? An International and Empirical Comparison*, 6 CHINA & WORLD ECON. 22 (2014); Guy L.F. Holburn & Bennet A. Zelner, *Political Capabilities, Policy Risk, and International Investment Strategy: Evidence from the Global Electric Power Generation Industry*, 31 STRATEGIC MGMT. J. 1290 (2010).

[15] Bala Ramasamy, et al., *China's Outward Foreign Direct Investment: Location Choice and Firm Ownership*, 47 J. WORLD BUS. 17, 18 (2012).

[16] Jing Li, et al., *Diplomatic and Corporate Networks: Bridges to Foreign Locations*, 49 J. INT'L BUS. STUD. 659, 660 (2018).

scholars have bothered to study a risk deemed nonexistent or minimal. Third, careful planning can often direct conflicts with host-state governments toward alternative dispute resolution mechanisms, such as investment arbitration, circumventing host-state courts.[17]

However, the global expansion of Chinese companies over the past two decades has raised questions about their use of host-state courts to safeguard investment interests. This issue is especially pertinent to Chinese investments in the United States, where a powerful and independent judiciary is available to counteract governmental mistreatment. Again, within the dual institutional framework, this chapter starts its inquiry by comparatively analyzing the Chinese and US institutions governing litigation against government agencies.

As just noted, the US institutions for judicial scrutiny of executive or legislative actions have been extensively studied.[18] While scholars disagree on the extent and merit of judicial deference to the actions of the other two branches,[19] few would dispute that the US judiciary offers a potential recourse for those with resources against the most egregious government mistreatment.[20] Moreover, social norms in contemporary United States encourage private parties to contest state actors who infringe on their legal rights and interests. Neoliberal ideology advocates for a legally restrained, small state, and the US legal culture portrays lawyers who challenge and defeat abusive government agencies in court as upholders of a high standard of professionalism.[21] In short, formal legal institutions in the United States are accessible to resourceful parties seeking review and rectification of wrongful government actions,

[17] *See, e.g.*, Anthea Roberts, *Incremental, Systemic, and Paradigmatic Reform of Investor-State Arbitration*, 112 Am. J. Int'l L. 410 (2018).

[18] For a list of notable works on judicial review of administrative actions, see David P. Currie & Frank I. Goodman, *Judicial Review of Federal Administrative Action: Quest for the Optimum Forum*, 75 Colum. L. Rev. 1 (1975); Eduardo Jordão & Susan Rose-Ackerman, *Judicial Review of Executive Policymaking in Advanced Democracies: Beyond Rights Review*, 66 Admin. L. Rev. 1 (2014); Martha Anne Humphries & Donald R. Songer, *Law and Politics in Judicial Oversight of Federal Administrative Agencies*, 61 J. Pol. 207 (1999).

[19] John F. Manning, *Constitutional Structure and Judicial Deference to Agency Interpretations of Agency Rules*, 96 Colum. L. Rev. 612 (1996); Humphries & Songer, *supra* note 18; Ronald J. Krotoszynski Jr, *Why Deference?: Implied Delegations, Agency Expertise, and the Misplaced Legacy of Skidmore*, 54 Admin. L. Rev. 735 (2002).

[20] Marc Galanter, *Why the "Haves" Come out Ahead: Speculations on the Limits of Legal Change*, 9 Law & Soc'y Rev. (1974).

[21] For a summary of the literature on cause lawyering, see Anna-Maria Marshall & Daniel Crocker Hale, *Cause Lawyering*, 10 Ann. Rev. L. & Soc. Sci. 310 (2014).

while informal US institutions place minimal normative constraints on private parties pursuing judicial remedies against state infringement.

In China, in contrast, both formal and informal institutions impede judicial resolution of grievances with government agencies. The Chinese government only began constructing an administrative law regime in the late 1980s, aiming to rationalize governance and maintain political control.[22] The administrative law system comprises a set of statutes, rules, and specialized judicial staff, supplementing several pre-existing Chinese institutions devised to address the inherent agency problem afflicting the vast apparatus of the authoritarian state. In addition to the nomenklatura structure that sets the major incentives for government officials, the powerful Central Commission for Discipline Inspection (CCDI) and the National Supervision Commission (NSC) play a prominent role in prosecuting the most severe violations of laws and party disciplines by state-affiliated actors. However, due to staffing shortages and information asymmetry, these institutions remain inadequate to hold lower-level officials accountable for wrongful acts. Conversely, a bottom-up petition system known as the "letters and visits offices" (or *xinfang* offices) allows citizens to selectively report official misconduct to higher officials or designated agencies.[23] Although they do not impose any temporal, procedural, or subject matter limit on the filing of complaints, the letters and visits offices have not offered an effective means to resolve disputes with governmental entities.[24] As will be detailed, the Chinese administrative law regime could serve to bridge the gap between the top-down supervisory institutions and the bottom-up petition system.

The first building block of China's administrative law regime is the Administrative Litigation Law (ALL), enacted in 1989 and significantly amended in 2014 and 2017. This statute enables individuals who are dissatisfied with concrete government malfeasance or nonfeasance to file a lawsuit in a People's Court. To process such claims, most Chinese courts have established administrative law divisions. Following the ALL, the central government has passed more

22 *See, e.g.*, Susan Finder, *Like Throwing an Egg Against a Stone? Administrative Litigation in the People's Republic of China*, 3 J. Asian L. 1 (1989); Randall Peerenboom, China's Long March Toward Rule of Law (2002); Ji Li, *Suing the Leviathan—An Empirical Analysis of the Changing Rate of Administrative Litigation in China*, 10 J. Empirical Legal Stud. 815 (2013).

23 Carl Minzner, *Xinfang: An Alternative to Formal Chinese Legal Institutions*, 42 Stanford J. Int'l L. 103 (2006).

24 *Id.*

substantive and procedural statutes aimed at rationalizing governance and curbing lower officials, including the State Compensation Law, the Administrative Reconsideration Law, the Administrative Punishment Law, and the Administrative Licensing Law. In brief, over two decades, these legislative efforts provided Chinese citizens with a set of formal laws to resist government mistreatment. In comparison with other East Asian countries, China was "ahead of its time" in terms of constructing a formal administrative law regime.[25] However, due to its reluctance to impose systematic judicial restraints on administrative discretion, the Chinese government has not enacted a comprehensive statute akin to the US Administrative Procedure Act (APA).

Moreover, significant gaps persist between the Chinese administrative laws on paper and their actual implementation. Although Chinese courts are formally authorized to restrain abusive local officials, judges often exercise considerable caution in doing so. Given the relatively low status of the Chinese judiciary within the state power hierarchy, it was not uncommon for defendant administrative departments to refuse cooperation during trials and enforcement of judgments.[26] For most victims of government mistreatment, taking government officials to court has been likened to "throwing an egg against a stone."[27] In the 2010s, however, the administrative law regime underwent substantial reforms, making it easier for private parties to address grievances against government officials.[28] Additionally, victims with significant interests at stake but few alternative resolution options, as well as those facing an end-game scenario (i.e., not expecting any future interactions with the defendant government actor), have become less hesitant to sue.[29] Nevertheless, compared with US courts, the Chinese judiciary generally offers less powerful and effective remedies against official malfeasance.

Concurrent with the development of the formal administrative law regime, the informal institutions in China pertaining to dispute

[25] John Ohnesorge, *Administrative Law in East Asia: A Comparative-Historical Analysis*, *in* COMPARATIVE ADMINISTRATIVE LAW: RESEARCH HANDBOOKS IN COMPARATIVE LAW 78 (Susan Rose-Ackerman & Peter L. Lindseth eds., 2010).

[26] Kevin J. O'Brien & Lianjiang Li, *Suing the Local State: Administrative Litigation in Rural China*, 51 CHINA J. 75 (2004).

[27] Finder, *supra* note 22.

[28] *See, e.g.*, Baogang Guo, *China's Administrative Governance Reform in the Era of "New Normal,"* 22 J. CHINESE POL. SCI. 357 (2017); Taisu Zhang & Tom Ginsburg, *China's Turn Toward Law*, 59 VA. J. INT'L L. 306 (2019).

[29] Ji Li, *Dare You Sue the Tax Collector? An Empirical Study of Tax-Related Administrative Lawsuits in China*, 23 PACIFIC RIM L. & POLICY J. 57 (2014).

resolution with state actors have remained relatively static. Chinese culture denigrates the escalation of conflicts, particularly with government officials, and litigation against government agencies bears complex social meanings and implications.[30] Though in limited circumstances, so-called "die-hard" lawyers might earn professional and social acclaim for zealously representing their clients in administrative cases,[31] the dominant social norms still encourage plaintiffs to reconcile and settle disputes with officials. In short, Chinese managers who are deeply ingrained in the home-state cultural and social context would strive to avoid seeking legal remedies for any losses caused by government malfeasance or nonfeasance. Therefore, they would have to "overcome some psychological barrier to sue the US government."[32]

To summarize, the Chinese government has established a formal administrative law system that enables aggrieved parties to seek legal recourse against official wrongdoing. However, despite notable improvement over the past three decades, the system still falls short of providing consistently reliable, independent, and effective remedies for government mistreatment. Moreover, informal institutions in China discourage the escalation of conflicts with state actors. In contrast, both formal and informal institutions in the United States facilitate the pursuit of legal recourse against government infringement on private rights. The diverging pulls of the home-state and host-state institutions should influence how Chinese companies seek judicial remedy for US government mistreatment. The following Section 6.2 explores the dual institutional effects with four detailed case studies.

6.2 FOUR CHINESE COMPANIES AND THEIR LAWSUITS AGAINST THE US GOVERNMENT

Litigating against the US government is no easy feat, even for well-established MNCs. Nonetheless, Chinese companies have been engaging in such litigation with increasing frequency. This part

[30] Ji Li, *Interactions Between Domestic Social Norms and International Law Over Trade Dispute Resolution*, *in* The Rule of Law at the National and International Levels: Contestations and Deference (Machiko Kanetake & André Nollkaemper eds., 2015).

[31] James Moliterno & Lan Rongjie, *The New-Breed, Die-Hard Chinese Lawyer: A Comparison with American Civil Rights Cause Lawyers*, 25 Wash. & Lee J. Civ. Rts. & Soc. Just. 99 (2018).

[32] Interview with a partner at the US office of a large Chinese law firm (November 19, 2021).

presents four case studies: Sany, Huawei, TikTok, and China Telecom. These companies were chosen for the following reasons. First, their lawsuits attracted extensive media coverage, so the archival data allows in-depth analysis. While several informants interviewed for this book are affiliated with these four Chinese companies, these case studies rely on publicly available information in order to preserve interviewee confidentiality. Second, the four companies differ in terms of sector, investment duration, and ownership structure, offering an opportunity to generate testable insights on their propensity to sue the US government. Third, several of their lawsuits have had far-reaching policy and jurisprudential repercussions. Finally, as will be demonstrated, the outcomes of the lawsuits exhibit considerable variation, underscoring the contingencies and uncertainties involved in pursuing legal recourse against US government mistreatment and the limitations of any attempted theorization or generalization.

6.2.1 Sany and Ralls Corporation

Sany Heavy Industry Group (Sany) was founded in 1989 and has experienced exponential growth over three decades, becoming the largest Chinese manufacturer of heavy machinery. In a recent industry ranking, Sany was placed second worldwide, surpassed only by Caterpillar.[33] Sany owns thirty foreign subsidiaries, and in 2006, it established a wholly owned US subsidiary (Sany Americas) on the outskirts of Atlanta, Georgia. Immediately thereafter Sany spent $60 million on an impressive office building in order to "show potential customers that we will be here for the long term"[34] and signed a memorandum of understanding with the State of Georgia to invest $100 million.[35] Sany executives were aware of the difficulties they would face when competing in a mature market fraught with "misconceptions about Chinese companies."[36] For instance, as the president of Sany Americas noted, "Many American clients and peer companies don't know that we are

[33] *Forbes: SANY Is China's Largest Heavy Equipment Company in 2021 and 2nd in the World* (May 18, 2021), at www.sanyglobal.com/press_releases/692/.

[34] James R. Hagerty & Colum Murphy, *Sany Tries to Gain Traction in the U.S.: Chinese Firm Comes to Georgia but Buyers Are Still Scarce*, WALL STREET J. (January 28, 2013), www.wsj.com/articles/SB10001424127887323706704578227702847406408.

[35] Tan Yingzi, *Sany Does Heavy Lifting in Pursuit of Growth in US*, CHINA DAILY (October 12, 2012), usa.chinadaily.com.cn/a/201210/12/WS5a2f399da3108bc8c6721e47.html.

[36] Tan Yingzi, *Sany's Bid to Usurp Caterpillar*, CHINA DAILY (October 16, 2012), www.chinadaily.com.cn/kindle/2012-10/16/content_15820378.htm.

a privately owned, publicly listed company," and some even considered "working with a Chinese company to be a taboo."[37] It took Sany Americas six years and several strategy shifts to gain traction in the US market and achieve profitability.[38]

In parallel to this Georgia investment, a senior executive of Sany overseeing its wind turbine business decided to explore the vast US market – a project that would prove more controversial. Sany invested in Ralls Corporation, a company incorporated in Delaware, and used it to purchase four US companies with the intent to develop windfarms in north-central Oregon.[39] The targeted sites are located in and around the "region of a restricted airspace and bombing zone maintained by the US Navy."[40] Unaware of any national security risk, Ralls failed to notify the Committee on Foreign Investments in the United States (CFIUS) prior to the transaction. After the closing and prompted by a US government official, Ralls filed a notice. CFIUS then determined that the transaction would impair US national security and issued interim mitigation orders restricting Ralls's access to the wind farm sites pending the president's final decision.[41]

Upon recognizing the seriousness of the situation, Ralls negotiated a sale of the assets at a significantly discounted rate to a US company, assuming the change of ownership would fully address the national security concern. However, CFIUS's interim orders prevented the sale from going through. Only then did the local managers inform Sany's Chinese headquarters about the trouble. With any possible sale of the assets blocked by CFIUS, Ralls had to find alternative solutions, and the search process clearly evidenced the influence of its home-state institutions. The executives initially contacted the commercial counselor at the US Embassy in Beijing, hoping that an insider might help.[42] Subsequently, Sany hired Wesley Clark, a former four-star general with thirty-eight years of service in the US Army, to lobby on its behalf. The managers were optimistic, because "according to the

[37] *Id.*

[38] *Id.*

[39] Ralls Corp. v. Comm. on Foreign Inv. in U.S., 758 F.3d 296 (D.C. Cir. 2014).

[40] *Id.*, at 304.

[41] *Id.*, at 302.

[42] Ya Tang, et al., *Sanyi Zhonggong: Wo Men Ru He Gao Ying Obama* [*Sany Heavy Machinery: How We Won the Lawsuit against Obama*], SHANG YE PING LUN [BUSINESS REVIEW] (August 5, 2016), www.ebusinessreview.cn/articledetail-286709.html.

Chinese way of thinking, a person of that stature should be able to turn things around."[43]

At the same time, the option of seeking legal recourse was being considered. The US lawyer for Ralls advised against litigation, yet the Sany manager, who had also invested his own money in the project, insisted on pursuing legal action as a last resort.[44] The board of Sany also considered the negative implications of being labeled a national security threat by the US government, which could thwart its long-term plan for global expansion.[45] To prepare for the possibility of legal action, Sany engaged one of the best US litigation boutiques. After all the alternative solutions failed, Ralls filed a legal complaint. Meanwhile, President Obama affirmed the CFIUS finding and ordered Ralls to divest itself of the US companies within ninety days. Furthermore, Ralls was required to have all its equipment dissembled by US-born American citizens within the given timeframe and obtain CFIUS approval for the sale of the assets to a third party.[46] Due to the onerous conditions, Sany anticipated losing its entire investment of at least $20 million.[47] Throughout the process, Sany received no explanation and was given no opportunity to rebut any incriminating evidence[48]; the agency never even inspected the site at issue before ordering the Chinese company to completely divest within a very short time. A little background may help readers understand the trouble Chinese investors have with CFIUS review.

The 1998 Exon-Florio amendment to the Defense Production Act authorizes the US president to block a covered transaction that threatens to impair US national security. Because this power is not time-barred, all covered foreign investments are exposed to the risk of a presidential veto.[49] To manage and mitigate the risk, foreign investors may seek a pre-transaction approval from CFIUS, which bars the

[43] *Id.*

[44] *Id.*

[45] *Id.*

[46] Ralls Corp. v. Comm. on Foreign Inv. in the U.S., 926 F. Supp. 2d 71, 80 (D.C. Dist. 2013).

[47] Jasmine Wang, *Sany Affiliate May Lose $20 Million on US Wind-Farm Ban*, Bloomberg (October 3, 2012), www.bloomberg.com/news/articles/2012-10-04/sany-affiliate-may-lose-20-million-on-u-s-wind-farm-ban.

[48] *Id.*

[49] Ji Li, *Investing Near the National Security Black Hole*, 14 Berkeley Bus. L.J. 1, 13 (2017).

agency's future review and investigation.[50] Thus, at its core, the CFIUS approval offers a safe harbor protection to a covered foreign investment,[51] and one may argue that a foreign investor assume the risk of adverse post-investment government actions by skipping the filing of a notice. That was indeed the reasoning of the trial court when it ruled against Ralls.

The lawsuit filed by Ralls claimed, among others, a violation of its due process right under the Fifth Amendment.[52] The D.C. District Court initially dismissed most of the claims as moot or for lack of subject matter jurisdiction,[53] and later tossed out the due process claim as well for failure to state a justiciable claim.[54] The trial judge's decision implicitly assumed foreign investors make rational decisions and that their decision not to file a prior notice with CFIUS had incorporated the risk of a subsequent presidential veto.[55] In other words, foreign investors who opt not to obtain a CFIUS approval merely acquired "contingent" property rights in US assets.[56] And legal professionals practicing in this area generally agreed with the District Court's logic.[57] Even Ralls's own lawyers were pessimistic about the outcome of the lawsuit.[58]

In a surprising turn of events, the D.C. Circuit reversed the lower court's decision.[59] The appellate judge rejected the argument that Ralls's due process claim was a nonjusticiable political question because the claim did not "encroach on the prerogative of the political branches," "did not require the exercise of non-judicial discretion," and was "susceptible to judicially manageable standards."[60] The D.C. Circuit found that Ralls was denied due process as it was neither informed of the

[50] *Id.*
[51] *Id.*, at 14.
[52] *Comm. on Foreign Inv. in U.S.*, 758 F.3d, at 315.
[53] *Id.*, at 306.
[54] *Id.*, at 307.
[55] *Comm. on Foreign Inv. in U.S.*, 987 F. Supp. 2d at 27.
[56] *Id.*
[57] *See, e.g.*, Daniel B. Pickard, Nova J. Daly & Usha Neelakantan, *The Ralls Case: Why CFIUS and the Court Got it Right*, 8 Glob. Trade and Customs J. 192 (2013); Jeremy Zucker & Hrishikesh Hari, *Gone with the Wind II: The Ralls Decision and Lessons for Foreign Investors*, 9 Glob. Trade and Customs J. 44 (2014); Jeremy Zucker & Hrishikesh Hari, *Gone with the Wind: The Ralls Transaction and Implications for Foreign Investment in the United States*, 8 Glob. Trade & Customs J. 182 (2013).
[58] Tang, et al., *supra* note 42.
[59] *Comm. on Foreign Inv. in U.S.*, 758 F.3d, at 315.
[60] *Id.*, at 307–13.

nature of the national security concern or the evidentiary basis for the determination, nor allowed a chance to rebut it.[61] As a result, the D.C. Circuit remanded the case to the District Court with instructions that Ralls be given access to the unclassified evidence on which the decision was based and an opportunity to respond to it.[62] The lower court was also instructed to fully adjudicate several other legal issues raised by the investor. After the defeat, CFIUS handed over three thousand pages of documents to Ralls. The two parties then negotiated an undisclosed settlement, under which Ralls was allowed to sell its investment at issue to desired purchasers.[63]

Viewed from a jurisprudential perspective, *Ralls* is no doubt a watershed case. The D.C. Circuit rejected the argument that foreign investors who skip the CFIUS filing, acting rationally with complete information, willingly assume the risk of expropriation. Instead, the court extended constitutional due process protection over foreign investors' US assets acquired through a covered transaction. This first lawsuit challenging CFIUS imposed a legal restraint over the nearly unlimited discretion of the federal agency. Though the full jurisprudential ramifications of the case and its precedential value were fleeting, as Congress later expanded the power of CFIUS and restructured the review process, *Ralls* illustrates how Chinese companies may incrementally alter the host-state legal landscape via lawsuits against US government agencies.[64] Moreover, as will be discussed in the next subsection, the case offered a legal basis for other Chinese companies to challenge the legality of CFIUS actions.

6.2.2 Huawei

Sany is certainly not the only Chinese MNC that felt prejudiced against by the US government. Huawei, another China-headquartered MNC with long-term US investments, better exemplifies the torturous experience of being caught in the crossfire of the superpower rivalry. As previously discussed, the company established its North American headquarters as early as 2001, and at one time had over a thousand US

[61] *Id.*, at 325.

[62] *Id.*

[63] Paul Welitzkin, *Lawsuit Settlement Seen as Unlikely to Affect CFIUS*, China Daily (November 11, 2015), usa.chinadaily.com.cn/epaper/2015-11/06/content_22387282.htm.

[64] Ji Li & Ruonan Tang, *Superpower Rivalry and the "Modernization" of Foreign Investment Risk Review*, 2023 U. Ill. L. Rev. 461, 479 (2023).

employees. Huawei was fully committed to expand in the US market, "no matter how long it takes."[65]

Like many other Chinese investors, Huawei sought to grow its US operations by acquiring local businesses and assets. However, its efforts were repeatedly obstructed by CFIUS. In 2008, Huawei partnered with Bain Capital to purchase 3Com, a US network security company. To allay potential US national security concerns, Huawei agreed to take less than 20 percent of the target company. Still, CFIUS objected to the deal, citing Huawei's national security risk. In 2010, Huawei completed a two-million-dollar acquisition of assets and employees from 3Leaf Systems, a firm specializing in server technology. Based on advice from its US lawyer, Huawei did not file a CFIUS notice, as it had acquired assets rather than a US business. However, CFIUS intervened again and instructed Huawei to divest. While Huawei initially pushed back by demanding a presidential decision on the matter, it ultimately decided to comply.[66]

As noted in Chapter 5, Huawei halted its US expansion plan after the House Permanent Select Committee on Intelligence released a report citing potential counterintelligence and security threats posed by Huawei's access to US telecommunications systems. Despite the setback, Huawei maintained a sizable presence in the US market and continued to invest in research and development and to serve several niche markets. Unlike Sany, Huawei did not litigate against the unfavorable CFIUS decisions or any other allegedly unfair treatment by US government agencies, due to fear of possible government retaliation that factored into in the decision-making process at the headquarters.[67] Instead, Huawei mainly relied on lobbyists and management localization to address political and regulatory risks.

However, the abrupt deterioration of US–China relations following the election of President Donald Trump in 2016 brought Huawei to the center of the geopolitical rivalry. In recent years, the US government has taken a myriad of actions aimed at ultimately "removing Huawei equipment from domestic and international telecommunications

[65] Shayndi Raice, *Small Deal Brings Scrutiny to Huawei*, Wall Street J. (November 18, 2010), www.wsj.com/articles/SB10001424052748703374304575622884122938068.

[66] *Huawei Backs Away from 3Leaf Acquisition*, Reuters (February 19, 2011), www.reuters.com/article/us-huawei-3leaf/huawei-backs-away-from-3leaf-acquisition-idUSTRE71I38920110219.

[67] William B. Plummer, Huidu – Inside Huawei 76 (2018).

networks."[68] These concrete measures have included "pursuing criminal charges against Huawei and its Chief Financial Officer, issuing visa restrictions for Huawei employees, banning trade in Huawei securities, and engaging in international efforts to convince foreign countries to ban Huawei from their networks."[69] As discussed in Chapter 5, the Trump administration began to sanction Huawei, prohibiting US companies from selling products or services to the Chinese company. The US government later tightened the rule and barred any company that uses American technology from trading with Huawei, thereby cutting off its supply of advanced chips.

Faced with this existential threat, Huawei's founder, Ren Zhengfei, assumed a more active role in designing and implementing counteractions. Instead of delegating to the local managers, Ren "enlisted an inner circle of Huawei board members to coordinate strategy," including the chief legal officer who, as noted in Chapter 5, is a self-taught Chinese intellectual property lawyer with no US legal training.[70] Recognizing the failure of the previous strategies that better fitted the home-state institutional context, Ren emphasized that "the right way forward" was to "adopt a Western mind-set to solve the issues we face in Western markets."[71] Litigation was considered a major countermeasure. Since 2020, Huawei has filed several lawsuits in US courts challenging various governmental actions by both the executive and legislative branches. The Chinese headquarters has always been in the backseat, making strategic decisions for the US affiliates, and the same top-down control permeated the decisions concerning US litigation to counter US government actions that threatened the entire business of the Chinese MNC.

One of Huawei's recent lawsuits illustrates its interactions with US government agencies. In 2017, Huawei shipped several pieces of equipment to California for certification testing. After testing, officials of the Department of Commerce (DOC) seized the equipment. At the agency's request, Huawei provided certain information for the

[68] Stephen P. Mulligan & Chris D. Linebaugh, Cong. Rsch. Serv., R46693, Huawei and U.S. Law 2 (2021), https://crsreports.congress.gov/product/pdf/R/R46693.

[69] *Id.*

[70] Dan Strumpf, *Huawei Founder Ren Zhengfei Takes Off the Gloves in Fight Against U.S.*, Wall Street J. (June 6, 2020), www.wsj.com/articles/huawei-founder-ren-zhengfei-takes-off-the-gloves-in-fight-against-u-s-11591416028.

[71] *Id.*

agency to investigate possible violations of the Export Administration Regulations (EAR) and requested that the agency make a determination and return the equipment if no violation was found. According to the DOC, "the normal processing time for such request is fewer than 45 days,"[72] yet it took no action for more than twenty months. After Huawei filed a lawsuit claiming that, among others, the agency's actions had violated the APA, the DOC agreed to release the equipment. Although the DOC provided neither "any basis for its decision to detain the equipment," nor any explanation for the extended delay, Huawei voluntarily had the case dismissed after receiving its equipment.[73]

Another high-profile lawsuit filed by Huawei challenged the constitutionality of Section 889 of the 2019 National Defense Authorization Act (NDAA) enacted by Congress, prohibiting any purchase by US government agencies of products from Huawei and working with other parties that use Huawei products or services. Huawei argued that Section 889 violates the Bill of Attainder Clause and the Due Process Clause of the Constitution. In its announcement of the action, Huawei emphasized that the US Congress did not afford it "the opportunity to defend itself," and it was "*compelled* to take this legal action *as a last resort*"[74] [emphasis added]. However, the District Court rejected the constitutional challenge, concluding that Congress acted within its powers by inserting the restriction in the NDAA.[75]

In late 2019, Huawei filed another lawsuit in the US Court of Appeals for the Fifth Circuit, seeking a judicial review of a rule and order by the Federal Communications Commission (FCC) that designated the company as a national security threat and prohibited American telecommunications operators from purchasing Huawei equipment or services.[76] The complaint alleged that the FCC order, among others, exceeded the agency's statutory authority, was arbitrary,

72 Huawei Technologies USA, Inc. v. U.S. Department of Commerce (D.C. Dist. June 21, 2019).

73 Huawei Technologies USA, Inc. v. U.S. Department of Commerce (D.C. Dist. Notice of voluntary dismissal filed on September 9, 2019).

74 *Why Has Huawei Filed a Lawsuit Against the US Government?* www.huawei.com/us/facts/question-answer/why-has-huawei-filed-a-lawsuit-against-the-us-government.

75 Huawei Technologies USA, Inc. v. U.S. Department of Commerce (D.C. Dist., 2019).

76 Huawei Technologies USA Inc. v. Federal Communications Commission (5th Cir. 2021).

capricious, and an abuse of discretion under the APA, and "violated the Constitution's Appointments Clause and statutory and constitutional due process protections."[77] In June 2021, the Fifth Circuit denied Huawei's petition for review. The court found that the FCC had acted within its broad Congress-granted authority and had expertise to make judgments about national security risks to the nation's telecom networks.[78] In summary, Huawei's lawsuits against the US government have largely been unsuccessful.

6.2.3 TikTok

In many ways, TikTok can serve as a poster child of how foreign investors should adapt to a host-country market. The founder of ByteDance, TikTok's Chinese parent, deliberately distanced the company from political matters.[79] Following the crackdown on Hong Kong's democratic movement, TikTok was among the first companies with direct ties to China to publicly exit Hong Kong.[80] To demonstrate its commitment to the US market, the company once appointed a former Disney executive to lead TikTok's global business.[81] In fact, at one point, "key personnel responsible for TikTok, including its CEO, Global Chief Security Officer, and General Counsel," were "all Americans based in the United States."[82] Also, to address potential data security concerns, TikTok stored its US user data "on servers located in the United States and Singapore."[83]

However, as one of the most successful Chinese-invested firms, TikTok found itself an unfortunate pawn in the great power game. On August 6, 2020, President Trump declared TikTok a risk to US national security, citing concerns that its China-based owner, ByteDance, could be manipulated by the Chinese government and grant it access to TikTok's US user data. Trump directed the Secretary of Commerce

[77] *Id.*

[78] *Id.*

[79] Michael Schuman, *Why America Is Afraid of TikTok*, ATLANTIC (July 30, 2020), www.theatlantic.com/international/archive/2020/07/tiktok-ban-china-america/614725/.

[80] Echo Wang, *TikTok Says It Will Exit Hong Kong Market Within Days*, REUTERS (July 6, 2020), www.reuters.com/article/us-tiktok-hong-kong-exclusive-idUSKBN2480AD.

[81] Brooks Barnes & Jack Nicas, *Disney's Head of Streaming Is New TikTok C.E.O.*, N.Y. TIMES (May 18, 2020), www.nytimes.com/2020/05/18/business/media/tiktok-ceo-kevin-mayer.html.

[82] *Why We Are Suing the Administration*, TIKTOK NEWSROOM (August 24, 2020), newsroom.tiktok.com/en-us/tiktok-files-lawsuit.

[83] *Id.*

to "identify a list of prohibited transactions with 'ByteDance … or its subsidiaries,' including TikTok,"[84] and ordered ByteDance to divest itself of TikTok's US operations by November 12, 2020, as approved by CFIUS.[85] In response to this existential threat, key US investors of TikTok attempted to broker an equity sale from its Chinese parent, ByteDance, to US companies.[86] However, during the negotiations, the Chinese government issued new restrictions on the export of artificial intelligence technology, effectively preventing ByteDance from selling its proprietary algorithms to any potential US buyer.[87]

Caught in the political vendetta between the United States and China and left with few other options, TikTok resorted to legal action after some initial hesitation.[88] In August 2020, shortly after the executive orders were issued, TikTok and its Chinese parent ByteDance filed a lawsuit in the Federal District Court in Central California, seeking a declaratory judgment that the executive order was unlawful and unconstitutional, as well as a judicial order invalidating it and enjoining its implementation.[89] The case, however, was not fully litigated. TikTok and ByteDance withdrew the action on September 18, 2020, by that time neither Trump nor the DOC had answered the complaint.[90] On that same day, the Secretary of Commerce published the prohibited transactions, and TikTok and ByteDance initiated an action in the D.C. District Court, alleging that, among others, the August 6 executive order was unconstitutional and ultra vires, and that the subsequent identification by the DOC of the prohibited transactions violated the APA. The plaintiffs sought a judicial order vacating the prohibitions, invalidating the executive order, and enjoining their

[84] TikTok Inc. and ByteDance Ltd. v. Trump (D.C. Dist. Ct.) (memorandum opinion, December 7, 2020).

[85] *Id.*

[86] Rolfe Winkler, et al., *General Atlantic, Sequoia Capital Are Key Drivers in Oracle Bid for TikTok*, WALL STREET J. (August 24, 2020), www.wsj.com/articles/general-atlantic-sequoia-capital-are-key-drivers-in-oracle-bid-for-tiktok-11598310734.

[87] Liza Lin, et al., *TikTok Deal Talks Are Snarled over Fate of App's Algorithms*, WALL STREET J. (September 2, 2020), www.wsj.com/articles/tiktok-deal-talks-are-snarled-over-fate-of-apps-algorithms-11598995674.

[88] Du Zhihang & Guan Cong, *TikTok Bu Ting Bu* [*TikTok Not To Stop*], CAIXIN WEEKLY (January 4, 2021), http://weekly.caixin.com/2021-01-02/101645960.html.

[89] Complaint filed by TikTok Inc. and ByteDance Ltd. against Donald Trump (Dist. Central CA), August 24, 2020.

[90] TikTok Inc. & ByteDance Ltd. v. Donald Trump (Dist. Central CA) (Plaintiffs' notice of voluntary dismissal without prejudice filed on September 20, 2020).

implementation.[91] Judge Nichols, who was nominated by President Trump, issued a preliminary injunction against the prohibitions that "threatened to irreparably harm the plaintiffs by banning TikTok from all US app stores."[92]

In addition to confronting the Trump administration directly, TikTok also mobilized its US users to challenge the ban in federal courts. It coordinated the litigation by several TikTok stars with large fan bases,[93] who filed a case in a federal District Court in Pennsylvania. They alleged that the TikTok ban violated the First Amendment and the International Emergency Economic Powers Act (IEEPA) by regulating informational materials.[94] On October 30, 2020, that court preliminarily enjoined all the prohibitions enumerated by the DOC. On November 12, 2020, the government appealed that injunction to the Third Circuit,[95] and soon thereafter the Secretary of Commerce agreed to comply with that injunction and suspend the enforcement of the TikTok prohibitions, "pending further legal developments."[96]

The parallel case in the D.C. District Court also resulted in favor of TikTok and ByteDance. Acknowledging the injunction issued by the court in Pennsylvania, Judge Nichols enjoined the rest of the prohibitions, finding that the plaintiffs "are likely to succeed on their IEEPA and APA claims," and the prohibitions, if enforced, would cause them irreparable harm.[97] In response, the US government appealed to the D.C. Circuit Court to vacate the injunction.[98]

TikTok and ByteDance also challenged CFIUS in the D.C. Circuit Court. They filed a petition on November 10, 2020 for judicial review of the presidential order regarding the acquisition of Musical.ly and "the related action of CFIUS, including its determination to reject

[91] Complaint filed by TikTok Inc. and ByteDance Ltd. against Donald Trump and the Department of Commerce (D.C. Dist. Ct.), September 18, 2020.

[92] TikTok Inc. and ByteDance Ltd. v. Donald Trump (D.C. Dist. Ct.) (memorandum opinion, December 7, 2020).

[93] Georgia Wells, *TikTok Stars Proved Key in Strategy to Fight U.S. Ban*, Wall Street J. (November 26, 2020), www.wsj.com/articles/how-three-tiktok-stars-beat-back-u-s-plans-to-ban-the-app-11606418513.

[94] Marland v. Trump, 2020 WL 6381397, at *14–15 (E.D. Pa. October 30, 2020).

[95] Notice of Appeal, ECF No. 55 (November 12, 2020); Marland v. Trump, No. 20-3322, ECF No. 1 (3d Cir. November 12, 2020).

[96] 85 Fed. Reg. 73191 (November 17, 2020).

[97] *Trump* (D.C. Dist. Ct.) (memorandum opinion, December 7, 2020).

[98] Appellate brief filed on behalf of the U.S. Government, Donald Trump v. TikTok Inc. and ByteDance Ltd. (January 15, 2021).

mitigation, truncate its review and investigation, and refer the matter to the president."[99] The plaintiffs claimed that the divestment order and CFIUS actions were ultra vires and violated the Due Process Clause and the APA, and amounted to unlawful taking under the Fifth Amendment.[100]

Interestingly, in their brief, TikTok and ByteDance relied on the ruling in *Ralls*, which imposes an obligation on CFIUS to inform the foreign investor whose acquisition was rejected of "the unclassified basis of its findings" and to offer the investor "the opportunity to respond before determining whether to issue a report to the President."[101] TikTok and ByteDance made it very clear that they would not have sought judicial intervention but for the divestment mandate that left them with no other options. And despite the petition, they "remain committed to reaching a negotiated mitigation solution with CFIUS satisfying its national security concerns."[102]

The Chinese company's US legal strategies proved to be highly successful, and after the courts enjoined the enforcement of the Trump ban, President Biden revoked it.[103] Hence, the US government voluntarily dismissed the appeal regarding the District Court's preliminary injunction.[104] Meanwhile, the D.C. Circuit Court held the case against CFIUS in abeyance, as the leadership at each of the constituting CFIUS agencies changed after Biden's election and, at the time of writing, negotiations were still ongoing to "determine whether the case may be resolved by mutual agreement."[105]

6.2.4 China Telecom

China Telecommunications Corporation (China Telecom) is one of the largest Chinese state-owned enterprises (SOEs) supervised by the State-Owned Assets Supervision and Administration Commission (SASAC) and one of the three dominant players in the sector of telecommunications. Founded in 2000, China Telecom has grown to

99 Petition for review filed by TikTok and ByteDance on November 10, 2020 (D.C. Cir. Ct.).

100 *Id.*

101 *Id.*

102 *Id.*

103 Exec. Order No. 14034, *Protecting United States Persons' Sensitive Data from Foreign Adversaries* (June 9, 2021).

104 Unopposed motion to voluntarily dismiss appeal, TikTok Inc. v. Joseph Biden (July 12, 2021).

105 Status report, TikTok Inc., et al., v. CFIUS (June 21, 2021).

become the world's largest fixed line and broadband operator,[106] with $71.5 billion in revenue and 400,945 employees worldwide. In 2021, it was ranked 126th on the Fortune Global 500 list.[107]

Since its inception, China Telecom has expressed interest in the US market, establishing a North American representative office in California in 2000.[108] In 2002, the US subsidiary was incorporated as China Telecom Americas and was licensed by the FCC to provide telecommunications services in the US market. That same year, China Telecom launched an initial public offering in the United States and became one of the first Chinese SOEs to list on a foreign securities exchange.[109] By 2005, China Telecom Americas had completed its nationwide telecom network in the United States, and since then, it has recorded an annual growth rate of 68 percent, making it the largest subsidiary of the state-owned Chinese company.[110]

In many ways the success of China Telecom Americas, owned by a central-level Chinese SOE in a sensitive sector, epitomized the trust and spirit of cooperation in US–China relations before the Trump presidency. However, as bilateral relations deteriorated, China Telecom Americas was among the first to suffer. The crisis began to brew in May 2019 when the FCC unanimously rejected the license application of China Mobile, another Chinese state-owned telecommunications company, to provide services in the US market. Among other reasons, the agency cited the risk of the Chinese government controlling the SOE to conduct espionage in the United States.[111] One of the commissioners noted that the same risk should apply to other Chinese firms in the same sector and suggested a review and revocation of approved licenses, including the one for China Telecom Americas. The US Justice Department and several other federal agencies made similar recommendations.

106 *Key Facts of China Telecom*, official website of China Telecom Americas, www.ctamericas.com/company/company-overview/.

107 *Global 500: China Telecommunications*, fortune.com/company/china-telecommunications/global500/.

108 *History of China Telecom Americas*, at www.ctamericas.com/company/history/.

109 Hudson Lockett & Tabby Kinder, *China Telecom Heads for $8.4Bn Shanghai Share Sale after US Ban*, Financial Times (July 23, 2021), at www.ft.com/content/6826e3e6-a5f9-4750-8cb6-1571aecf1f9f.

110 *History of China Telecom Americas*, *supra* note 108.

111 David Shepardson, *FCC Begins Process of Halting China Telecom U.S. Operations*, Reuters (December 10, 2020), www.reuters.com/article/usa-china-tech-idUSKBN28K2ER.

In December 2020, the FCC launched a revocation proceeding and concluded it with an order for China Telecom Americas to discontinue its US operations within sixty days. When the FCC commenced the revocation proceedings, China Telecom Americas filed a lawsuit in the Fourth Circuit, alleging that the agency's denial of a hearing was "arbitrary and capricious" and a violation of its due process rights. However, the court dismissed the suit for lack of jurisdiction since the FCC's proceedings were not final and thus not yet reviewable.[112]

During the proceedings, China Telecom Americas submitted extensive evidence about its independent operations in the United States and its trustworthiness. It also requested an evidentiary hearing, which the FCC denied for alleged lack of "substantial and material fact-based questions." Facing the immediate risk of losing all its US operations and having exhausted alternative remedies such as diplomatic assistance,[113] China Telecom Americas filed a complaint with the D.C. Circuit Court, seeking judicial review of the FCC order revoking its authorization to operate and an emergency stay of the order pending the review. The complaint alleged that the FCC violated the APA and its due process rights by refusing to hold a public hearing, and that its decision was arbitrary and capricious. The complaint also claimed that the commissioners failed to act impartially, as evidenced by their publicly expressed desire to terminate the Chinese firm's right to operate in the US market. However, the D.C. Circuit promptly sided with the FCC.[114]

The US government's tough approach toward China Telecom was not limited to the revocation of its license to provide telecommunications services. Prior to that, President Trump had issued an executive order that forced the delisting of several Chinese companies whose securities were traded on US securities markets. As one of the targeted firms, China Telecom was delisted from the New York Stock Exchange. Because the companies are also listed in Hong Kong, the delisting has had little financial ramifications since investors can simply swap their equity interests traded on the US exchange for shares traded in Hong Kong. While China Telecom petitioned the US exchange to

[112] China Telecom (Ams.) Corp. v. FCC, 2021 U.S. App. LEXIS 13848.

[113] *Zhongguo Shangwu Bu: Zhongfang Jiu Meiguo Chexiao Zhongguo Dianxin Meizhou Gongsi Paizhao xiang Meifang Tichu Yanzheng Jiaoshe* [*Ministry of Commerce of China: China Lodged Solemn Representations with the United States over the Revocation of the License of China Telecom Americas*], Reuters (October 28, 2021), https://cn.reuters.com/article/china-telecom-us-license-1028-idCNKBS2HI0ZY.

[114] *FCC*, 2021 U.S. App.

reconsider the order for delisting, it did not challenge the delisting in a US court.[115]

To summarize, the four prominent Chinese companies differ in many key aspects, such as the duration of their US investment, size of their US business, sector of investment, and ownership type of the investors. However, a common theme can be detected. In all four cases, the Chinese companies used litigation against the US government as a last resort, seeking legal recourse only when substantial interests were at stake. Nonetheless, significant inter-firm variations exist in their attitudes toward and use of US litigation against perceived host-state government bias. Huawei and Sany responded differently to alleged arbitrary intervention by CFIUS at around the same time (i.e., the order for Ralls to unwind the wind farm deal and the order for Huawei to divest from 3Leaf). In both cases the transaction had been consummated before the Chinese investor was ordered to divest. Sany filed a lawsuit against CFIUS and President Obama, despite professional legal advice against doing so, while Huawei reluctantly complied with the agency order after a transient show of resistance.[116] Moreover, the case studies show little evidence that ownership type of Chinese investors makes a significant difference, as both Huawei and China Telecom Americas, despite their different ownership structures, sued the FCC when the agency excluded them from the US market. Section 6.3 will analyze the insights from the case studies with more expansive survey data.

6.3 LITIGATION BY CHINESE COMPANIES AGAINST THE US GOVERNMENT

The four case studies may convey the impression that Chinese investors find themselves frequently ensnared in the US–China rivalry and often resort to legal action within the United States to safeguard their interests. However, such high-profile lawsuits do not necessarily reflect the prevailing attitudes and actions of Chinese companies when confronted with perceived mistreatment by the host-state government. In fact, according to the CGCC survey conducted in 2020,

[115] Chong Koh Ping & Alexander Osipovich, *NYSE to Delist Chinese Telecom Carriers After Rejecting Appeals*, Wall Street J. (May 7, 2021), www.wsj.com/articles/nyse-to-delist-chinese-telecoms-carriers-after-rejecting-appeals-11620394719.

[116] *Huawei Resisting Calls to Divest 3Leaf*, Reuters (February 14, 2011), www.reuters.com/article/huawei-3leaf/huawei-resisting-calls-to-divest-3leaf-idINN1417564220110215.

when US–China relations were arguably at their lowest point in four decades, only 40 percent of the Chinese companies reported experiencing unfair government treatment in the United States. While this percentage is disconcertingly high, it still constitutes a minority of Chinese companies with direct investments in the United States. For the majority of such firms, mistreatment by the host-state government remains only a potential threat.

It is important to note that self-selection bias may also distort the survey results, particularly in the context of Chinese companies operating in the United States. Presumably, those that have experienced mistreatment by the US government are more likely to exit the US market, leaving behind Chinese investors who may be either excessively optimistic or relatively insulated from escalating geopolitical risks. This self-selection dynamic could yield a low percentage of respondents reporting unfair treatment by the host-state government.

To better understand Chinese companies' litigation preferences when treated unfairly by a US government body, I incorporated a generic hypothetical question in the survey questionnaires administered from 2014 to 2017. This question inquired about the potential coping strategies Chinese companies would contemplate *if* subjected to unjust treatment by a US government entity, with legal recourse being one of the available options. Utilizing this data, the first portion of this section will scrutinize the revealed preferences of Chinese companies concerning the prospect of suing the US government. To further examine inter-company variations in litigation preferences, this analysis will employ the 2017 survey data, when selection bias was less of a concern, as the Trump administration had not yet implemented its anti-China policies. The second part of this section will briefly assess a limited dataset derived from the 2022 survey that pertains to the actual coping measures Chinese investors adopted in response to inequitable treatment by US regulatory agencies, with a particular analytical emphasis on litigation.

6.3.1 Legal Actions against US Government Mistreatment

In contrast to China, the United States features formal legal institutions that may provide foreign investors with a viable recourse against government mistreatment, and US social norms impose no constraints on pursuing legal action against government agencies. Consequently, to what extent would Chinese companies consider litigation when they perceive unfair treatment by the host state? According to the survey

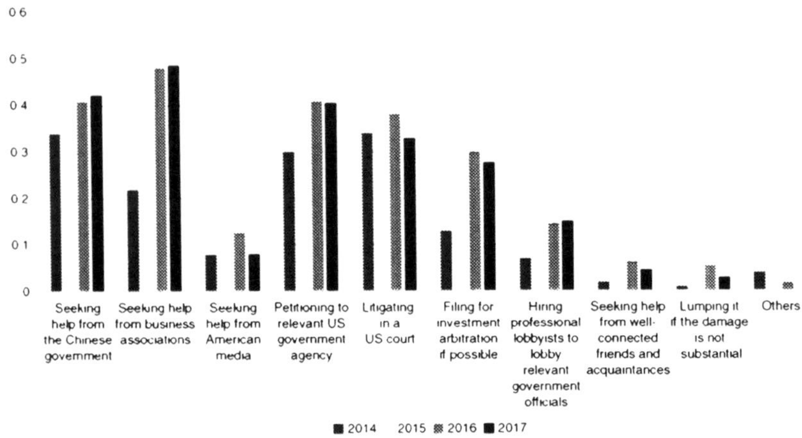

Figure 6.1 Contemplated reactions to perceived unfair treatment by US government [Survey question: What actions would your company consider taking if treated unfairly by a US government body? (multiple choices allowed)]
Note: 70 responses to the question in the 2014 survey; 89 responses to the question in the 2015 survey; 110 responses to the question in the 2016 survey; 173 responses to the question in the 2017 survey.

data (see Figure 6.1), about 30 to 40 percent of the Chinese investors would contemplate taking legal action.

Under the principle of separation of powers, a primary function of the US judiciary is to safeguard against abuses by the executive and legislative branches. However, US judges typically exercise considerable caution and deference in reviewing administrative actions,[117] thereby raising the bar for those seeking to challenge a US government body in court. While Chinese managers may be deterred in actual cases, their intuitive reaction to hypothetical official mistreatment in the United States demonstrates confidence in the host-country judiciary. Indeed, according to a recent study, Chinese investors hold key US institutions that facilitate free market capitalism in high regard, including the judicial system,[118] which they perceive to be both independent and impartial.[119] This adaptation to the host-state institutional environment probably explains why 30 to 40 percent of the Chinese managers, while generally averse to the notion of suing government officials in their home state, would

[117] Valley Forge Christian Coll. v. Americans United for Separation of Church & State, Inc., 454 U.S. 464, 474 (1982).
[118] Li, *supra*, note 2.
[119] *Id.*, at 73.

consider challenging the US government in court.[120] Equally intriguing is the question concerning the remaining 60 to 70 percent who would mentally rule out litigation if treated unfairly by a US government body. What factors may explain the inter-company variations?

To investigate the question, I ran a series of statistical tests using the 2017 survey data. The selection is for two reasons. First, the 2017 sample is larger than those in the other years in which the same question was posed.[121] Second, Chinese investment in the United States was expanding in 2017, with few, if any, firms exiting prior to the abrupt downturn of US–China relations that occurred following Trump's election. Consequently, for testing the hypotheses of this chapter, the 2017 data is less distorted by the selection effect lurking behind the more recent data. To perform the statistical tests, I created a dummy dependent variable that equals one if a survey respondent selected "litigating in a US court" as a potential reaction to "unfair" government treatment, and zero otherwise. Below is a list of factors that might be associated with this litigation preference (see Table 6.2 in the Appendix for the summary statistics).

6.3.1.1 *Factors Potentially Associated with the Litigation Preference*

State ownership. Though the case studies have indicated otherwise, state ownership of Chinese investors could play a role in their varying preferences to pursue legal action against government officials in the United States. As noted, due to growing geopolitical tensions, Chinese SOEs are often targeted in US administrative and legislative actions; however, it remains unclear how they might respond with lawsuits. On the one hand, Chinese SOEs exercise greater control over their overseas investments,[122] including decisions regarding US litigation, as demonstrated in Chapter 4. This rigid hierarchical control could serve as a conduit for home-state institutional influence over litigation preferences. Within the home-state context, executives of Chinese SOEs share a sense of being an integral part of the state apparatus, which may militate against administrative litigation. However, when the alleged wrongdoer is a foreign government locked in a fierce conflict with China, pressing legal charges against it may earn Chinese managers political credit back home. Also, as previously noted, state-owned

[120] Li, *supra* note 22, at 815.

[121] Though the question was asked in the 2019 survey, for reasons unrelated to the research, the choice litigation was excluded.

[122] Li, *supra* note 2.

Chinese firms may discount the cost of litigation due to the multi-agency problem. Overall, a clear unidirectional hypothesis regarding the propensity of Chinese state-owned companies to sue the US government is lacking. Additionally, there is no evidence to suggest that US courts discriminate based on a corporate party's ownership type,[123] and Chinese investors, regardless of their ownership structure, have expressed confidence in the US judiciary.[124] To test the indeterminate effects of state ownership, I propose a working hypothesis that state-owned Chinese companies are more likely to contemplate litigation if mistreated by the US government.[125]

Cultural difference. In China, suing the government became legally permissible only in the late 1980s, and the process is shaped by a set of formal and informal institutions that regulate business-state relations and dispute resolution.[126] Particularly, as discussed earlier, Chinese social norms attach complex but generally derogatory meanings to suing government officials, and depending on the context, such a lawsuit might be interpreted as an insult to the defendant or a sign of plaintiff's incompetence. In contrast, challenging government agencies in court carries no social stigma in the United States. Comparing data between the two countries illuminates the significant institutional difference. While hundreds of thousands of US taxpayers initiate legal proceedings against federal and state tax agencies annually without exhibiting serious concern about government retaliation or judicial bias, only a few hundred lawsuits are filed each year against tax agencies in China, most of which occur in end-game scenarios where substantial interests are at stake, and the plaintiff anticipates no future interactions with the defendant tax agent following the lawsuit.[127] To evaluate possible effects of the cultural and normative differences, I again employ the measure of varying cultural challenges facing Chinese companies in

[123] *See, e.g.*, Kimberly A. Moore, *Xenophobia in American Courts*, 97 Nw.U. L. Rev. 1497 (2002); Kevin M. Clermont & Theodore Eisenberg, *Xenophilia or Xenophobia in US Courts? Before and After 9/11*, 4 J. Empirical Legal Stud. 441 (2007).

[124] Li, *supra* note 2, at 97.

[125] I use the same dummy variable adopted in prior chapters, i.e., the dummy takes the value of one if a Chinese government entity owns more than 50 percent of a Chinese investor's equity interest, and zero otherwise. Dirk Holtbruegge, *Political Strategies of Chinese Firms in Germany: An Institutionalist Perspective*, 13 Int'l J. Emerging Markets 1438 (2018).

[126] Li, *supra* note 22.

[127] Li, *supra* note 29.

the United States.[128] Presumably, all else being equal, Chinese companies that are more rooted in their home-state normative environment would be less inclined to consider litigating against the US government.

Size of US investment. The financial resources available to a Chinese company could influence its propensity to pursue legal action against the US government. While US courts are relatively accessible to all with justiciable claims, litigation in the United States can be costly, particularly when it involves government entities. As the case studies indicated, only sizable Chinese companies may possess the financial means to mount a successful legal challenge against perceived mistreatment by US officials.[129] Thus, one might observe a positive correlation between the litigation preference and the size of a Chinese company's US operations.

Listing status. The listing status of a Chinese investor may also influence its inclination to litigate against the host-state government for mistreatment. First, as previously discussed, the variable may serve as an alternative proxy for the investor's resources. Publicly traded Chinese companies, due to their ability to raise capital, are better equipped to mount an effective legal challenge against the US government. Second, all else being equal, publicly traded companies tend to be more transparent, and their management may be less concerned about public scrutiny resulting from litigation against the US government. Third, initiating legal proceedings against a US government body could significantly impact the stock price of a publicly traded company, and therefore, a listed Chinese company may be more hesitant to consider such a remedy. These hypotheses suggest disparate associations between a Chinese company's listing status and its inclination to sue a US government entity.

In-house legal capacity. As shown in Chapters 4 and 5, the presence of professional US legal managers alters the allocation of decision-making power concerning US litigation and impacts the litigation experiences of Chinese companies. It is therefore plausible that this same factor may influence the propensity to sue the US government. On the other hand, given that conflicts with US government agencies are relatively rare but highly consequential, US in-house counsel, who typically

[128] As discussed in prior chapters, I created a dummy that equals one if a Chinese responding firm reported that cultural differences pose a major challenge to its US business, and zero if otherwise.

[129] As in prior chapters, I used the US revenue of a Chinese MNC's US subunit as the primary proxy of its resources.

handle routine corporate legal matters, may have only a marginal role in resolving such disputes. As illustrated by the Huawei case, the headquarters formulated its litigation strategies against the US government after the decision to seek legal recourse. Moreover, testing the variable in this context can further enrich our understanding of in-house legal management at Chinese MNCs.[130]

Sectoral regulation. In heavily regulated sectors, Chinese companies interact more frequently with US officials, often on matters vital to the companies. These interactions may give rise to two divergent hypotheses. On the one hand, repeated interactions may facilitate dispute resolution and the building of trust, both of which would generally prevent litigation. On the other hand, frequent interactions may amplify the damages of official bias, thus increasing the inclination to litigate in US courts.[131]

Investment duration. The duration of a Chinese company's operations within the US institutional context may serve as a second-order indicator of the degree of normative adaptation. Those companies that entered the US market earlier may have internalized host-state norms and be less apprehensive about "offending" the host-state government or facing retaliation. In addition, as mentioned in previous chapters, investment duration is an important control variable that may correlate with other factors, such as state ownership and size of US investment.[132]

130 To test the indeterminate effect, I include the dummy variable that equals one if a Chinese firm has employed an in-house legal manager licensed to practice US law and zero otherwise.

131 I use the dummy variable described in prior chapters that analyzed the 2017 survey data. It equals one if a responding firm operated in eight heavily regulated sectors either at the federal level or at the state or local level, or both: mining, utilities, construction, information, finance and insurance, real estate development and rental, health care, and public administration, and zero otherwise. Some may not consider real estate and rental industry as heavily regulated. I create an alternative dummy that excludes that sector and rerun all the tests using the alternative dummy. All the regression results remain largely the same.

132 A control is added to robustness tests to address possible respondent bias. Though the survey questionnaire inquired about the Chinese firms' contemplated reactions to unfair government treatment, the data may nonetheless reflect the preferences of the individual survey respondents. Although the survey questions were written in Chinese and targeted at senior executives of the CGCC member companies, producing a sample of similar national background, stature, and scope of management experiences, their tenure in the United States may vary significantly. Those who relocated to the United States years ago may have adapted to the host-country

US market importance. Not all Chinese companies prioritize the US market; those that regard it as more important may have strong incentives to adapt. For instance, a US general counsel for a Chinese company observed that her employer derived greater profits from the US market than from the home market, leading the headquarters to fully commit to expanding in the United States; and the managers respected her professional opinions.[133] However, as shown in previous chapters and exemplified by the Huawei case, the importance of the US market might also induce heightened headquarters control that impedes local adaptation. Moreover, a Chinese company that deems the US market crucial may not casually exercise the exit option even if mistreated by the US government. In such a situation, litigation against the government wrongdoer might be justified for the long-term benefits, as illustrated by the decision of Sany's managers to challenge the CFIUS decision.[134]

6.3.1.2 *Analysis of Test Results*

The test results indicate that publicly traded Chinese investors are more inclined to litigate over US government mistreatment (see Table 6.3 in the Appendix).[135] This finding may be attributed to the greater transparency of listed companies. In the context of superpower rivalry, listed Chinese companies may have less to fear from the publicity and disclosure arising from legally challenging the US government, as they have been reporting material corporate information pursuant to securities regulations. For example, it is likely easier for such firms to produce evidence of commercially driven corporate governance and transactions to rebuke claims of national security threat or political agency. Conversely, non-listed Chinese firms may prefer alternative dispute

environment. Meanwhile, the tenure may correlate with the other interested variables such as state ownership and investment size. Thus, I add to the robustness tests a control variable measuring the length of the responding manager's stay in the United States. The variable is calculated by subtracting the year when the manager started to work in the United States from 2017, the year of the survey. So, the variable equals zero for those who moved to the United States in 2017. The results from the robustness tests remain largely the same.

133 Interview with general counsel of the US subsidiary of a large Chinese MNC (August 12, 2022).

134 To assess this hypothetical connection, I included in the tests the scale measure of US market importance described in earlier chapters.

135 To test the hypotheses articulated in Subsection 6.3.1.1, I conducted a series of logit regression analyses using a binary dependent variable that measures whether a Chinese company would contemplate pursuing legal relief for US government bias.

resolution for fear that any improper information disclosure may jeopardize their relationship with the home-state government. A former Huawei executive commented on the impossible task of full disclosure for Chinese companies caught in the crossfire of the US–China rivalry.

> Huawei was acting out of fear of going sideways of the Chinese government, of opening up another can of worms. Any information Huawei might provide—however innocent or innocuous, such as the names of the Founder's superiors when in the military—could be considered controlled information by the Chinese government, just as they would have been by the US government.[136]

A lawyer who represents Chinese companies in their dealings with US sanctions alluded to the dual institutional pressure in explaining his clients' reluctance to legally challenge the sanctions in US court. Such litigation would require extensive discovery and public disclosure of corporate information that could implicate the Chinese government in a negative light. The lawyer summed up his clients' fear, stating, "The US government can hurt us [with sanctions], but the Chinese government can destroy us."[137]

Moreover, investment duration is positively associated with the preference to sue. The longer a Chinese company has been operating in the United States, the more likely it is to perceive any unfair US government treatment as unjustified and consider resolving grievances with the host state through legal means. Also, as just noted, Chinese investors long immersed in the US normative environment may have adapted and rationalized legal challenges to official mistreatment. However, the finding is not robust across all model specifications.

None of the other variables is significant. While the limited sample size cautions definitive inference from the null results, three variables deserve further discussion. First, state ownership is insignificant, and given the magnitude of the error term, enlarging the sample size is unlikely to change this result. As noted, the home-state institutions regulating SOEs are highly complex when it comes to litigation against government agencies. This complexity obscures any significant unidirectional association between the ownership structure of a Chinese state-owned investor and its proclivity to sue the US government. Of course, when official bias does occur in the United States against

[136] Plummer, *supra* note 67, at 132.
[137] Interview with a partner of a large US law firm (June 8, 2020).

state-owned Chinese companies, their reactions may very well differ from the privately owned Chinese firms, given the hierarchical corporate control of the former, the severe agency problem, and the geopolitical complexity.

Second, cultural difference is not significant. Although social norms differ greatly between the two countries regarding legal challenges against government entities, suing the US government is a high-stakes decision where cool-headed cost-benefit calculation prevails. As demonstrated by the case studies, all four Chinese companies, despite their differences in connections to the home state, pursued legal strategies when the actions of the US government threatened their key interests. In other words, the high coercive pressure of formal host-state institutions on Chinese companies diminishes or obscures the influence of informal home-state institutions.

Third, internal legal capacity is insignificant. Suing the US government is a serious endeavor; as illustrated by the case studies, the headquarters typically take charge, sidelining US in-house counsel. Based on the preliminary test result, the presence of professional legal managers at the US subsidiaries fails to modify the executives' preferences to mount judicial challenges to US government mistreatment.

To summarize, the statistical tests have identified preliminary associations between the litigation preference and Chinese investors' listing status and investment duration. In contrast, state ownership, cultural difference, and internal legal capacity were found to be insignificant. As demonstrated by the case studies, conflicts with the US government can have substantial impacts on the companies, sometimes even threatening their survival (e.g., Huawei and TikTok). In this issue area, the coercive isomorphic pressure of the host-state institution may eclipse any effect of the ownership-differentiating home-state institutions and the social norms governing litigation against government officials.

6.3.2 Litigation against Unfair Treatment by US Regulatory Agencies

According to the data from 2014 to 2017, litigation is one of the top three non-commercial coping strategies that Chinese companies would consider if mistreated by a government entity in the United States. However, contemplating legal action against the US government cannot be equated to actual litigation, and we know nothing about the likelihood of mistreated Chinese companies pursuing legal recourse in the United States. Moreover, little has been done to explore the use of litigation relative to other coping strategies, including commercial ones. As just mentioned, Chinese investors may adjust their operations in response to host-state mistreatment, such as by exiting the US market. The 2022 survey data shed light on these questions. Again, due to the tensions between the United States and China and the pandemic, the sample size is smaller than in previous years. Moreover, the self-selection dynamic skews the data in such a way that mistreated Chinese investors are likely under-represented in the sample. Consequently, the analysis suggests the lower bound of the actual figure.

Based on the 2022 survey data, around 12 percent of Chinese companies that participated in the survey reported experiencing unfair treatment by a US regulatory agency.[138] It is important to note that the 2022 survey question specifically focused on "US regulatory agency," as opposed to the more general term "US government entity" employed in previous surveys. This change in terminology for the 2022 survey reflects the CGCC's objective of gathering information on Chinese investors' regulatory compliance in the United States. The emphasis on regulatory agencies, combined with the self-selection of Chinese companies (i.e., those most mistreated having exited the US market and thus being absent from the data), results in a relatively low percentage of reported unfair treatment.

Chinese companies encountering unfair treatment by a US regulatory agency are more inclined to adopt coping measures that are commercial in nature (see Table 6.1). The survey data reveals that approximately 36 percent of the responding companies opted to downsize their US business, while an equal percentage chose to alter their business direction in response to the unfair treatment. Taking into account that one out of the eleven respondents decided not to take any action, it is reasonable to draw a preliminary conclusion that, when confronted with mistreatment by a regulatory agency in the United States, Chinese companies are more likely to exit or forbear than to pursue legal resistance.

Nonetheless, litigation stands out as one of the most widely employed strategies, alongside appealing to higher ranking US officials and engaging in lobbying efforts. Specifically, around 27 percent of Chinese companies that have experienced unfair treatment have pursued legal

[138] Among the firms that responded to the 2022 CGCC Survey, ninety-five answered the survey question: "Has your firm ever been treated unfairly by a U.S. regulatory agency?" Twenty respondents skipped the question.

TABLE 6.1 Reactions to unfair US government treatment [survey question: If your firm has been treated unfairly by a US government regulatory agency before, which of the following actions did your firm take? (multiple choices allowed)]

Response options	Responses	
	%	No.
We did not do anything	9.09	1
We downsized our US business	36.36	4
We changed business direction	36.36	4
We negotiated with the agency informally and settled the dispute	0.00	0
We requested a hearing and presented our position	9.09	1
We filed a lawsuit in US court against the agency	**27.27**	**3**
We communicated our complaint to higher ranking officials in the agency	27.27	3
We filed an administrative appeal	18.18	2
We sought help from the Chinese government	0.00	0
We engaged in lobbying	27.27	3
We filed an insurance claim to cover the damage (we had purchased insurance to cover investment risks)	0.00	0
We filed an investment arbitration against the US government (we had taken measures to avail ourselves the option of investment arbitration)	0.00	0
We sought help from US media	9.09	1
We sought help from Chinese media	0.00	0
We sought help from business or industrial associations	18.18	2
We sought help from well-connected friends and acquaintances	9.09	1
	Answered	11

Source: 2022 CGCC Survey.

recourse. This finding aligns with the revealed preference illustrated in Figure 6.1. In contrast, none of the surveyed Chinese companies opted to seek assistance from the Chinese government. This may reflect the increasingly tense US–China rivalry since the 2017 survey was conducted. Prior to that time, the two governments had maintained predominantly cooperative relationships and established mechanisms for addressing significant bilateral issues, such as biased implementation of policies and regulations. Against this backdrop, soliciting diplomatic assistance may have aided mistreated Chinese companies.[139] However, given the current political climate, where a bipartisan consensus perceives China as an existential threat, rational Chinese investors are likely to avoid this strategy. Additionally, the Chinese government has explicitly advised mistreated Chinese companies to exhaust legal remedies before seeking diplomatic intervention.[140] Moreover, the most frequently considered non-commercial response to unfair treatment by the US government, seeking support from business associations, was employed by only about 18 percent of the sample. Although the dataset is limited, the overall analysis suggests that litigation plays a pivotal role in how Chinese companies address disputes with host-state government entities.

6.4 CONCLUSION

As geopolitical tensions between the world's two largest economies escalate, Chinese companies operating in the United States face an increasingly complex and hostile regulatory environment. The confluence of suspicion, prejudice, Sinophobia, political maneuvering, and legitimate policy concerns heightens the probability of conflicts between Chinese companies and US government agencies. Given their limited political leverage, Chinese companies may perceive the US judiciary as the sole viable forum for resolving such conflicts. Some prominent Chinese companies have already tested the robustness and extent of US judicial protection, and their approaches to US courts and legal strategies have reflected subtle dual institutional influence. Nonetheless, all the case studies have yielded the same outcome: Chinese companies will undertake legal actions against US government mistreatment if their vital interests are at stake.

139 Li, *supra* note 1, at 387–88.
140 *Id.*, at 397–98.

The survey data presented in this chapter confirmed a nuanced picture of contemplated reactions to US government mistreatment and revealed significant inter-company variations in the propensity to seek legal relief. Statistical tests have identified associations between the litigation preference and factors such as Chinese companies' listing status and duration of US investment. The high coercive pressure of the host-state institutions governing disputes with US government entities probably outweighs and obscures the influence of Chinese companies' home-state institutions. Amid the ongoing geopolitical confrontation, legal recourse plays a crucial role in protecting Chinese companies against discriminatory actions by the US government.

The findings contribute to several other important literatures and policy debates. First, the tectonic shifts in the global geopolitical order have considerably complicated the business environment for MNCs. To manage heightened political risk, they may increasingly depend on host-state courts, particularly those in developed countries – yet few empirical studies have explored this topic. This chapter narrows that gap with preliminary evidence regarding Chinese companies' variable inclination to combat official mistreatment in US courts. Second, much research has examined the management of US–China relations, which Secretary Blinken has described as "the biggest geopolitical test of the twenty-first century."[141] While US law obviously plays a central role in these intricate relations, the litigation of such laws by Chinese parties has received insufficient scholarly attention. As the case studies have demonstrated (e.g., TikTok), US and Chinese foreign policies, especially those involving transnational economic actors, may not achieve their intended objectives if policymakers fail to consider the potential for judicial intervention sought by these actors. This chapter contributes to the understanding of the adjudicatory aspect of the rapidly evolving and highly impactful US–China relations. Third, as evidenced by the *Ralls* case and the *TikTok* case, lawsuits filed by Chinese companies are incrementally altering US law, and some of the changes have the effect of extending legal protection to politically marginalized groups, and thereby potentially fostering an unintended long-term effect of strengthening the rule of law in the United States.

[141] Lara Jakes & Michael Crowley, *The Crisis That Defined Blinken's First Year*, N.Y. Times (February 6, 2022), www.nytimes.com/2022/02/06/us/politics/antony-blinken.html.

APPENDIX

TABLE 6.2 Summary statistics

Variable	Mean	Standard deviation	Min.	Max.	Number of observations
Size of US investment	2.452	1.610	1	5	188
State ownership (50%)	0.393	0.490	0	1	191
US market importance	2.136	1.021	1	4	198
Listing status	0.484	0.501	0	1	184
Sectoral regulation	0.381	0.487	0	1	210
US in-house legal capacity	0.284	0.452	0	1	190
Duration of US investment	9.239	9.114	0	36	201
Cultural challenge	0.304	0.461	0	1	191
Tenure of respondent	5.561	6.199	0	35	173

Source: 2017 CGCC Survey.

TABLE 6.3 Test results (dependent variable: would contemplate litigation if treated unfairly by a US government body)

Variable	Model 1	Model 2	Model 3	Model 4
State ownership	0.963	1.131	1.174	1.176
	(0.399)	(0.511)	(0.537)	(0.540)
Cultural challenge	1.493	1.379	1.421	1.382
	(0.563)	(0.539)	(0.566)	(0.552)
US in-house legal capacity	1.195	1.078	1.017	1.041
	(0.492)	(0.462)	(0.493)	(0.508)
Investment duration	1.035*	1.037*	1.033	1.037
	(0.021)	(0.021)	(0.024)	(0.025)
Listing status	2.118*	2.332**	2.576**	2.781**
	(0.830)	(0.938)	(1.092)	(1.213)
US market importance		0.789	0.782	0.793
		(0.171)	(0.175)	(0.178)
Size of US investment			0.994	0.989
			(0.148)	(0.148)
Sectoral regulation				0.672
				(0.278)
Constant	0.202***	0.301**	0.298*	0.315*
	(0.074)	(0.164)	(0.180)	(0.191)
Pseudo R^2	0.052	0.063	0.066	0.071
N	149	146	142	142

Note: Data source 2017 CGCC Survey; logit model; odds ratio reported.

CONCLUSION

China's extraordinary economic growth has prompted Chinese businesses to expand globally, and the United States had been a preferred investment destination until Trump's trade war triggered a seemingly unstoppable deterioration of US–China relations. The intensifying superpower rivalry has caught Chinese companies operating in the United States off guard,[1] and some have taken the exit option. However, despite the increasingly adverse business environment, many Chinese companies with long-term US operations are reluctant to withdraw from the lucrative and strategically important market. Some have even expanded their US investments, defying the popular expectation of a swift economic decoupling.[2]

Due to its potential impacts, China's global expansion has spawned many heated policy and scholarly debates,[3] yet its legal aspect has

[1] Ji Li, *In Pursuit of Fairness: How Chinese Multinational Companies React to U.S. Government Bias*, 62 Harv. Int'l L. J. 375, 376 (2021).

[2] *See, e.g.*, Jing Yang, *Fast-Fashion Giant Shein Plans U.S. Expansion as Sales Climb*, Wall Street J. (September 15, 2022), www.wsj.com/articles/fast-fashion-giant-shein-plans-more-u-s-distribution-centers-as-sales-climb-11663236002; Fan Feifei, *Pinduoduo's Temu to Expand in North America*, China Daily (Feb. 14, 2023), www.chinadaily.com.cn/a/202302/14/WS63eadecca31057c47ebae977.html.

[3] *See, e.g.*, Andrew Scobell, *Perception and Misperception in US–China Relations*, 135 Pol. Sci. Q. 637 (2020); Ka Zeng, et al., *Bilateral Tensions, the Trade War, and US–China Trade Relations*, 24 Bus. & Pol. 399 (2022); David Shambaugh, China Goes Global: The Partial Power (2013); Mark Wu, *The "China, Inc." Challenge to Global Trade Governance*, 57 Harv. Int'l L.J. 261 (2016); Deborah Brautigam, The Dragon's Gift: The Real Story of China in Africa

remained under-explored. How do Chinese companies cope with their host-state legal systems, particularly the intricate, stringent US legal system, in their transnational fields? To answer this question, I devised an analytic framework of dual institutional influence. Transnational actors such as multinational companies (MNCs) are subject to pressure from their home-state and host-state institutions that encompass both formal rules and informal social norms. When the institutions are worlds apart, as is the case between China and the United States, the varying balance of the institutional pulls modifies the Chinese companies' internal legal capacity building, their choice of US legal representation, consumption of legal services, and litigation preferences and experiences in US courts. Drawing on multiyear survey data, interviews, and legal archives, this book presented empirically rich illustrations of Chinese companies' adaptation to the US legal system.

Let me highlight some of the key findings. Despite the ever-present legal risks, most Chinese MNCs have not established full-time legal management positions at their US subsidiaries. Among those that have done so, a significant minority have filled the positions with expatriates or laypeople. While cost considerations partially account for this variation, home-state institutional influence is evident, with state-owned Chinese investors being more inclined to rely on expatriates or non professionals to oversee their US legal affairs. Meanwhile, Chinese investors that are culturally adaptive tend to recruit local lawyers as US legal managers. The same for Chinese companies that are sued more frequently in the United States, suggesting that they yield organizationally to coercive host-state institutional pressure.

Regardless of their in-house legal capabilities, Chinese companies have to rely on external lawyers to navigate the complex US legal system. Their US lawyer selection also bears evidence of dual institutional influence. Notably, state-owned Chinese investors are more sensitive to legal fees, attentive to a US lawyer's government background, and receptive to headquarters' recommendations. Meanwhile, Chinese companies facing significant cultural differences opt for US lawyers with a Chinese background, who can more effectively bridge the

(2009); Ping Deng, *The Internationalization of Chinese Firms: A Critical Review and Future Research*, 14 INT'L J. MGMT. REV. 408 (2012); CHING KWAN LEE, THE SPECTER OF GLOBAL CHINA: POLITICS, LABOR, AND FOREIGN INVESTMENT IN AFRICA (2018); Jessica Chen Weiss, *A World Safe for Autocracy: China's Rise and the Future of Global Politics*, 98 FOREIGN AFF. 92 (2019); Matthew S. Erie, *Chinese Law and Development*, 62 HARV. INT'L L.J. 62 (2020).

institutional gaps. However, these preferences will likely have no more than marginal impacts on the mature US legal services market. With limited legal budgets, Chinese companies generally lack bargaining power vis-à-vis US service providers, so the market, not the companies' preferences, sets the conditions for their legal service consumption.

Varying dual institutional influences also shape Chinese companies' dispute resolution and litigation in the United States. Like their local counterparts, many Chinese investors premise litigation decisions on monetized cost-benefit analysis. However, a minority still adhere to home-state norms, preferring settlement over litigation to avoid supposed reputational damage. Yet this normative aversion to litigation fails to reduce the number of lawsuits, for the underlying cultural divergence gives rise to misunderstandings, incorrect expectations, and other sources of high transaction cost that result in more conflicts and lawsuits. Consequently, Chinese companies facing cultural challenges in the United States are more likely to experience US litigation. Their litigation experiences are largely reactive, as Chinese companies tend to appear in US courts as defendants rather than as plaintiffs. Additionally, state-owned Chinese companies, subject to a unique home-state institutional setting, typically centralize decision-making power regarding US litigation and at the same time have to defend more federal lawsuits.

However, the dual institutional influences manifests differently when Chinese companies address disputes with the US government. Caught in between the superpower rivalry, Chinese companies operating in the United States must cope with a heightened risk of being mistreated by US government entities. While case studies indicated varying home-state institutional influence in this context, Chinese companies converge in the pursuit of legal recourse when their substantial business interests are at stake. The coercive pressure from formal US institutions governing high-stakes dispute resolution trumps any influence of relevant home-state institutional factors, such as rules regulating Chinese SOEs and social norms discouraging lawsuits against state actors.

Viewed as a whole, these empirical findings elucidate the varying dual institutional influence on Chinese companies' interactions with the US legal system. Home-state institutions notably modify the preferences and organizational arrangements of Chinese companies operating in the United States. Yet these preferences and arrangements may not impede their adaptation, let alone make a substantial local impact, in subject areas featuring high coercive pressure from host-state institutions or powerful local actors. Meanwhile, the institutional heterogeneity gives rise to disputes and prevents their efficient resolution, leading to more lawsuits for certain Chinese companies operating in the United States.

To what extent are these findings unique to Chinese companies operating in the United States? One reasonably speculates that Chinese MNCs differ from those based in other countries. Chinese companies now dominate the Fortune Global 500 list, outpacing US firms.[4] And Chinese outbound foreign direct investment surpasses that of all other developing countries.[5] However, when investing in industrialized countries like the United States, Chinese MNCs have to surmount formidable institutional hurdles. Most MNCs, including those from other major developing countries like India and Brazil, are headquartered in democratic states with vibrant civil societies. In contrast, China remains a steadfast authoritarian regime where its laws and courts, despite changes in recent decades,[6] have maintained their politically instrumental and socially subordinated role.[7] These institutional features may differentiate Chinese MNCs from those of most other countries. The findings in this book offer some supportive evidence. For instance, compared with their privately-owned counterparts, state-owned Chinese companies express a stronger preference for US lawyers with some government experience and their headquarters assert more control over decisions regarding US legal matters.

This book also contributes to several broad theoretical and policy debates. First, the dual institutionalist framework, applicable to all research about transnational actors, contributes to the vast institutionalist literature. It adds to the scholarship of new institutional economics by analyzing informal institutions along with formal rules and that of sociological institutionalism by focusing on MNCs' varying preferences and actions within a transnational field featuring multiple actors with diverging and competing interests, values, rules, and norms.[8] Second,

[4] Yangpeng Zheng, *In a First, China Has More Companies on Fortune Global 500 List than the US*, South China Morning Post (July 22, 2019), www.scmp.com/business/companies/article/3019632/first-china-has-more-companies-fortune-global-500-list-us.

[5] Deepti Aggarwal & Cara Lyttle, *FDI in 2021: Outbound Investment*, Investment Monitor (August 19, 2022), www.investmentmonitor.ai/fdi-data/fdi-in-2021-outbound-investment/.

[6] Taisu Zhang & Tom Ginsburg, *China's Turn Toward Law*, 59 Va. J. Int'l L. 306 (2019).

[7] *See, e.g.*, Ji Li, *The Power Logic of Justice in China*, 65 Am. J. Compar. L. 94 (2017); Carl Minzner, *China's Turn against Law*, 59 Am. J. Compar. L. 935 (2011).

[8] See Chapter 1 for discussion about the neo-institutionalist literature.

this book enriches the scholarship of legal pluralism that explores issues arising from "a situation in which two or more laws (or legal systems) coexist in (or are obeyed by) one social field (or a population or an individual)."[9] Scholars of this camp, traditionally preoccupied with case studies in domestic settings, have begun to recognize the importance of applying the pluralist framework to "studying law on the world stage."[10] This book takes a major step in that direction and makes the case that legal pluralism will greatly benefit from theoretical insights of institutionalism and applying a mixed method to explore transnational actors. The third contribution is to the existing literature on MNCs' litigation in host countries, which has largely focused on the liability of foreignness,[11] bias against foreign litigants in US courts,[12] and evolving US jurisprudence.[13] The framework elaborated in this book connects the dual institutional tensions faced by MNCs, regardless of their countries of origin, to their preferences and behavior in resolving legal disputes in host states, particularly those states with a robust judiciary that might potentially protect foreign-invested businesses.

Fourth, this book enlarges the growing body of scholarship on Chinese state-owned enterprises (SOEs), a pillar of China's state capitalism and a distinguishing factor in Chinese outbound investment.[14] The findings have revealed unique patterns in how state-owned Chinese MNCs develop internal US legal capacity, engage US lawyers, and litigate in US courts. These important aspects of Chinese SOEs have, until now, largely escaped systematic research. Although SOEs were once thought

[9] Ralf Michaels, *Global Legal Pluralism*, 5 ANN. REV. L. & SOC. SCI. 243, 245 (2009).

[10] Paul Schiff Berman, *The New Legal Pluralism*, 5 ANN. REV. L. & SOC. SCI. 225, 227 (2009).

[11] *See, e.g.*, Utpal Bhattacharya, et al., *The Home Court Advantage in International Corporate Litigation*, 50 J.L. & ECON. 625 (2007).

[12] *See, e.g.*, Kevin M. Clermont & Theodore Eisenberg, *Xenophilia or Xenophobia in US Courts? Before and After 9/11*, 4 J. EMPIRICAL LEGAL STUD. 441 (2007); Kimberly A. Moore, *Xenophobia in American Courts*, 97 NW.U.L. REV. 1497 (2002).

[13] *See, e.g.*, Paul Hoffman & Beth Stephens, *International Human Rights Cases Under State Law and in State Courts*, 3 UC IRVINE L. REV. 9 (2013); Beth Stephens, *Translating Filartiga: A Comparative And International Law Analysis of Domestic Remedies for International Human Rights Violations*, 27 YALE J. INT'L L. 1 (2002); Jeffrey Davis, *Justice Without Borders: Human Rights Cases in US Courts*, 28 LAW & POL. 60 (2006).

[14] *See, e.g.*, Alessia A. Amighini, et al., *Do Chinese State-Owned and Private Enterprises Differ in Their Internationalization Strategies?* 27 CHINA ECON. REV. 312 (2013); Li-Wen Lin & Curtis J. Milhaupt, *We Are the (National) Champions: Understanding the Mechanism of State Capitalism in China*, 65 STANFORD L. REV. 697 (2013).

to be transitory, it has become clear that they will persist and play a significant role in the global economic order. As a result, these important yet overlooked aspects warrant scholarly scrutiny.

Fifth, this book broadens our understanding of the impacts of China's growing outbound investment on the legal profession and the legal service market in the United States and other countries.[15] It presented empirical evidence linking the domestic legal environment to the way some Chinese corporate clients approach lawyers in their host countries. Specifically, their lawyer selection preferences reflect how they interact with legal professionals in the domestic setting. While the Chinese legal market is undergoing dramatic changes, the status of lawyers remains lower than their counterparts in the United States, and clients typically underappreciate the value of quality legal services.[16] The influence of such a mindset, however, has insignificant impacts on a large, mature legal service market like that of the United States. Of course, peripheral players may feel the need to adjust their practices, as demonstrated by fee caps some small law firms have to install when serving Chinese clients.

Finally, this book provides valuable insights into the ongoing debates about US–China relations and China's foreign direct investment. Amid the escalating superpower rivalry, MNCs based in both countries face increasingly hostile laws and regulatory actions. In the current political climate, Chinese companies in the United States that anticipate substantial losses due to government mistreatment often seek legal recourse, as exemplified by Huawei's lawsuits against the US government. These companies represent an important constituency strongly motivated to preserve the status quo of the bilateral relations, and US courts provide them with a crucial, and sometimes the only viable, platform to do so. Collectively, Chinese companies' pursuit of US judicial remedies has become an integral part of the complex, impactful US–China relations, as the lawsuits introduce contingencies to the foreign policies of the two superpowers and influence the trajectory of US jurisprudential development in relevant subject matter areas. This book sheds light on this important yet unexplored topic.

Despite all these contributions, this first systematic effort to examine Chinese companies in the US legal system is not without limitations.

[15] For a review of the vast literature on the corporate in-house movement and other relevant topics of the US legal profession, see Sections 2.1 and 3.1.

[16] Ji Li, *Meeting Law's Demand: Chinese Multinationals as Consumers of US Legal Services*, 46 YALE J. INT'L L. ONLINE 72, 77 (2021).

Larger samples will certainly help by allowing the testing of additional variables. For instance, state ownership of Chinese investors could be further divided by the administrative level of the government owners (central versus provincial), which may reveal under-explored nuances regarding the state ownership effect. Also, personal information of the managers may explain a part of the varying interactions between Chinese companies and the US legal system. Moreover, the empirical findings of this book raises new, important questions. How do lawsuits involving Chinese companies unfold in US courts? To what extent do Chinese litigants settle, and what considerations do they take into account? Are US judges biased against Chinese litigants? What new legal issues do Chinese companies raise in US courts, and how does the resolution of these issues impact US law and US–China relations in the long run? Does the ownership structure of Chinese companies matter in all these aspects? This book marks only the beginning of a long exploratory journey, and its main purpose would have been served if it could spark readers' curiosity and inspire further investigation into these important questions.

INDEX

CAMBRIDGE STUDIES IN LAW AND SOCIETY

Books in the Series

Diseases of the Will: Alcohol and the Dilemmas of Freedom
Mariana Valverde

The Politics of Truth and Reconciliation in South Africa: Legitimizing the Post-Apartheid State
Richard A. Wilson

Modernism and the Grounds of Law
Peter Fitzpatrick

Unemployment and Government: Genealogies of the Social
William Walters

Autonomy and Ethnicity: Negotiating Competing Claims in Multi-Ethnic States
Yash Ghai

Constituting Democracy: Law, Globalism and South Africa's Political Reconstruction
Heinz Klug

The Ritual of Rights in Japan: Law, Society, and Health Policy
Eric A. Feldman

Governing Morals: A Social History of Moral Regulation
Alan Hunt

The Colonies of Law: Colonialism, Zionism and Law in Early Mandate Palestine
Ronen Shamir

Law and Nature
David Delaney

Social Citizenship and Workfare in the United States and Western Europe: The Paradox of Inclusion
Joel F. Handler

Law, Anthropology, and the Constitution of the Social: Making Persons and Things
Edited by Alain Pottage and Martha Mundy

Judicial Review and Bureaucratic Impact: International and Interdisciplinary Perspectives
Edited by Marc Hertogh and Simon Halliday

Immigrants at the Margins: Law, Race, and Exclusion in Southern Europe
Kitty Calavita

Lawyers and Regulation: The Politics of the Administrative Process
Patrick Schmidt

Law and Globalization from Below: Towards a Cosmopolitan Legality
Edited by Boaventura de Sousa Santos and César A. Rodríguez-Garavito

Public Accountability: Designs, Dilemmas and Experiences
Edited by Michael W. Dowdle

Law, Violence and Sovereignty among West Bank Palestinians
Tobias Kelly

Legal Reform and Administrative Detention Powers in China
Sarah Biddulph

The Practice of Human Rights: Tracking Law between the Global and the Local
Edited by Mark Goodale and Sally Engle Merry

Judges beyond Politics in Democracy and Dictatorship: Lessons from Chile
Lisa Hilbink

Paths to International Justice: Social and Legal Perspectives
Edited by Marie-Bénédicte Dembour and Tobias Kelly

Law and Society in Vietnam: The Transition from Socialism in Comparative Perspective
Mark Sidel

Constitutionalizing Economic Globalization: Investment Rules and Democracy's Promise
David Schneiderman

The New World Trade Organization Knowledge Agreements: Second Edition
Christopher Arup

Justice and Reconciliation in Post-Apartheid South Africa
Edited by François du Bois and Antje du Bois-Pedain

Militarization and Violence against Women in Conflict Zones in the Middle East: A Palestinian Case-Study
Nadera Shalhoub-Kevorkian

Child Pornography and Sexual Grooming: Legal and Societal Responses
Suzanne Ost

Darfur and the Crime of Genocide
John Hagan and Wenona Rymond-Richmond

Fictions of Justice: The International Criminal Court and the Challenge of Legal Pluralism in Sub-Saharan Africa
Kamari Maxine Clarke

Conducting Law and Society Research: Reflections on Methods and Practices
Simon Halliday and Patrick Schmidt

Planted Flags: Trees, Land, and Law in Israel/Palestine
Irus Braverman

Culture under Cross-Examination: International Justice and the Special Court for Sierra Leone
Tim Kelsall

Cultures of Legality: Judicialization and Political Activism in Latin America
Javier Couso, Alexandra Huneeus, and Rachel Sieder

Courting Democracy in Bosnia and Herzegovina: The Hague Tribunal's Impact in a Postwar State
Lara J. Nettelfield

The Gacaca Courts, Post-Genocide Justice and Reconciliation in Rwanda: Justice without Lawyers
Phil Clark

Law, Society, and History: Themes in the Legal Sociology and Legal History of Lawrence M. Friedman
Edited by Robert W. Gordon and Morton J. Horwitz

After Abu Ghraib: Exploring Human Rights in America and the Middle East
Shadi Mokhtari

Adjudication in Religious Family Laws: Cultural Accommodation, Legal Pluralism, and Gender Equality in India
Gopika Solanki

Water on Tap: Rights and Regulation in the Transnational Governance of Urban Water Services
Bronwen Morgan

Elements of Moral Cognition: Rawls' Linguistic Analogy and the Cognitive Science of Moral and Legal Judgment
John Mikhail

Mitigation and Aggravation at Sentencing
Edited by Julian V. Roberts

Institutional Inequality and the Mobilization of the Family and Medical Leave Act: Rights on Leave
Catherine R. Albiston

Authoritarian Rule of Law: Legislation, Discourse and Legitimacy in Singapore
Jothie Rajah

Law and Development and the Global Discourses of Legal Transfers
Edited by John Gillespie and Pip Nicholson

Law against the State: Ethnographic Forays into Law's Transformations
Edited by Julia Eckert, Brian Donahoe, Christian Strümpell and Zerrin Özlem Biner

Transnational Legal Ordering and State Change
Edited by Gregory C. Shaffer

Legal Mobilization under Authoritarianism: The Case of Post-Colonial Hong Kong
Waikeung Tam

Complementarity in the Line of Fire: The Catalysing Effect of the International Criminal Court in Uganda and Sudan
Sarah M. H. Nouwen

Political and Legal Transformations of an Indonesian Polity: The Nagari from Colonisation to Decentralisation
Franz von Benda-Beckmann and Keebet von Benda-Beckmann

Pakistan's Experience with Formal Law: An Alien Justice
Osama Siddique

Human Rights under State-Enforced Religious Family Laws in Israel, Egypt, and India
Yüksel Sezgin

Why Prison?
Edited by David Scott

Law's Fragile State: Colonial, Authoritarian, and Humanitarian Legacies in Sudan
Mark Fathi Massoud

Rights for Others: The Slow Home-Coming of Human Rights in the Netherlands
Barbara Oomen

European States and Their Muslim Citizens: The Impact of Institutions on Perceptions and Boundaries
Edited by John R. Bowen, Christophe Bertossi, Jan Willem Duyvendak, and Mona Lena Krook

Environmental Litigation in China: A Study in Political Ambivalence
Rachel E. Stern

Indigeneity and Legal Pluralism in India: Claims, Histories, Meanings
Pooja Parmar

Paper Tiger: Law, Bureaucracy and the Developmental State in Himalayan India
Nayanika Mathur

Religion, Law and Society
Russell Sandberg

The Experiences of Face Veil Wearers in Europe and the Law
Edited by Eva Brems

The Contentious History of the International Bill of Human Rights
Christopher N. J. Roberts

Transnational Legal Orders
Edited by Terence C. Halliday and Gregory Shaffer

Lost in China? Law, Culture and Society in Post-1997 Hong Kong
Carol A. G. Jones

Security Theology, Surveillance and the Politics of Fear
Nadera Shalhoub-Kevorkian

Opposing the Rule of Law: How Myanmar's Courts Make Law and Order
Nick Cheesman

Ironies of Colonial Governance: Law, Custom and Justice in Colonial India
James Jaffe

The Clinic and the Court: Law, Medicine and Anthropology
Edited by Ian Harper, Tobias Kelly, and Akshay Khanna

The World of Indicators: The Making of Government Knowledge through Quantification
Edited by Richard Rottenburg, Sally E. Merry, Sung-Joon Park, and Johanna Mugler

Contesting Immigration Policy in Court: Legal Activism and Its Radiating Effects in the United States and France
Leila Kawar

The Quiet Power of Indicators: Measuring Governance, Corruption, and Rule of Law
Edited by Sally Engle Merry, Kevin E. Davis, and Benedict Kingsbury

Investing in Authoritarian Rule: Punishment and Patronage in Rwanda's Gacaca Courts for Genocide Crimes
Anuradha Chakravarty

Contractual Knowledge: One Hundred Years of Legal Experimentation in Global Markets
Edited by Grégoire Mallard and Jérôme Sgard

Iraq and the Crimes of Aggressive War: The Legal Cynicism of Criminal Militarism
John Hagan, Joshua Kaiser, and Anna Hanson

Culture in the Domains of Law
Edited by René Provost

China and Islam: The Prophet, the Party, and Law
Matthew S. Erie

Diversity in Practice: Race, Gender, and Class in Legal and Professional Careers
Edited by Spencer Headworth, Robert L. Nelson, Ronit Dinovitzer, and David B. Wilkins

A Sociology of Constitutions: Constitutions and State Legitimacy in Historical-Sociological Perspective
Chris Thornhill

A Sociology of Transnational Constitutions: Social Foundations of the Post-National Legal Structure
Chris Thornhill

Genocide Never Sleeps: Living Law at the International Criminal Tribunal for Rwanda
Nigel Eltringham

Shifting Legal Visions: Judicial Change and Human Rights Trials in Latin America
Ezequiel A. González-Ocantos

The Demographic Transformations of Citizenship
Heli Askola

Criminal Defense in China: The Politics of Lawyers at Work
Sida Liu and Terence C. Halliday

Contesting Economic and Social Rights in Ireland: Constitution, State and Society, 1848–2016
Thomas Murray

Buried in the Heart: Women, Complex Victimhood and the War in Northern Uganda
Erin Baines

Palaces of Hope: The Anthropology of Global Organizations
Edited by Ronald Niezen and Maria Sapignoli

The Politics of Bureaucratic Corruption in Post-Transitional Eastern Europe
Marina Zaloznaya

Revisiting the Law and Governance of Trafficking, Forced Labor and Modern Slavery
Edited by Prabha Kotiswaran

Incitement on Trial: Prosecuting International Speech Crimes
Richard Ashby Wilson

Criminalizing Children: Welfare and the State in Australia
David McCallum

Global Lawmakers: International Organizations in the Crafting of World Markets
Susan Block-Lieb and Terence C. Halliday

Duties to Care: Dementia, Relationality and Law
Rosie Harding

Insiders, Outsiders, Injuries, and Law: Revisiting "The Oven Bird's Song"
Edited by Mary Nell Trautner

Hunting Justice: Displacement, Law, and Activism in the Kalahari
Maria Sapignoli

Injury and Injustice: The Cultural Politics of Harm and Redress
Edited by Anne Bloom, David M. Engel, and Michael McCann

Ruling Before the Law: The Politics of Legal Regimes in China and Indonesia
William Hurst

The Powers of Law: A Comparative Analysis of Sociopolitical Legal Studies
Mauricio García-Villegas

A Sociology of Justice in Russia
Edited by Marina Kurkchiyan and Agnieszka Kubal

Constituting Religion: Islam, Liberal Rights, and the Malaysian State
Tamir Moustafa

The Invention of the Passport: Surveillance, Citizenship and the State, Second Edition
John C. Torpey

Law's Trials: The Performance of Legal Institutions in the US "War on Terror"
Richard L. Abel

Law's Wars: The Fate of the Rule of Law in the US "War on Terror"
Richard L. Abel

Transforming Gender Citizenship: The Irresistible Rise of Gender Quotas in Europe
Edited by Eléonore Lépinard and Ruth Rubio-Marín

Muslim Women's Quest for Justice: Gender, Law and Activism in India
Mengia Hong Tschalaer

Children as 'Risk': Sexual Exploitation and Abuse by Children and Young People
Anne-Marie McAlinden

The Legal Process and the Promise of Justice: Studies Inspired by the Work of Malcolm Feeley
Jonathan Simon, Rosann Greenspan, Hadar Aviram

Gift Exchanges: The Transnational History of a Political Idea
Grégoire Mallard

Measuring Justice: Quantitative Accountability and the National Prosecuting Authority in South Africa
Johanna Mugler

Negotiating the Power of NGOs: Women's Legal Rights in South Africa
Reem Wael

Indigenous Water Rights in Law and Regulation: Lessons from Comparative Experience
Elizabeth Jane Macpherson

The Edge of Law: Legal Geographies of a War Crimes Court
Alex Jeffrey

Everyday Justice: Law, Ethnography, and Injustice
Sandra Brunnegger

The Uncounted: Politics of Data in Global Health
Sara L. M. Davis

Transnational Legal Ordering of Criminal Justice
Gregory Shaffer and Ely Aaronson

Five Republics and One Tradition
Pablo Ruiz-Tagle

The Law Multiple: Judgment and Knowledge in Practice
Irene van Oorschot

Health as a Human Right: The Politics and Judicialisation of Health in Brazil
Octávio Luiz Motta Ferraz

Shari'a, Inshallah: Finding God in Somali Legal Politics
Mark Fathi Massoud

Policing for Peace: Institutions, Expectations, and Security in Divided Societies
Matthew Nanes

Rule of Law Intermediaries: Brokering Influence in Myanmar
Kristina Simion

Lactation at Work: Expressed Milk, Expressing Beliefs, and the Expressive Value of Law
Elizabeth A. Hoffmann

The Archival Politics of International Courts
Henry Redwood

Global Pro Bono: Causes, Context, and Contestation
Edited by Scott L. Cummings, Fabio de Sa e Silva and Louise G. Trubek

The Practice and Problems of Transnational Counter-Terrorism
Fiona de Londras

Decoupling: Gender Injustice in China's Divorce Courts
Ethan Michelson

Anti-Constitutional Populism
Martin Krygier, Adam Czarnota and Wojciech Sadurski

Lawyers in Conflict and Transition
Kieran McEvoy, Louse Mallinder and Anna Bryson

The Ghostwriters: Lawyers and the Politics behind the Judicial Construction of Europe
Tommaso Pavone

The Sentimental Court: The Affective Life of International Criminal Justice
Jonas Bens

Practices of Reparations in International Criminal Justice
Christoph Sperfeldt

Seeking Supremacy: The Pursuit of Judicial Power in Pakistan
Yasser Kureshi

The Power of the Jury: Transforming Citizens into Jurors
Nancy S. Marder

Undue Process: Persecution and Punishment in Autocratic Courts
Fiona Feiang Shen-Bayh

Discounting Life: Necropolitical Law, Culture, and the Long War on Terror
Jothie Rajah

Clean Air at What Cost? The Rise of Blunt Force Regulation in China
Denise Sienli van der Kamp

Law and Precarity: Legal Consciousness and Daily Survival in Vietnam
Tu Phuong Nguyen

Prosecutors, Voters and The Criminalization of Corruption in Latin America: The Case of Lava Jato
Ezequiel A. Gonzalez-Ocantos and Paula Muñoz Chirinos

Entangled Domains: Empire, Law and Religion in Northern Nigeria
Rabiat Akande

The Social Constitution: Embedding Social Rights Through Legal Mobilization
Whitney K. Taylor

Out of Place: Fieldwork and Positionality in Law and Society
Edited by Lynette J. Chua and Mark Fathi Massoud

Negotiating Legality: Chinese Companies in the US Legal System
Ji Li